MALPRACTICE:
Managing Your Defense
2nd Edition

Raymond M. Fish, PhD, MD
Melvin E. Ehrhardt, MD, JD
Betty Fish, MSW

Medical Economics Books
Oradell, New Jersey 07649

Library of Congress Cataloging-in-Publication Data

Fish, Raymond M.
  Malpractice, managing your defense. Second Edition

  Spine title: Malpractice defense.
  Includes index.
  1. Physicians—Malpractice—United States—Trial
practice.   2. Trial practice—United States.
I. Ehrhardt, Melvin E.   II. Fish, Betty.   III. Title.
IV. Title: Malpractice defense.   [DNLM: 1. Malpractice.
W 44 F532M]
DF8925.M3F57   1990   346.7303′32′0269   84-1132
                         347.3063320269

ISBN 0-87489-545-6

Medical Economics Company Inc.
Oradell, New Jersey 07649

Printed in the United States of America

Contents

About the Authors

Raymond M. Fish, PhD, MD, has served both as an expert medical witness in court and as a consultant in planning and developing defenses against malpractice charges. A fellow of the American College of Emergency Physicians, he practices at the Burnham City Hospital Trauma Center in Champaign, Illinois, and is clinical instructor in emergency medicine at the University of Illinois, Champaign-Urbana. He is also adjunct professor of electrical and bioengineering at the University of Illinois, and has designed a cardiotachometer for NASA's Manned Spacecraft Center and invented an audio instrument for the U.S. Public Health Service that lets the blind "see" in two dimensions.

Melvin E. Ehrhardt, MD, JD, "emergency department physician at United Samaritans Medical Center, Logan Campus, Danville, Illinois," director of the Emergency Care Center of the Mennonite Hospital, Bloomington, Illinois, has taught both clinical and medicolegal courses at the University of Illinois Medical School, Champaign-Urbana. His writings include three texts for continuing education on medical evidence, handbooks on malpractice, the chapter on legal implications in a textbook on surgery, and computer programs on issues of informed consent and abuse. He has lectured widely to in-service training groups of physicians, nurses, paramedics, and medical records personnel, and has conducted courses for attorneys at the Illinois Continuing Legal Education Seminars. He has consulted extensively in legal preparation and has served as an expert medical witness in malpractice court cases.

Betty Fish, MSW, ACSW, is a psychotherapist in private practice. She has experience counseling individuals, couples, and families. As both a professional counselor and a doctor's wife, she has an insider's perspective on how stress affects every member of a medical family.

Acknowledgments

One of the most interesting aspects of writing this book was the varied response from those we asked to review the manuscript.

Some thought the book would cause health-care practitioners to put too much trust in insurance company attorneys and their motives. The practitioners should have more to say about how a malpractice case is run, they said. One physician, who has successfully defended himself several times in court, even suggested that a defense attorney is unnecessary.

Others felt the book would cause practitioners to place too little trust in insurance company attorneys. All arrangements should be left to the defense attorney, they said, because health professionals don't understand the law and therefore can't effectively help develop a defense strategy.

Some said the book unfairly categorized patients and their attorneys as beasts of prey; others said it was too complimentary to plaintiffs' attorneys and the legal system in general.

This divergence of opinions is not surprising. The reviewers are involved in law and medicine—professions that approach and analyze problems quite differently. Yet without exception every one of them submitted suggestions that were both useful and greatly appreciated. We included many of these opposing points of view throughout the book as a means of providing perspective on how various issues are perceived and handled by each side.

We especially want to thank Mr. Jack E. Horsley for his many helpful suggestions for the second edition of this book. We would also like to thank for their help on the first edition, Sue Bartlett; Donald Bartlett, MD; Paul Fish, JD; Rochelle Hochman; Sidney Hochman, MD; Joyce Lohman, PhD; Tim Lohman, PhD; James D. Rogers, MD; the Honorable Judge Robert Steigmann, JD; Wayne B. Wheeler, MD, JD; Cathy Zalar; Joe Zalar, MD; Phillip C. Zimmerly, JD; and Mary Lee Casio, RN.

Foreword from First Edition

What should you do when you're sued for malpractice? First, inform your insurance company. Second, read this book!

You haven't been sued yet? Reading this book could decrease your worry about malpractice and might lessen your likelihood of committing malpractice. This is a doctor's book. Doctors who are sued will find it a valuable guidebook. Doctors interested in how malpractice law can affect them should read it.

It's about time there was a textbook for physicians that describes the way the litigation war is fought, its implicit dangers, and the fair defenses.

Today's physician faces the risk that treatment of a patient might result in bad publicity, a long lawsuit, hostile depositions, and a public trial, followed by financial loss that could exceed insurance and consume all assets accumulated over a lifetime. No wonder malpractice litigation provides an omnipresent background of anxiety in today's practice of medicine.

To the doctor who has worked diligently and in good faith to diagnose and treat a patient, a subpoena in a malpractice suit is seen as an unfair, catastrophic criticism of his or her medical judgment. It may never happen to you. But it has happened to many. It usually doesn't result in an extreme outcome. But it could. Every doctor should be prepared for a lawsuit.

Our legal process is an advocacy system. Lawyers on each side of a suit advocate their client's position; each side is represented by hired guns. It's the American way. This book gives practical advice, examples, and an analysis of how you may be attacked—and how you can defend yourself.

This book doesn't make anxiety or danger disappear; neither does it prevent negligence or vexatious litigation. But it prepares you to handle these occurrences. It tells you what to do so you can meet the unpleasant with confidence based on educated maturity. The worst fears are a lesser burden when understood.

Many issues covered in this book are controversial and could be inflammatory. Yet the authors present both sides frankly and without pulling punches.

It's a pleasure to see a good book like this written by experts who spend their professional time in the trenches dealing with the problems they write about. Both Raymond Fish and Melvin Ehrhardt are nationally recognized emergency physicians who have spent years helping very sick and traumatized patients, teaching doctors and lawyers the issues of medical malpractice, and serving as expert witnesses and defense consultants. Betty Fish, a social worker and counselor, gives this book the wisdom of a professional who knows how to bring discipline to conflict, realistic thinking to panic, and quiet assessment in the face of hostility.

We are fortunate that such a learned group of authors have shared their insight with us.

Marshall B. Segal, MD, JD

Foreword

More and more practicing physicians are now (or are more likely soon to be) involved in the malpractice crisis. That's not just talk—it's a harsh reality. Lawyers can't attend to doctors' defenses without knowledgeable help from the physicians themselves. Some are misled by the idea that managing the defense is solely in the province of attorneys, but this isn't true. Management involves putting together all the elements necessary to resist the claims of self-seeking patients who sue their doctors. Such suits are too often lacking in substantial merit. Erring physicians must be brought to the fullness of responsibility, but unfortunate doctors, free from fault, are caught in the same net as the ones who make mistakes—they too must defend themselves.

No one is better qualified to make cogent suggestions addressing physicians' management of their own defense than Dr. Raymond M. Fish, Dr. Melvin E. Ehrhardt, and Betty Fish. The authors' prowess has been proven by the valuable counsel in the first edition of this work. Subsequent developments and the pressing need for updating and bringing into current focus the wise recommendations in the first edition make this book timely, helpful, and of marked value to practicing physicians.

Doctors contribute to their own defense by managerial suggestions. Although doctors must avoid seeking to manage matters relating to trial tactics and rules of legal procedure and in-court handling of the defense, their special knowledge of the medical aspects as well as the actual facts makes contributing to the management feature important. But doctors must also be mindful of the rules of law that will increase the worth of their management contributions. The authors of this work deal with this feature informatively. For example, their careful delineation of the change in the rule speaking to the required standard of care is significant. Traditionally, doctors were required to comply with the professional standard adopted by reputable physicians at the time *and in the community involved*. Now it is assumed that patients in peninsular areas are entitled to the same treatment as ones in sophisticated metropolitan centers. Sometimes this seems attenuated but the authors explain in lucid terms why this modification was adopted by the courts. Improvements in communication, as well as the mobility of physicians who train in large city hospitals, practice in small communities, and transfer to other large cities, are cited as reasons for scrubbing what the authors call correctly "the locality rule."

This work is replete with similar supported suggestions to assist doctors in managing their own defense. It is also strengthened by the clarity of the authors' stressing that this purpose shouldn't invade lawyers' area of expertise. They emphasize that attorneys are the experts in such matters. Attorneys guide doctors in building a defensive presentation that will comprise a combination of the law and the facts. Without doctors' contributions, however, the latter element may well be insufficiently included in the final tapestry that brings to the jury the most convincing defense. This book rivets with equal effectiveness on the help doctors can furnish in coordinating the contributions that will be made by experts engaged to testify for the defense. These are only two facets of the practical aspects of this significant work.

To see this book come to fruition is a special pleasure for me, for its was my honor to review the first draft of the manuscript. It was plain to me then that this work is something that every physician should own, read, and absorb. That initial reaction in the nascent stages of this work is confirmed by my careful reading of the completed book.

Doctors owe it to themselves, the courts, their communities, and their associates to own, study, and be guided by the knowledgeable presentations in *Malpractice: Managing Your Defense*. This excellent guide is indispensable to practicing physicians. If adopting the convincing course so expertly brought together in this book is widespread in the national medical community, it may well contribute effectively to changing the malpractice crisis into a malpractice chapter only. Wise management by doctors of their own defense, in concert with the legal expertise of attorneys, will make a marked dent in the incidence of that burgeoning phenomenon—the specious malpractice suit.

I recommend this book without reservation and with enthusiastic pleasure.

Jack E. Horsley, A.B., LL.B., J.D.

Introduction: If the suit fits, how to bear it

If you find yourself in—or feel you are about to be put in—a malpractice suit, this manual is tailor-made for you. It tells you what to do at every step along the unfamiliar path of litigation. It gets and keeps you in step with your lawyer and other allies all along the way.

This book is not guaranteed to prevent lawsuits against you. It does not detail all the landmarks of good medical and legal practice. (Those details can be drawn from the many good references included at the end of this book to help avoid future mistakes.)

This is rather a map that pinpoints and moves you through the legal and personal difficulties you will face if and when you are charged with professional malpractice. It directs the medical professional already being sued through the strange forest of legal forms and strategies with specific, practical pointers.

The journey begins at the first sign of a charge against you, and takes you 1-2-3 through preparing, presenting, and paying for your case. Medial facts and legal citations are carefully chosen and provided to help the accused health practitioner get equipped for the legal process and carry out an effective defense.

Your case is not unique. You are not alone. Here is a solid body of evidence and witnesses for and from hundreds of physicians, nurses, physicians' assistants, nurse practitioners, paramedics, pharmacists, dentists, physical and respiratory therapists, psychotherapists, risk managers, hospital administrators, and emergency medical technicians who care for patients and share your risks.

This journey is not an escape. It does not deny or try to throw a cape over the real problems that come from taking the risks of medical and surgical practice. It is not about going bare—taking your chances out there when the legal elements beat upon you. You will need the protection of an insurance policy.

When the lawsuit is already upon you, this owner's manual shows you how to bear it, defend yourself in it, and make positive changes in your life and practice as a result of it.

As the physician moves in practice through the stages of diagnosis, treatment, and follow-up, so this book will take you through the 1-2-3, before-during-after, preparation-presentation-payment stages of the legal process in claims of malpractice. The office or operating room in this case is the courtroom. This book contains the tools you will need and the steps you will likely need to take to operate best on your own case.

Step 1 sets you on the map by showing where and why malpractice suits appear, and how you might head one off in your case.

Step 2 takes you through the stop and go signs, the people who may be involved, who you should talk to, and who to avoid once you hear that you are in a lawsuit.

Step 3 leads you through the first legal moves.

Step 4 prepares you for the plaintiff's attorney and tactics.

Step 5 helps get your lawyer and you together and moving.

Step 6 is the final set of preparations you need to make before presenting your case.

Step 7 presents the keys to a deft deposition—your "day in court" that could save you from having to face a jury.

Step 8 puts you on the stand face-to-face with judge, jury, and attorneys and lays out for you the art of testifying.

Step 9 takes you into the anatomy of a trial—what is there and how it works.

Step 10, 11, and 12 are definite defenses that can be and have been successfully used to defend health practitioners and bring to light patients' contributions to bad outcomes in large numbers of common malpractice accusations, to involve other responsible defendants in the liability, and to counter certain specific charges you may face or need to anticipate.

Step 13 discusses counter suits.

Step 14 starts to lead you out of the malpractice maze by showing when and how to settle out of court.

Step 15 is the win-or-lose payoff of settlements and legal fees, with tips on how to make the most of your malpractice insurance and protect your assets if the costs exceed your coverage.

Step 16 shows you how to bear the stress and anxiety that your family and you may have to handle throughout this experience.

Through each step along this lonely ordeal, this book accompanies you with both psychological and legal resources you may need to tap. This is not a legal textbook, but it seeks to give you enough legal grounding to stand firm in your own defense on someone else's turf. Bombarded as you are with regulations from hospitals, insurance companies, and governmental agencies on how to handle treatment and reporting of diseases, disabilities, consent, confidentiality, and all the other parts of current medical practice, it would be impossible for you to keep up as well with all the latest legal, social, and administrative developments. This book seeks to offer the factual material you will most need as you move from the discipline of medicine into law.

Law and medicine differ not only in subject matter but also in style. Therefore, as we move through the legal procedures, language, and definitions, we will also examine the mind-sets of judges, juries, patients, and attorneys you will meet at the various steps along the way, and show you what to do and say. Controversy is likely to be unfamiliar and distasteful to you as one whose profession is pledged to healing. In contrast, attorneys are most comfortable in this setting of opposition and conflict. This manual is designed to help you understand and withstand the charges and tactics of the opposing attorney, and to counter them to your own advantage.

"Too often the first time a physician comes into contact with the way the legal mind works is when an opposing attorney asks questions during a deposition," warn Barry Gold and Stu Chapman. "From then on, a doctor may start playing a guessing game."[48]*

From here and now on, you can stop guessing and start playing with the best evidence and tactics, and to your best advantage. Here is a set of directions to get you off on your best foot and guide you through the steps that you must take to make it through the maze and pitfalls of a malpractice contest.

---

*All references to printed resources and case citations will be numbered where they appear throughout the text to correspond to their complete alphabetical listings at the end of the book; case citations will be distinguished by a "c" preceding their numerical designation in the text.

PREPARING YOURSELF AND YOUR EVIDENCE

Where and why the malpractice suit appears

"How's the lawsuit coming?" That may be how you first hear you're being sued. What do you say? What do you do?

Before you do anything, realize that you may not know what to do. You may not believe it can happen to you. Believe it. It can. If you've already been served papers charging you with malpractice, have just heard a rumor that a suit is coming, or have only been threatened with one, you are not alone.

Three out of five obstetricians and gynecologists have been sued at least once. Walsh and Walker, in a study of litigation in the United States, reported that one of ten dentists will be sued each year, and one of every four physicians will be sued before retirement.[177]

Before you say anything about the reality or rumor of your lawsuit, you ought to know why it is happening. Why? It comes with the times and the territory.

These are litigious times. The public is suited for lawsuits. The average citizen is understandably aware of and concerned about personal rights. People have come to expect a high degree of performance from systems and persons they see as designed to serve them. Unfortunately, many patients don't take care of themselves and don't cooperate with treatment. They may seek to shift the burden of fault, loss, and cost to someone else. That transmission takes place more and more in the courtroom.

Today there seem to be few loyalties, little appreciation for a job well done over many years, and a weakening of the bond of allegiance and friendship between a patient and doctor. Workers, including professionals, are commonly fired when financial times are difficult, regardless of long dedication to their companies and colleagues. The medical professional is less susceptible to being fired, but more likely to be sued and abandoned.

The US is now lawsuit territory. Each year, twice as many new lawyers as physicians will enter their fields. Suits charging negligence have become a real problem and threat for manufacturers, engineers, architects, entrepreneurs, and even lawyers.

While there was one claim for every 11 physicians in 1986, one in every 17 veterinarians was sued for malpractice.[210] Any health professional may be sued for malpractice.

Between 1983 and 1985 the cost of physicians' malpractice premiums doubled—from $1.7 billion to $3.4 billion. By 1986, 37 out of every 100 physicians had been sued at least once, while 64% of OBGs had been sued, leading some to think "MD" stands for malpractice defendant.[107]

In 1988, South Florida attorneys filed a large number of lawsuits in anticipation of a pending tort reform bill being considered. A 52-year-old physician who had been served with five malpractice suits in 10 days suffered a massive stroke and died.[234] Legal charges are a constant threat to all who work in the medical field, no matter how careful and responsible the practitioner is. Mistakes will happen; they just happen to be less tolerated and more costly in the territory of medicine.

This book's first step is a survey of the territory, a look at why and where your lawsuit appears. Step 2 tells you who to start talking to about it. Step 3 sets out your first legal moves. Before you move, look and listen.

DO AND DON'T ROOTS OF MALPRACTICE SUITS

Malpractice suits arise from two basic roots. The first reveals what the practitioners do as wrong or harmful. But the other root is concealed: It bears fruit from what the practitioners don't do. One is *mal*practice; the other is *non*practice. Here are the common forms in which they may appear:

Rare cases. Obscure conditions and unusually complicated cases can make diagnosis and treatment difficult and lead to bad decisions. In such cases, few practitioners perform well alone. You would have been wise to call in a consultant, had you recognized the need for one. You did what you thought best, yet you are sued because someone expected better.

Bad labels.   Watch how you identify a disease. Tempers can flare when a condition is labeled neurotic in origin, especially if the workup to exclude organic disease is obviously inadequate.

Alcoholic content.   Another cause of malpractice is the effect of alcohol. Drunk patients often feel no pain, will not cooperate with a physical examination, and will not tell you what happened to them. They may be verbally abusive. But if you threat them, the law requires that you give competent care, no matter how difficult and frustrating that may be.

Verbal abuse.   Words can hurt you; they can hurt others too. Watch what you say to patients and families. Those who are hurt or displeased by what you say may be stimulated to bring suit against you. This problem occurs when the health-care provider is insensitive or curt at a time of grief, pain, or stress. Some of us can be downright rude. When we are, we may be in for a rude awakening from the patient's lawyer. Verbal abuse is not sufficient reason for a suit, but it will cause your treament to be examined. If flaws are found, a suit will likely follow.

Silent treatment.   Your failure to talk may also motivate a patient to sue. The hasty physician who leaves it to a nurse to explain the diagnosis, treatment, prognosis, and follow-up may be followed up with a hasty lawsuit from a patient who feels ignored and uninformed. Let patients vent their understandable anger at the disease, and they may not need to transfer their rage, shame, or blame to you.

Bill collection.   If pushing for payment of your bill adds to a patient's discomfort, the injured party may push back with a malpractice "bill." If a patient and you are facing a complication in treatment, you must tell your patient what the problem is, or at least that you are trying to determine the cause and will discuss it when you know more. If you know what the complication is, tell what must be done to correct it. Even if the patient or family does not request a consultant, get one anyway. This shows your concern, may help the patient, and will make further complications and loss of faith in your treatment less likely. If correcting the problem is costly, don't reduce your fee. That can be taken as an admission of guilt. Instead, you might be able to arrange financial assistance for the family through a social worker. You can assure the patient that you're in no hurry to collect. You certainly should not push for payment, but you must give a reasonable bill for your services.

Sexual abuse. One case of "treatment" that moves from negligence into abuse is the doctor who engages in "sexual therapy." This is a particular problem in psychotherapy with a vulnerable patient. Most people and juries agree that a therapist who has sexual relations with a susceptible patient is taking unfair advantage. Nevertheless, a small minority of therapists do engage their clients in sexual activity.[132,150] One therapist, for example, induced a patient to leave her husband, become his mistress, and turn over her savings to him. His actions were judged to constitute negligent treatment.[204] A similar case found a psychiatrist who acted as a sex therapist guilty of assault as well as negligence.[c163] Another such case involved a third party, and a hospital as accomplice: A widower successfully sued the hospital where his late wife was "treated" sexually by a therapist who had promised to marry her once she was released. The doctor broke his promise, the woman committed suicide, and the husband got $28,600 in damages from the hospital.[c8]

Physical abuse. Two psychotherapists who beat[c1] and tortured[c78] patients to bring out their anger and hidden identities were sued for malpractice. Many states have outlawed abuses of mental patients. In Illinois, for example, mistreatment is defined as the infliction of any mental, physical, or verbal abuse, including unnecessary restrictions and unreasonable use of force. And the penalty for abusing a mental patient is up to $1,000 and up to six months in prison.

Failing the physical. What we don't do can be just as damaging as what we do. Some of us will not examine patients with chest or abdominal pain or a sore throat. We tell them over the phone to take two aspirin, go to bed, and come see us at our convenience. Such practice is common because we can almost always get away with it. Some patients seem to get better no matter what we do. If a serious problem develops, however, one of its side effects may be a malpractice suit. Treating a patient without having done a thorough physical examination is unacceptable by medical or legal standards.

Out of practice. Along with sloppy practices, out-of-date practices hold up the other leg of negligence. We all make mistakes. Some of us say or do things we know are wrong. Some of us don't know we are wrong. None of us devotes enough time to learning: no one ever

6

knows enough. But some of us are way behind the times. Some are still prescribing chloramphenicol for sore throats, ampicillin for infections that are probably caused by staph, and Quaaludes for simple "nervousness." Although such practices were acceptable 20 years ago, they are now known to be harmful. In 1983, the New York Health Commissioner estimated that one of every ten practicing physicians in that state was incompetent or impaired.[11] Nevertheless, the probability of being sued for libel or slander (see Step 11) keeps health-care professionals from exposing the known incompetence of their peers.[62]

Out of touch. A major reason for so many malpractice suits is that we doctors are getting out of touch with our patients and colleagues. We're losing our honored place in this society. Our fellow physician, William Bauer, tells us not to blame all our problems on lawyers, but to see their roots in these real shortcomings in our own profession and practice:

- Snobbery toward patients and co-workers.
- Criticism of other doctors in front of patients.
- Failure to respect nurses and other health-care professionals.
- Lack of review and reporting of substandard conduct.
- Pursuit of money, power, and prestige.[20]

Pursuit of the deep pocket. The pursuit of money leads to the pursuit of the deep pocket that physicians are supposed to have. Doctors have been portrayed in some law schools as rich and callous pirates out to profit from other people's misery. So some attorneys set out to get into that deep pocket and share the treasure.[83] Many lawbooks, journal articles, and seminars instruct attorneys on how to get into the doctor's pocket and win a large malpractice award.

This book is not a legal text with a lock and key for your pocket. If you are innocent of malpractice, it will help you prove it. If you are guilty, it will not help you hide it. This book will, however, help you prevent the prosecuting attorney from making you appear a callous, incompetent, dishonest, greedy, and lazy villain who did someone in and deserves to pay for it. The legal concepts, terms, resources, and procedures you need will be provided along the way.

The first step, before you begin to talk about and carry out your defense, is to look for the four pillars upon which a malpractice case must rest. Absence of any one of them will collapse the case.

THE 4 PILLARS OF MALPRACTICE

1. Duty. The plaintiff must first demonstrate that a duty existed that obligated you to treat the injured party. Your duty is easy to demonstrate if the patient has begun treatment in your care. If there is no established practitioner-client relationship, the lawsuit against you will be dismissed.

2. Dereliction. The plaintiff must demonstrate that you were derelict or negligent in performing the duty owed. You must meet the standard of care, which is the degree of ability and skill maintained by other practitioners in your field. Experts and colleagues may be called to measure the standard of care in your case.

3. Damage. Evidence must show that harm and damage actually befell the patient. Deterioration in the patient's condition is not enough. The condition may have grown worse in spite of, rather than because of, your efforts. In any case, evidence of the damage must be presented.

4. Cause. Your practice or negligence must be shown to have been a direct, proximate cause of the patient's damages. Expert testimony and the "but for" and "substantial factor" tests can be used to connect you to the damages.[89,113] The "but for" test requires the patient to show the injury wouldn't have occurred but for your actions.[c178] The "substantial factor" test must prove what you did to be a substantial factor causing the damage.

LOSS OF CHANCE INSTEAD OF CAUSATION

In recent years the "loss of chance" doctrine has been applied in many jurisdictions when causation could not be proven. This doctrine, which is most obviously applicable in myocardial infarction cases, is related to the plaintiff's loss of chance of recovery. Under this doctrine the patient's damages were not the probable result of negligence. Instead, *the loss of chance of recovery (or survival) was the result of negligence.*[236]

Application and acceptance of the loss of chance doctrine varies throughout the country. In some jurisdictions it must be proven that it is more likely than not the patient would have recovered or survived with proper treatment. Damages may be reduced by some percentage related to the probability the patient would have recovered with treatment.

THE TOP 10 MALPRACTICE CLAIMS

Here are the top 10 claims allegations for 1986:

Allegation	Number	Average Cost
1. Surgery—Postop Complications	1,019	$ 50,006
2. Improper Treatment—Birth Related	518	119,249
3. Failure to Diagnose Cancer	376	102,072
4. Surgery—Inadvertent Act	262	51,033
5. Failure to Diagnose—Fracture/ Dislocation	228	46,726
6. Improper Treatment—Drug Side Effect	211	51,842
7. Failure to Diagnose—Infection	208	76,614
8. Surgery—Inappropriate Procedure	208	46,619
9. Improper Treatment—Infection	195	57,836
10. Improper Treatment— Fracture–Dislocation	193	50,286
Total: Top 10 Allegations	3,418	
Total: All Allegations	6,935	

Postoperative complications accounted for the greatest number of malpractice claims against physicians insured by St. Paul Fire and Marine Insurance Company in 1986. Birth-related complications accounted for the highest cost per claim.[229]

THE TREND TOWARD MISDIAGNOSIS SUITS

"One of the biggest shifts in types of malpractice cases over the past half dozen years has been to problems of misdiagnosis," notes Peter Sweetland, president of doctor-owned Medical Inter-Insurance Exchange of New Jersey and an administrator of the Physicians Insurance Association of America. "In the past, claims almost always related to surgical problems. Now, more and more, the primary-care physician is being exposed to as big a claim when it's alleged that he could have caught something early and perhaps prevented death or debilitating injury."

A prime example is missing the early indications of cancer and failing to recognize the need for a consult with or a referral to a specialist at an early stage. OBGs are also more in the malpractice spotlight these days as a result of what insurers call neurologic-deficit cases—birth-related defects.

Joseph B. Nardi, president of the medical services division of St. Paul Fire and Marine Insurance Company, is among those who report a tremendous increase in malpractice claims in this area. Nardi says prenatal and postnatal specialties are emerging, and medical science is growing increasingly sophisticated. "But as medical specialists become better," he adds, "people tend to have higher expectations, and we see more claims." St. Paul insurance underwriter John Rolig agrees with this, and cites complaints stemming from emergency-room care as another major trouble spot.

What other situations are putting doctors in jeopardy? Failure to keep up, for one. Like failure to refer or consult, failure to be aware of new treatments that might have helped can trigger a lawsuit.

Be aware, too, that far more physicians are willing to testify as expert witnesses today than they were years ago, according to famed malpractice lawyer Melvin Belli. Computers enable plaintiffs' lawyers to do a far better job of research in less time, Belli notes.

Medicine's team approach will also increase the "sue everybody" trend because it makes pinpointing blame extremely difficult.

9 CLUES TO SUIT-PRONE PATIENTS

You may already be aware of an unsatisfied patient who may start a lawsuit. Even if you can't forestall a suit, these clues can help you defend yourself against legal action by spotting patients most prone to sue.

Review your medical records for any of the common warning signs uncovered by investigators for St. Paul Fire and Marine Insurance Company in clinics of 20 to 200 doctors across the country:

1. Patient returns within three months of the initial visit for management of a condition that might suggest adverse effects of prior management.
2. Patient suffers cardiac or respiratory arrest. If the patient survives, the record should be analyzed to determine whether the patient can attribute any present or future injury to the arrest, can assert that the arrest was possibly iatrogenic or preventable, or can claim that the injury would have been mitigated by more timely and appropriate response.
3. Patient dies. All death cases should be analyzed for potential liability, excluding exceptional circumstances such as patients receiving planned terminal care.

4. Laceration, perforation, tear, or puncture of an organ or a body part occurs during an invasive procedure and requires surgical intervention for repair.

5. Unanticipated transfer of a patient to an acute-care facility (or of a hospitalized patient to intensive care).

6. The medical record doesn't show that proper instructions have been given to the patient or to members of the family.

7. The patient's family complains. This identifies people who may be prone to sue for an actual or perceived physical injury or emotional trauma.

8. Incomplete or nonexistent evidence of informed consent to certain diagnostic and therapeutic procedures.

9. Medical record is incomplete. The entry for each patient visit should contain at a minimum: date and time, department (if departmentalized), provider name and designation, chief complaint, purpose of visit, diagnosis or medical impression, studies ordered, therapies administered, disposition, recommendations, instructions to patient, and signature of practitioner.

LAST TIPS BEFORE THE FIRST STEP

Before stepping into the legal arena, you need more than a look at the warning signs already identified. You also need to listen for some final words of warning that might give you a last chance to head off a lawsuit.

"I'm going to sue you!" You may hear these dreaded words from an angry patient or family member. They frequently come from someone who is drunk. Your first defensive reaction may be silence and withdrawal. Once a lawsuit has actually been filed, you should say nothing to the patient or family. Let your attorney do all of the talking for you.

If a suit has not yet been filed against you, however, withdrawal may be the worst medicine. An outburst threatening legal action may be a plea for help, and you might be able to help. Talk about it. Part of practicing your profession is explaining to patients what has happened to them. If a problem arose in treatment or recovery, the complication can be explained. Most patients are understanding and fair. They may just want to know what is happening. They may well see the reasoning behind what you say. Just state the facts and tell why you thought that what you did seemed best at the time.

Don't admit guilt or wrongdoing. Be honest, but don't blame yourself. Occasionally a patient will contact a lawyer, and continue to talk with you. So don't damage yourself by saying more than you should. In one case, a dermatologist told a patient that cancer might develop as a result of burns received during X-ray therapy; the patient responded by successfully suing the radiologists for the mental anguish of "cancerphobia."[c63]

On the other hand, don't let "patientphobia" keep you from talking or acting where needed. One counselor who failed to warn a woman of his client's death threats against her was sued for negligence when his client killed the woman.[c188] In an analysis of more than 300 psychotherapy malpractice cases, one third revealed negligent treatment, many with the charge of no treatment at all.[125]

Don't jump to the conclusion that you are liable for any and every unexpected bad result. Malpractice doesn't exist just because of a bad result, an incorrect diagnosis, or a better course of action that wasn't taken.

Nevertheless, being dishonest is grist for the legal mill. Never exaggerate a patient's injury to "help" obtain insurance payments. If you overstate the extent of the disability, you may come to regret it when the patient later blames you for the injury. Understating a disability to help yourself or the patient's employer could also land you in court.

Whatever the threat, if you have not yet been sued, keep talking to the patient and the family to help them understand what has happened and what can be done in the future. As with every one of your patients, continue to give your best treatment.

But once a suit has been filed naming you as the defendant, immediately refer the plaintiff to another doctor for continuing care. Don't discuss the case unless your lawyer is present.

"May I see your medical records?" You may learn that a case is pending or possible when someone asks to see your medical records.

Don't try to hide them. Hospital charts are extremely easy for anyone to examine, and copy machines work all night long. The patient's attorney may already have a copy of your records in hand.

Don't "doctor" your records. It's wrong. Besides, handwriting and chemical analysis can show that changes were made at different times, by different pens, and by different people.[72] One physician had already won his case, but it was later found that one page of the medical record was on a form that hadn't been manufactured until several years after the notes were supposedly written on it. A new trial was ordered.[c99]

Don't make the mistake of failing to add or do something you find is necessary. You may make additional notes in the chart at any time, if you label them as such and indicate the time and date of the entry. If a charge against you is pending or only possible, such notes accurately added to the record now can avert a greater loss later.

"The consequence of my action is many times the consequence of my inaction," warns William D. O'Riordan, president of Crisis Communications Corporation, a California-based service to help doctors avoid lawsuits. "From my past family practice and present practice in emergency medicine, I realize that taking those three minutes to look in the chart and record something that is missing, or mistated, could save me from being taken away from my practice for three months in a trial."

Fundamentally, accurate and timely records are a reflection of good medical practice.

"How's the lawsuit coming?"   This may be, as was said at the start, your first and last warning that a legal battle is brewing for you. It's not the end of your life or practice, as we will see in the steps ahead. If you can't head it off at this first step, the next steps can help you meet it head on—and defeat it.

Stop and go signs: who to talk to

Once notified that you are being sued, don't talk to anyone but your insurance carrier and your attorney: Talk through your attorney. Consider the notification the equivalent of being read your legal rights: "Anything you say may be held against you." Before saying a word to anyone, remember this:

STOP TALKING TO

The patient. Once a lawsuit starts, your patient becomes a plaintiff, and you stop being the doctor and become the defendant. Don't talk to the patient or family. It's too late. If they wanted to talk to you, they would have done so. They have chosen to talk to an attorney, so you should also talk through an attorney.

You may be able to get your insurance carrier's lawyer to talk to their lawyer. Don't try to do it yourself. Everything you say will be remembered and can be held against you. You are not yet prepared to talk about your case. The next four steps will help prepare you to talk about it. You will do your talking with the aid of your attorney.

Friends of theirs. Friends and distant relatives of the patient may question you about the case. They have no right to hear about it from you. This is true whether a lawsuit is possible or not—or already in process. If the patient wants them to know about his or her personal business, the patient can inform them directly.

You do and should, however, have something to say to them. Don't be curt or nasty. Be nice. With great courtesy tell the concerned friends and relatives this: "It is my practice never to discuss any patient's case with anyone but the spouse or parents. I would like to tell you about it, but I am not sure the patient would approve. I just want you to know that I must hold this confidentiality out of my respect for my patient's privacy and feelings." Take the conversation as an opportunity to show compassion for the patient, no matter what happened. Your comments may actually help cool their anger.

Friends of yours. "How's the lawsuit coming?" a friend may ask you at a party. You're in good company, among allies. Those who want to hurt you aren't there: they can't hear. This person wants to help you, and you need help. You may feel the need to let someone know your side of the story, especially someone on your side. Opening up to a friend may help you emotionally now, but it can harm you legally later.

It's not good to speak to anyone about the case who doesn't have a right and need to know about it. Stories and rumors move quickly and easily get distorted as they spread. The less you contribute to the spreading, the better. Your answer to your friend's question should be, "Anybody can file a lawsuit."

Other patients. You may be tempted to make comments about a case to other patients, especially if they ask. If the fact that you are being sued for malpractice has been printed in the local newspaper, you may feel the need to start defending your practice immediately, especially since you've begun to fear that other patients may quickly become uneasy. Don't do it. Neither a newspaper nor a patient's bedside is the place to try your case.

When asked by one patient for information about another, invoke patient privilege. Simply explain that any information given by a patient to a physician, nurse, or other health-care provider—or to an attorney for that matter—is privileged, private, and secret. Do not admit guilt or even say that things did not go well. Just say that you cannot discuss another patient's case with anyone else.

You can say, "Yes, I am being sued. Anyone who takes care of patients is likely to get sued. Many of the best physicians in the country get sued, along with architects, accountants, engineers, attorneys, business people, and most anyone else you can think of."

Your patient's lawyer. If a suit has begun, or even if talk with a lawyer has begun, it is time to refer to "your patient's lawyer" as "the plaintiff's attorney." This legal counsel may call to invite you to discuss the case for the purpose of avoiding a lawsuit, stating that if you can explain things or work out your differences, then a charge will not have to be filed against you. Articles in some medical journals have encouraged health professionals threatened with legal charges to attend such "pretrial conferences." Here are three reasons why you should say no to such an overture:

1. Malpractice insurance policies often prohibit such conferences and cancel coverage if you speak to a plaintiff's attorney.
2. You might make admissions or inaccurate statements, not having yet had a chance to review the case with your own attorney.
3. You would be giving the opposition information that could arm their attack and crack your defense. You may think you have such a strong defense that letting the accusers know what you've got will make them back off immediately. But you may actually be showing them where to attack.

Let your insurance carrier be your emissary. This will not only indicate your innocence; it will also show them that you're not willing to give up information so freely and easily.

In any case, you don't want to let them know any more than they already know. Don't give them any more ammunition than they already have. If they're really calling for a truce, let your insurance company's appointed messenger meet them for you.

Don't, however, try to prevent those who are about to charge you from getting access to information that doesn't belong to you. You can't camouflage your charts. You can't put "top secret" on your medical records. They are the property of the hospital. Your patient's lawyer already may have seen a copy of your charts, and now wants—and has the right—to legally obtain the original record as evidence when the court battle begins. You have no legal right to prevent anyone authorized by a patient from examining the medical record.

In some hospitals, the attending physician is always consulted before a record is released. This policy alerts the physician that a case is under evaluation.

The plaintiff's attorney will want to examine, and later bring to court, the original medical record. The "best evidence rule" states that the most reliable evidence must be obtained and presented in court. A photocopy doesn't show as clearly as the original any erasures, different colors of ink, and other subtleties. In court, the original must be produced, or its absence must be explained.[56] This rule applies to hospital records as well as private office records.

Your records should have been made at or near the time care

was rendered. A request for office records should be promptly handled through your attorney. Do not ignore the request—or it will be brought up later in court to embarrass you.

News reporters. If your case is being publicly exposed and, you feel, maligned or misrepresented, you may be tempted to give the other side of the story to the news media.

The first problem with releasing information to the media is that you really can't speak in public about a patient's case. That information is privileged, except in court under certain circumstances.

The second problem is the risk of being sued for slander, even if what you say is true.

The third problem is that anything you say may be distorted, improperly summarized, or misquoted.[165]

You might try to protect yourself against being misquoted by asking that you be allowed to read your story before it is printed. Sometimes the opportunity to review a newspaper story is promised, but because of deadlines the opportunity to proofread the material is lost, and the article appears without your getting the chance to catch any errors.

Co-workers. Doctors, nurses, and other hospital and office staff have no right or need to learn about the case from you. You can gain nothing by talking to them. They may be friends or relatives of the plaintiff or of other defendants. They will likely be, by their chosen profession, sympathetic to anyone suffering from injury or illness. They could take, report, and distort any remarks you make, and make them marks against you in court.

Co-defendants. It is common for more than one health-care professional to be sued in the same case. For example, a patient may bring suit against a surgeon, an anesthesiologist, several nurses, and the hospital because of an injury that occurred during surgery.

If you know that others are also being charged in your case, your first inclination may be to talk to your fellow defendants. But watch out. Don't assume that the others will cooperate with you in your defense. Cooperative strategies are usually complex and must be worked out carefully with your lawyers.

If a co-defendant asks to discuss the case with you, say that you don't yet have a good understanding of how the case should be handled, and suggest that you both meet with your attorneys to plan your joint strategy.

If pushed to talk in private, you should say you've promised that your attorney would be present at all talks concerning the case. If your "friend" objects to this action, the co-defendant may have some ulterior motive.

Co-defendants' attorneys. Speaking to the lawyers or insurance carriers of those being charged with you can also be risky. They may try to place all the blame on you. Refer all overtures and questions from representatives of other defendants to your lawyer. You and your attorney should try to cooperate with the other defendants and their attorneys. The best forum for a mutually beneficial defensive effort is a session in which all parties to the defense are involved.

Potential co-defendants. All the co-defendants may not be apparent at the beginning of a malpractice charge. If you don't know who else might be involved, here are some clues that point to those most likely to be charged:

You can be held legally responsible for the actions of those who are responsible to you and even for those who replace you. This legal doctrine is described as vicarious liability. It can hold you accountable, indirectly, yet legally, for the actions of others. Under this doctrine, called _respondeat superior_ ("let the master answer"), you are responsible for civil wrongs, including malpractice, committed by your employees.

You can incur vicarious liability when your patients are taken care of by another practitioner, whether a partner or not. You may, of course, have another practitioner care for your patients while you vacation or are unavailable for a short period of time. But you must know that the replacement is competent to handle the kinds of problems you do. If you're a specialist, your replacement should be, if possible, a specialist of the same type.

You must make available to your replacement all records and information relevant to your patients. You can be held liable for any damages if you are negligent in not leaving the proper information for when you're gone, or in not providing a competent practitioner in your place.

Even when your substitute is able and well-informed, you may still be held liable for negligence if he or she can be shown to be your employee, rather than an independent contractor.

If you leave instructions telling your replacement how to do certain things, that person is not an "independent" contractor. For example, you may say that Ethel Jones always develops chest pain on Saturday evenings because she gets drunk, that she should be given

Demerol for her pain, and that no workup should be done. If these instructions are followed, and the patient dies of a myocardial infarction, you then are liable because your instructions prevented your replacement from exercising independent judgment.

An emergency department recently was visited by a woman in her 50s with vague chest pain. Her electrocardiogram was normal, as was her physical examination. The attending doctor, her usual physician, told the doctor on emergency duty that the woman was a complainer and often had pains like this. She was sent home.

She returned the next night, feeling worse. Her electrocardiogram showed definite signs of a myocardial infarction. While in the emergency department, she developed bradycardia and hypotension—a slow heart rate and shock. Fortunately, promptly administered treatment saved her life.

In this real situation, the physician who saw the patient the first night was unduly influenced by instructions from her regular doctor. If she had gone home and died, her attending physician might have been held liable, even though he didn't see her that night.

The relationships that can invoke the doctrine of vicarious liability are complex, constantly changing, and different in various states. Your attorney will have to research the most recent law in your state if such issues become important to you.

An example of the complex laws governing vicarious liability is the case of Fure v. Sherman Hospital. In this instance, two physicians were shareholders in a medical corporation. The court held that the physician-shareholder who did not treat the patient could not be held personally liable for the malpractice of the other physician-shareholder. If they had been partners, the nontreating physician would have been financially responsible.[45]

It used to be said that in the operating room the surgeon was the "captain of the ship." The surgeon told all the assistants what to do—and was responsible for what they did. But this old concept of single command is changing into a chain of responsibility.

In most states, the anesthesiologist is no longer seen to be under the control of the surgeon, and so is personally responsible for negligence. Nurses are likewise becoming accountable for their actions. Of course, the hospital that employs the nurses is also responsible for their actions.

The surgeon, however, is usually still considered responsible for the acts of nurse anesthetists. In one case, a surgeon was held not liable for the negligent administration of a drug by a nurse because the surgeon was not in the operating room at the time. The courts said that the surgeon would have been liable if he had been present when the drug was given.[191]

In some cases surgeons may be held responsible for the negligent acts of anesthesiologists under the "captain of the ship" doctrine because the surgeon has the right to cancel a case if anesthesia problems develop. Anesthesiologists also have the responsibility to cancel a case when it is felt the risks of anesthesia are too great. Also, the chief of anesthesiology may be found liable for anesthetic problems because the chief is usually hired to assure safe and adequate anesthesia practices.[138]

START TALKING TO

Your insurance company's attorney. The greatest danger in communicating with your insurance company's lawyer is that you may not do enough of it. As Steps 3-6 will make clear, a long-term cooperative effort with your chief defender is essential if you want a good chance of winning your case. Develop an early, close, continual, and complementary relationship with your insurer's attorney so you have full understanding and trust in his or her actions on your behalf.

If you disagree with how the case is being handled, discuss your differences directly with the company's lawyer. Try to resolve your problems without outside interference. If you can't come together because of personality conflicts or clashes over defense methods, seek legal advice from someone else. You certainly should get another lawyer if you're being sued for more than your policy will pay, or if the insurer's lawyer lets you know the company will not pay.

You could be denied insurance benefits if you fail to report your case as soon as you know about it. Talk to your insurers immediately after you hear you're being charged with malpractice. Other reasons policies do not pay in certain cases are given in Step 15.

Your own lawyer. Turning to an attorney of your own is certainly permitted. The issue is whether it's necessary. If you feel the assigned lawyer isn't doing a good job, you may want to talk to another attorney. You may be tempted to talk to any lawyer who is handy—the one who handles your other legal needs, or a friend who practices law. Don't do it. It won't help. If you really need help, you need a lawyer who is an expert on malpractice.

20　　　　　　　　　　*PREPARING YOURSELF AND YOUR EVIDENCE*

You should certainly consider retaining your own private attorney in addition to the one supplied by the insurance carrier if you're being sued for more than your policy will pay.

You might find yourself in the position of wanting to change a clause of your malpractice insurance policy while a case is pending. This issue usually arises with a question about settlement. You may object, for example, to a clause stating that your case can be settled without consulting you or obtaining your permission. You can talk about it with the lawyer your insurance carrier provided to represent you. That lawyer, however, can't represent you in any dispute between you and the insurance company the lawyer is working for; that would amount to a conflict of interest.[168]

Some attorneys contend that there is no conflict of interest— that the attorney employed by the company has a sole obligation and loyalty to the defendant and cannot be controlled by the company. Others disagree.

In any case, you need to talk first, forthrightly, and at each step along the way of your defense to the lawyers chosen for you or chosen by you to make your case.

There are six good reasons to turn to your own attorney. We have already identified three:

1. The claim exceeds your coverage.
2. The insurer disclaims liability to your case.
3. The insurer suggests a quick, cheap settlement.
4. You can't get along with the assigned attorney.
5. You doubt the attorney's competence in your case.
6. You suspect the attorney is not on your side.

You need an attorney who is with you, with it on the case, and competent, and a company willing to go with you all the way. Some law firms readily review a malpractice suit and evaluate how well the defense attorney is handling it. If you need it, get backup defense.

You do need a lawyer on your side. A few brave physicians have defended themselves in court against malpractice claims. Dr. James D. Rogers of Joliet, Illinois has had five such suits, and he won them all. Over 40% of Illinois physicians are sued each year, and about 75% of those suits are resolved without finding physician fault. So, Dr. Rogers, who has won 100% of his suits, has fared better than the physicians who were defended by attorneys.

Other physicians have not done so well when defending themselves. There are a number of reasons why handling your case without a lawyer is too risky:[284]

1. Conducting a defense requires legal skill, knowledge of legal procedures, and legal judgment. These are generally acquired only through legal experience.

2. Emotional involvement can cloud the judgment of anyone trying to manage his case alone.

3. A conflict may arise in the juror's eyes when the physician who is supposed to be a caring patient advocate aggressively cross-examines witnesses.

4. Some judges have a bias against persons who defend themselves. At least one lawsuit (not involving medical malpractice) has been summarily ruled against without even hearing the arguments in the case.[153]

With the best lawyers on hand, you can begin to get the best evidence in hand. Along with your legal defenders, there is only one other source where you may find teammates to talk to about your case—your hospital.

Your hospital administrators. If the malpractice you're being charged with happened at a hospital where you practice, the administrators should be informed, through or with your attorney, of the pending lawsuit. The responsibility of a hospital for the patients in its care has been established by a large number of court decisions. Many legal precedents make hospitals accountable for the actions of even nonemployees and independent contractors who work within their jurisdiction.

There is often joint liability when a health-care practitioner is sued for actions that occurred in a hospital. For that reason, there's no use in the hospital and the practitioner blaming each other for what happened. Also, nothing pleases a plaintiff's attorney more than having defendants provide evidence against other defendants.

The responsibility of hospitals for patients within their walls has been established slowly over the years. Formerly, hospitals were considered charitable institutions in which physicians completely controlled what was done to patients, at least in theory. The hospitals were immune to lawsuits.

Hospitals are no longer protected from legal charges, though claims to such immunity are still occasionally made, as in the recent case of a hospital in Georgia.[c118] Today it is generally recognized that nurses and other hospital employees have the ability and the responsibility to recognize and correct improper care when they see it.

Probably the best known decision that increased the hospital's responsibility for patient care is Darling v. Charleston Community Hospital. In this case there was obvious evidence of impaired blood flow and infection in a football player's leg caused by a tight cast. The nurses caring for the patient informed hospital administration of the questionable care. Hospital bylaws permitted the administration to require specialist consultation in cases of questionable care. The plaintiff suffered for two weeks before being transferred to another hospital. He eventually lost his leg. The hospital was held independently responsible for the damages because it did not follow its own bylaws when it failed to have a consultant called in.[79]

Because it is an employer, the hospital is responsible for the acts of nurses, orderlies, maintenance personnel, and physicians who are employees. Hospitals have also been held responsible for the acts of physicians who were independent contractors. This accountability occurs when the "doctor holds himself out to the public in such a manner as to cause the patients to assume that he was acting on the hospital's behalf." Thus, it seemed to the patient that the doctor was an agent of the hospital. Also, physicians have been judged to be employees, and not independent contractors, when the hospital has controlled the way in which they practiced. In addition, because physicians must conform to hospital regulations and standards, some courts find hospitals liable for the acts of any doctor practicing in the hospital.[c62]

The public has come to recognize that hospitals have independent status and institutional authority. The hospital employs many physicians, nurses, administrators, therapists, and other personnel. Patients entering a hospital believe that the *hospital* will care for them, not that nurses and other hospital personnel are acting independently to provide their care.[c11,c19]

Patients going to a hospital emergency department also believe that the hospital is accountable. In many cases plaintiffs tried to hold hospitals responsible for negligent acts of emergency physicians. If the physician is an employee of the hospital, the hospital is clearly liable. If the physician is an independent contractor, the situation is less clear. Some courts have held that the main consideration is to what extent the hospital controlled the way the physician worked.[239]

Another consideration is whether it is made clear to the patients that the physicians are an independent group of practitioners having little connection with the hospital. This "independence" is hard to maintain when the physicians are practicing in the hospital, working under hospital bylaws, and ordering procedures performed by nurses and technicians who are controlled by hospital protocol. Nonetheless, there are cases in which doctors working in hospital emergency rooms were judged to be independent contractors.[c13]

In one case, in which emergency physicians were independent contractors, the Ohio appellate court nevertheless ruled that the hospital could be liable for the negligence of those doctors. The court stated that the hospital could not insulate itself from liability for negligent acts that occur in its emergency room. The hospital was a full-service institution, of which the emergency unit was an integral part. Since the hospital held itself out as a full-service provider, it couldn't deny responsibility for the failures of its emergency physicians.[c99]

Another hospital was held liable for a doctor acting as an independent contractor as the aftermath of a patient being admitted to the hospital from its emergency department for treatment of a nosebleed. Over the next six days he developed delirium tremens and turned violent. The emergency physician was summoned to the patient's room. Drugs were administered. The patient later suffered a cardiac arrest and died. Both the physician and the hospital were sued for wrongful death.

The appellate court said the hospital could be found liable for the negligence of the physician. Applying the theory of ostensible (implied) agency, the court held that the physician was an apparent agent of the hospital because the hospital held out the physician as its employee by providing his services for dealing with emergencies within the institution.[c35]

Accordingly, nursing supervisors can be held responsible for their individual acts. The employer will be responsible for the supervisor's acts under the principle of *respondeat superior*. A supervisor will usually not be held liable for the negligence of the nurses being supervised, because the supervisor is not their employer. But an overseer would be held liable if the supervisor knew that the nurse assigned to a task was incompetent to perform it.[219]

Teaching institutions also are responsible for the decisions of their students. In such a case, a first-year psychiatry resident released from the ward a patient who had been considered a suicide risk. The court determined the resident at that point in training was not able to make such decisions without supervision.[c47]

Although federal, military, veterans, and public health service hospitals were immune to negligence suits prior to the Federal Tort Claims Act of 1946, that act makes it possible to impose liability on the federal government for negligent acts of hospital employees and independent-contractor physicians working in its hospitals. The negligent act must have been performed as part of the health-care professional's official duties. But the government is protected from liability in certain situations, including intentional acts.

As noted earlier, hospitals are liable for the damages caused by their employees. If the hospital, however, was not negligent and paid damages, it may sue the employee to recover those damages. This doctrine of "subrogation" says that the party who has paid an obligation that the negligent person should have paid, has a right to be reimbursed by the negligent person.

Whether you are an employee or consider yourself an independent practitioner working within a hospital, you and your attorney should be talking and working with hospital administrators at the first hint of a legal problem. As in dealing with other defendants and their attorneys, it's best to communicate with hospital administrators with the full knowledge, approval, and assistance of your attorney.

If you think of anyone else you may need or want to talk to, talk it over first with your attorney.

First legal moves and papers

The first reaction to receiving a legal summons is often panic. For a health professional, the panic can be compounded by tension and depression over the threatened loss of money, pride, prestige, and patients. If a newspaper publicizes a claim against you, the loss in patients may be immediate.

Don't panic. A legal paper may seem like a fatal missile dropped in your lap. Receive it instead as a messenger, a first chance to meet the one who is charging you.

FIRST NOTICE: HOW TO TAKE IT

Call your carrier.   Being served a summons or subpoena marks the first step of a lawsuit. You get it from a lawyer, and you must get a lawyer to respond. When you're served papers, immediately notify your insurer, and do nothing without your carrier's orders. You have a "carrier," so don't try to be your own messenger.

Notifying your carrier when papers are served may not be soon enough. Many malpractice insurance policies state that the physician must immediately notify the insurance company of any incidents that might result in a later lawsuit. Failure to do so could, according to the wording in some policies, eliminate the carrier's responsibility related to the suit. One of us did report an incident in which a suit was threatened, though there could not have been much in the way of damages. Detailed documentation that would have been helpful in defending the case was obtained by the insurance company. Until the statute of limitations ran out, the company periodically sent questionaires concerning the incident. The incident had to be listed as an open case when insurance was applied for with another carrier.

It is valuable to investigate and document cases in a timely fashion because it is *common* in defending malpractice cases to find that no one can adequately remember what happened by the time the suit is filed.

First move, first mistake? Before you examine any papers served against you, examine the serving. Expect and look for mistakes on the part of the plaintiff's attorney. If you receive a legal document, note when and how it was served. If done too late or improperly you can use this to your advantage. Write down when, how, and by whom the papers were served. Describe the person who gave them to you. With that information, your attorney can determine if the serving was in time and in order. If not, you must document the errors. If you find mistakes in the first move against you, document them. But don't tell the opposition. Turn instead to your lawyer and to other defensive resources.[3]

Don't take it personally. Nothing personal is meant by these papers. The patient probably hasn't even seen them, much less read and approved them. The legal phraseology is fairly standard. The papers sent to you use words and phrases made relevant to your case by a few words filled in, much like a lease with blanks filled in.

Read it carefully. Documents, forms, and legal procedures vary from state to state. Your attorney will handle all the documents described in this chapter, but will need your help. You have an indepth knowledge of medicine and of your particular case and can therefore be of great assistance to your attorney. As a defendant, it's in your own best interest and for your own peace of mind to find out and understand everything that's going on with your case and to work with your lawyer in handling the forms. That means reading every document and form.

Stay civil, not criminal. A medical malpractice case is a civil lawsuit, not a criminal case. Your opponents are suing to get your money, not to put you away. In criminal cases, guilt must be proven beyond a reasonable doubt; in your civil case guilt may be proven by a preponderance of evidence. In a criminal case, the defendant is accused of violating a written law; in your case, you are charged with failing to perform up to the accepted standard of care. Because the burden of proof is less for civil than for criminal cases, absolute proof is not needed in malpractice litigation.

The forms we are about to view are the means by which civil charges of negligence are made. The information they contain will be used to establish and present your guilt. They are important to you, even if the opposing attorney doesn't seem to treat them seriously. Make sure you and your attorney do.

Stay on time.   It's common for attorneys to put off preparing their cases until shortly before they come to court. Two of us have been asked to consult or testify in several malpractice cases when the trial was only a few weeks away. The attorneys had little understanding of the medical background relevant to the case. There was no well-planned strategy.

Such last-minute, unorganized legal scrambling occurs with both prosecution and defense attorneys. If that is your situation, you and your attorney should be quick to notice it. A fair settlement might be made with little further wasted time and expense, if the opposing attorney can be shown that he or she has a lot of work to do in order to understand and prepare the case against you. And you, of course, should get your own case in order and on time.

One well-known case had been under investigation for eight months. The week before the statue of limitations (the deadline for filing a suit) would have run out, the plaintiff, who had suffered a broken arm after a cardiac arrest, filed a complaint listing as defendants the cardiologist who had read the electrocardiogram, the radiologist who read the X-ray, and others who were indirectly involved with the case. The inappropriateness of this last-minute, frantic charging allowed the defendants to succeed in a countersuit.[68]

The case also serves as a warning to all health practitioners, showing just how vicious—not to mention unappreciative—some "patients" can be. Consider what happened:

The plaintiff had suffered a massive myocardial infarction. He collapsed at home, then in the emergency department sustained a cardiac arrest. At some point during his resuscitation, he suffered a fracture through the surgical neck of the left humerus. It was in satisfactory position, so no realignment was needed. He recovered, and then sued everyone connected with saving his life.

Resuscitation was unknown thirty years ago. It is more than taken for granted today. If miracles are now expected of you as a healer, you should at least expect a lawyer to meet minimal legal procedures and schedules. If the lawyer is late or incorrect, note it.

As you begin to move through the first legal steps and papers, remember that they're not deadly. You're not being called on for resuscitation. You'll only be called on to research your case to the best of your ability.

FIRST PAPERS: HOW TO HANDLE THEM

Here are descriptions of the first legal papers you'll probably see— and how to deal with them:

Attorney's lien. This is the notification that the plaintiff's attorney will get a contingency fee. Sometimes the defendant first learns about the malpractice case by receiving a notice of the attorney's lien.

Although a lawyer has been engaged, a suit may not have begun. You may still have time to get your insurance carrier to communicate with the plaintiff's attorney and settle the case without a suit being filed. Some attorneys will use the lien as a quick and inexpensive way to get a settlement without ever involving the courts.

Summons. Used to inform the defendant that an action has been started, the summons is usually physically given to the defendant. In some jurisdictions, it may be given to an adult member of the defendant's family, left at the defendant's home, or mailed to the defendant. It may require the defendant to appear at a certain time and place to answer the complaint in the action.

Complaint. Also known as a petition, the complaint lists the allegations made against the defendant. It contains the *ad damnum* clause, which specifies the amount being sought. This amount is usually much greater than it should be. Certainly, no one will ask for less than they think they should get. Additional factors discovered during investigation of the case, or further deterioration of the patient, may make the high claim seem more reasonable by the time the case goes to trial.

The complaint may contain a summary of the case. It may also list the various legal theories (reasons for suing) on which the case is based. Possible theories of action include negligent treatment, lack of informed consent, and breach of contract.

The complaint usually contains a large number of allegations, and it can be amended. Often, many of the charges are insignificant or untrue. They may be included to confuse or enrage you. During the trial, plaintiff's attorneys usually concentrate on very few of the allegations made in the complaint.[133] The skillful attorney will be fully prepared to pursue these points at great length.

How do you know which points to be able to discuss? You must be prepared to defend yourself on every specific claim. You should, however, concentrate on those areas that state how you came to injure the plaintiff.

Pretrial motions.   Instead of answering the complaint, your lawyer may file motions with the court. These motions are an effort to end the lawsuit immediately. Such motions can claim, for example, that you were improperly served notice of the suit, that the action was brought in the wrong court, or that the statute of limitations had run out. Sometimes the plaintiff's attorney can correct the mistake.

Demurrer.   As a motion to dismiss the case, a demurrer states that even if all of the claims are true, the plaintiff still has no right to sue you. It asserts that the complaint does not demonstrate a reason why damages should be paid. It may, for example, point out that the complaint does not declare that you directly caused the plaintiff's injury; therefore, you cannot be charged as the defendant.

Answer.   The answer is a document written by your attorney in response to the complaint. You should help your attorney prepare the answer. To do so, write an answer to each point in the complaint.

Interrogatory.   In some states, a list of questions, referred to as an interrogatory, may be used in any civil case. Its purpose is similar to that of a deposition: to obtain information relevant to the lawsuit before a trial begins. The interrogatory is useful to the plaintiff's attorney in asking questions that require the defendant to make investigations in order to answer. A physician may be asked, for example, how many times he or she had performed a certain operation.

Verification.   This is the act and fact of signing a statement such as a complaint, answer, or deposition. Verification is thus a confirmation of the correctness and authenticity of a document. So be especially careful in reading any paper before you sign it. It will be used in court.

Counterclaims.   A counterclaim may be included in the answer to claim payment for services provided to the patient. Such an action may be unwise, depending on the overall strategy of the case.

Impleader. The answer may contain an impleader or third-party complaint. The impleader is a complaint against some other party believed to be responsible (at least in part) for the patient's damages. The new party brought into the suit may be hospital personnel, the hospital itself, physicians, the manufacturer of equipment involved in the injury, or anyone else.

A patient with a cast, for example, may develop circulatory impairment because of swelling inside the cast. And the swelling could lead to permanent damage. In one such case, the nurses involved noticed that the plaintiff's fingers were blue and swollen, yet they failed to notify the patient's doctor. It was determined that the hospital, but not the doctor, was responsible for the patient's injury.[c166] In this case, if the patient's attorney had not originally named the hospital as a defendant, the physician sued would have needed an impleader in the answer. This impleader would have named the nurses and their employer, the hospital, as defendants in the case.

Another case of one practitioner naming another as a defendant is the nurse-anesthetist who feels under the control of the surgeon. The Ohio Supreme Court recently found that a surgeon did control a nurse-anesthetist. The nurse was an employee of an anesthesia group. Nevertheless, the court felt that the surgeon was responsible for the nurse's actions under the doctrine of *respondeat superior*. The nurse was judged to be a borrowed (loaned) servant.[c15]

The court emphasized that it did not want to revive the "captain of the ship" doctrine, under which surgeons are responsible for everything that occurs in the operating room. The facts, nevertheless, indicated that the surgeon actually was directing the actions of the nurse-anesthetist.

The Darling case established that nurses must observe the care being given, and also brought up the concept of nurses reporting negligent medical care to others.[c53] If there are no established protocols for reporting, a nurse is unfairly caught in the middle when given inappropriate orders. Accurate notes can help the nurse in such situations, but they don't solve the problem completely.

The Darling case also paved the way for the introduction of certain documents as evidence. In Illinois, where that case was tried, admissible evidence now includes the American Hospital Association's standards for hospital accreditation, the bylaws of the hospital being sued, and hospital regulations of the State Department of Public Health under the State Hospital Licensing Act.[275] Similar standards are gradually being accepted in federal and other state courts.

Courts are frequently finding hospitals responsible for the actions of private contractors such as emergency physicians. Courts have felt that institutions are not simply physical facilities where physicians practice, but rather hold themselves out as able to render quality medical care. Emergency physicians who are independent contractors are increasingly seen as being in an ostensible agency situation. Under ostensible agency, a hospital is vicariously liable for negligent acts of a physician if the patient believes the physician is an agent of the hospital.[c119] Ostensible agency has served as a basis of hospital liability, even when specific private contract provisions exempted the hospital from liability for the negligence of emergency physicians.[c81,248] Ostensible agency has been recognized in some cases, but not in others, so it is best to check recent decisions in your state.

Legal measures of joint responsibility. Two legal tests help determine which parties are responsible when there are one or more defendants.[143] The "but for" (or "sine qua non") test for causation applies when there is one defendant. The plaintiff must prove that "but for" the negligence of the physician, the damage would not have been done. The "but for" principle does not require that the physician's act be the only cause, nor even the last or nearest cause of the patient's injury. It is enough if the act concurs with some other cause acting at the same time which in combination brings about the injury. Therefore the act of the physician need not be "the" proximate cause, but simply "a" proximate cause of the injury.

If the "but for" test were applied in cases involving multiple defendants, each defendant might escape responsibility because the conduct of another defendant would have been sufficient to produce the same result. Therefore, when multiple defendants are involved, attorneys use the "substantial factor" test. The "substantial factor" test asks whether or not one's negligent conduct was a substantial factor in causing an injury or death. If the plaintiff would have been injured or would have died despite the conduct of the defendant, then the conduct of the defendant was not a substantial factor. Two or more defendants' actions can be substantial contributing factors in bringing about death or injury.[143]

Demand for a bill of particulars. This document can be sent by the defendant to the plaintiff's attorney asking for specific information about the claims made in the complaint. The demand for a bill of particulars is often served after the initial answer to the complaint has been given. When received by the defendant, the bill of particulars will define more precisely the issues in the case.

Pleadings. These are formal allegations by the plaintiff and the defendant that set forth their claims and defenses. They include the complaint, the answer, the counterclaims, and the bill of particulars. The pleadings set general limits on the scope of the case, though they can be amended.

Once the pleadings are complete, either party may request that the judge settle the case on the basis of the pleadings alone. Called a motion for judgment on the pleadings, this request is seldom made—and is usually unsuccessful.

Summary judgment. A motion for summary judgment can be made at any time before as well as during the trial. A summary judgment is a decision by the court that there is no provable case against the defendant. Such a judgment is not based on an analysis of the facts, but upon a showing by the defendant of an absence of facts that could be used against him. There may be, for example, no proof that he caused the patient's injury.

Knowing the purpose of those forms will help you prepare your case so that all facts, theories, and witnesses are known prior to the trial date.

While surprise witnesses and dramatic new information can occasionally appear, as happens in some movies, your preparation should be so thorough that the trial is only a presentation to the jury of known material.

With an understanding of the content and intent of the forms and procedures up to the point where the legal contest begins, you're ready for the next step: facing the specific charges and those who make them.

Checking the charges

A defendant in a malpractice case faces two kinds of charges: legal and financial. The latter are no less vital than the former. For the plaintiff's lawyer they are inseparable. So let's look at the payoff system behind the attacker, and then check the legal charges.

ADDING UP THE TAB

Contingency fee. Free legal services may motivate a patient to sue. Common practice in malpractice cases is for an attorney to charge the plaintiff nothing if the case is lost, but to collect a fraction of the settlement if it's won. In some cases, the plaintiff's attorney can come away with several hundred thousand dollars as the agreed-upon "fraction" of the settlement. With such carrots held before them, the lawyers can be highly motivated.

Such big money and motivation are made possible by the contingency fee system. Although the patient eventually may have to pay the costs of carrying out the lawsuit, the fee-free chance of legal help makes making a charge most attractive.

But you and other potential defendants have no contingency-plan option. The law generally considers it illegal for doctors and other professionals to work on a contingency-fee basis.

Doctors, for example, can't set their fees as expert witnesses on a percentage of a potential malpractice award. A surgeon can't offer

34

to charge no fee for an operation if a patient dies, but then to take a percentage of the patient's future earnings if that patient survives. In contrast, a disabled patient can fairly win support for life from a malpracticing surgeon, but the winning attorney will often take one-third of the award.

Under the contingency-fee system, millions of dollars each year go to lawyers involved in malpractice litigation. Health-care costs are increased because physicians have high malpractice premiums to pay, and they order more tests and X-rays than are necessary. These costs are then passed on to patients.

Nevertheless, the contingency-fee system is not likely to be changed. It benefits lawyers and patients. And it even benefits you as a health-care practitioner by holding down the number of malpractice suits filed because lawyers won't invest their time and money to conduct a case unless there's a good chance of winning.

The leading argument for the contingency is that many plaintiffs could not otherwise afford to fight for their rights in court. A retort is that such plaintiffs could still afford good counsel if there were a ceiling on the contingency fee. A 1980 Florida law was passed to promote "reasonable" payments to plaintiff's attorneys who win cases. Section 768.56 of the Florida statute states that "the court shall award a reasonable attorney's fee to the prevailing party in any civil action which involves a claim for damages by reason of injury, death, or monetary loss on account of alleged malpractice." The law does not, however, clearly define a reasonable payment. After the law went into effect, a circuit judge awarded $4.4 million in fees to a plaintiff's attorney in one case.[3]

High cost of incompetence.   When a practitioner is shown to have acted incorrectly, what is done to correct that incompetence? Usually nothing. Lawsuits are often conducted to show that the practitioner made a mistake, or was not careful. If the practitioner is shown to be incompetent in general, even that fact does not change the situation, because lawsuits result only in monetary compensation.

When a doctor loses a malpractice case, he or she does not lose the license to practice medicine, and is not ordered by the court to seek further training.

No periodic testing is required to maintain a physician's license. Patients would benefit if some minimal standards of knowledge were required for doctors and other health professionals who want to keep their licenses year after year. This testing could be done with minimal expense by making every physician take an examination periodically, as if trying to become certified. Such exams already exist and are periodically updated by each of the specialty boards. But taking them is not required.

General practitioners, for example, could be required to take the Family Practice Board test. Physicians working in operating rooms would take the Surgery Boards. Those in emergency rooms would have to pass the written test for certification by the American Board of Emergency Medicine.

In one of the rare examples of disciplinary action, a physician was found guilty of gross negligence after performing a tonsillectomy and adenoidectomy on a four-year-old boy. The mother claimed she called the physician because the boy was bleeding at home after the operation, and was told to bring the child to the office in the morning. She followed those instructions, and the boy collapsed and died while being examined by the physician. He denied being told the child was bleeding. An action was filed with the Board of Medical Quality Assurance in California. The panel found him guilty and imposed, but stayed, a penalty of suspension from practice for six months and probation for one year.[c3]

The end product of a malpractice suit is the exchange of money, not the rehabilitation of the practitioner.

Physicians are not in power. The ability to give and revoke licenses lies in state governments. Individual physicians or peer review committees can find physicians to be incompetent, but they have a hard time doing anything about it. And, they sometimes get sued in the process of trying to reform or remove an incompetent physician.[75]

"Physicians have repeatedly demonstrated that they will diligently and aggressively perform the peer review function while at the same time brining to it an expertise and knowledge which enhances the quality of the process..." Despite this record of achievement in the peer review process, organized medicine continues to be denied a truly meaningful role within the primary area of conduct control, namely the state's discipline system, and the status of a physician's professional license under the law of the state. Physicians must continue their efforts to achieve this role under our law.[195]

How payments are set: What are the damages? A patient has the legal right to be compensated for injuries and suffering resulting from negligence. Damages are determined by considering a number of items. Original medical bills must be taken into account, as must subsequent bills resulting from further injury. The value of lost time and wages must be calculated, and the patient may be compensated for pain, suffering, mental anguish, and loss of consortium. Punitive damages may be awarded if there was an element of malicious intent or fraud on the part of the practitioner. (Most malpractice insurance policies won't pay punitive damages.)

The cost of death. Relatives may sue for monetary loss caused by the patient's "wrongful" death, as well as for the patient's pain, suffering, loss of services, and expenses.[3]

If a person is not expected to be gainfully employed, however, it is unreasonable to award damages for lost wages.[c82] A $475,000 damage award for the wrongful death of a 57-year-old man was not supported because he lacked earning capacity due to prior disability. In another case, a patient who had been diagnosed as a paranoid schizophrenic was killed after being permitted to leave a Veterans Administration hospital. Damages for subsequent services and nurture to his family could not be recovered in the resulting wrongful-death suit they entered.[c176]

Have your attorney check into current state laws concerning who may file a wrongful death suit. For example, in Florida the *only* person who can file a wrongful death suit is the personal representative who sues on behalf of the estate and all of the beneficiaries, including the children of the patient.[4]

Minus consortium. Price tags have also been put on loss of consortium, the various services of a spouse. These include companionship, sexual relations, and material services. Also considered in such cases are expenses incurred because of the spouse's injury.[c57]

The state of Michigan has recognized damages claimed for loss of parental consortium. In a case in which a parent was negligently injured, it was determined that a child deserves love, comfort, and various services from a parent. The child may also suffer emotional problems because of the loss of a parent's love and affection.[c18] Massachusetts is the only other jurisdiction to recognize this cause of action.[c64] Others have declined to recognize parental consortium and have suggested that their legislatures rule on the subject.[203]

In one suit against physicians for the wrongful death of his wife, a man claimed damages for loss of consortium, and the court would not allow the fact that the man had remarried to be brought up in the courtroom.[c40]

What price pain and suffering? Some people think that awards for pain and suffering are unfairly low; others believe they're ridiculously high.

"Pain and suffering" is a legal phrase sometimes used to cover all intangibles. It may not be possible to literally equate the phrase to the words as used in medicine, but the medical meaning of the terms will be considered below.

"Pain" is subjective. An unbearably excruciating pain to one person may be tolerable to another.

When the cause of the pain is removed, a person may continue to suffer.[105] So suffering may be decreased if you know your pain is not of a serious or permanent nature. Conversely, the suffering due to pain may be increased if you believe it to be the sign of a serious condition.[47]

Collecting for pain and suffering is big business. A Florida state constitutional amendment that would limit pain-and-suffering damages to $100,000 was to be decided in the November 8, 1988 election. Legal professionals decided that the best strategy to keep voters' attention away from the issue of the cap was to keep silent about the issue. Therefore lawyers and the Florida Bar Association delayed a $600,000 television advertising campaign for personal injury cases until after the election.[84]

ANTICIPATING CHARGES

Unfortunately, no meter can be applied to determine if patients are undergoing pain. An emergency physician sees many people who are experiencing both pain and suffering. Fewer than one percent of the patients seen suffering the severe pain of an acute myocardial infarction cry or scream. Many who come for emergency care saying they're in severe pain, particularly those who scream and cry the loudest, are often found sleeping if given no medication and left alone for 30 minutes.

While some patients minimize their pain and suffering, others deliberately exaggerate their symptoms, or malinger. Thus, it's often difficult, if not impossible, to examine a patient and tell how much pain he or she is having.

How much more difficult must it be to sit in court and obtain a measure of past pain and suffering? The situation is clouded even more because the patient is seeking compensation based on the amount of pain and suffering. Pain is "sold" to the jury. Jurors then determine the dollar value of suffering.

The law compensates plaintiffs for pain, suffering, and, less frequently, mental anguish. These terms have special meanings.[122] Pain is a sensation we're all familiar with. The initial perception of pain is fairly constant from one individual to another. Reactions of individuals to pain, however—how they cope with it, and what the pain means to them—vary greatly. Thus, physical pain can invoke anxiety and various forms of behavior.

One of the great teachers of emergency medicine, Peter Rosen, advises physicians to periodically scan the "emergency" waiting room, looking for a patient who is sitting quietly. This patient is often seriously ill. The patient who is screaming may not be very sick. The loud patient at least has a lot of energy to spare.

The patient's pretraumatic personality plays a larger role in his "suffering" than in his perception of pain. Suffering includes anxiety, insomnia, fear, and emotional upset, and may persist after the original pain has ended. The psychological implications of a traumatic event may be more important than the actual physical injury. A person may feel a loss of health, youth, or self-image due to a limp or disfigurement. This loss can lead to posttraumatic stress disorder. Many people with stress disorder have dreams in which they relive their traumatic experiences.[258] If a patient had problems from an even remotely similar injury, or if there are compensation payments to be settled, the stress disorder may be prolonged.[288]

Measuring mental anguish medically. "Mental anguish" is the term applied to the discomfort associated with a sense of alienation. It can occur after disfiguring injuries, such as loss of facial features. When connected with a physical injury, the mental anguish legally includes both the mental sensation of pain and the accompanying feelings of distress, fright, and anxiety.

Psychotherapists are often hired by plaintiffs or defendants to evaluate psychic trauma.[214] This evaluation can occur in tort (civil wrong) cases, including malpractice suits.

When acting as an expert witness, a psychotherapist should limit testimony to determining and presenting the facts of the case. The witness should try to learn about any mental and physical problems the patient may have had prior to the alleged psychic trauma, the traumatic event itself, and the condition of the patient since the trauma.

The therapist who examines a patient in a psychic trauma case may give an informed opinion concerning causal relationships.[113] However, proving that psychic trauma caused a certain physical or emotional problem is difficult. Any therapist who claims that such a causal relationship exists can and should be cross-examined closely. It's more appropriate for the court, guided by expert testimony, to decide causal relationships.

Psychological labeling. A jury may be impressed when a therapist puts a label on the patient's symptoms, making things look definite. If labeling is attempted, your defense must do five things:

1. Ask the psychotherapist to define the label, which is, in effect, a diagnosis.
2. Verify the existence and definition of the diagnosis in the *DSM—III (Diagnostic and Statistical Manual of Mental Disorders of the American Psychiatric Association—Third Edition)*.[64]
3. Point out to the jury how the patient does not fit the diagnosis, if that is the case.
4. Show the jury, if true, that the diagnosis is often associated with compensation-related cases or malingering. Such diagnoses include traumatic neurosis and causalgia.
5. Remind the jury of other causes contributing to the condition, such as pre-existing problems, and failure to seek treatment early enough or at all.

The *DSM—III* is recognized by many psychiatrists, psychologists, and social workers as the definitive book on the characteristics of psychiatric conditions. It lists diagnostic criteria and serves as a necessary reference for anyone involved in a case in which a psychiatric problem is an issue. Although well known and often quoted, it is not completely accepted by all authorities. The conditions it and other texts cite as sometimes associated with malingering or the seeking of compensation are at other times real.

The *DSM—III* states that a posttraumatic stress disorder is "the development of characteristic symptoms following a psychologically traumatic event that is generally outside the range of usual human experience." Characteristic symptoms include re-experiencing the traumatic event and withdrawal from the external world. Watch out for a claim of such rare and extreme signs of stress in patients and in any legal charges made against you.

Under the *DSM—III* definition, a posttraumatic stress disorder would not result from such common experiences as loss of a loved one, illness, or monetary loss. It may result, however, from assault, rape, military combat, or torture. Rarely will events like automobile accidents produce a posttraumatic stress disorder.

The traumatic event may be re-experienced in dreams or wakeful states of remembering. In addition to nightmares, symptoms of the posttraumatic stress disorder include autonomic arousal (hyperalertness, insomnia), impaired memory, difficulty in concentrating, depression, anxiety, aggressiveness, and impulsive behavior. If symptoms begin within six months of the trauma and don't last more than six months, remission is likely.

The *DSM—III* warns that malingering should be suspected when there is:

1. A medicolegal context, such as when a lawyer requests a medical examination of one of your patients.
2. A discrepancy between claimed and observed disability.
3. Lack of cooperation with evaluation or treatment.
4. An antisocial personality disorder.

Circumstantial evidence may sometimes be used to disprove proximate cause in cases of trauma-induced stress disorder. In the case of Cohen v. Weber, for example, an instrument fell into a patient's bronchus during root canal work. She claimed this kept her from seeing a dentist for four years, and that the delay adversely affected her dental condition and caused further loss of teeth. But the defense established that the patient had a history of dental neglect. The court ruled that the alleged malpractice did not proximately cause the pain, suffering, and further loss of teeth. The (circumstantial) evidence of prior neglect "proved" that she would not have gone to a dentist even if the accident had not occurred.[c48]

ANSWERING CHARGES

Seeing your defense in the right perspective requires that you have a firm understanding of (a) the difference between malpractice and criminal cases, and (b) the four pillars necessary to uphold a malpractice charge.

A preponderance of evidence.   The degree of proof required in a malpractice suit is not as demanding as the proof required in a criminal case. In a criminal action, allegations must be verified "beyond a reasonable doubt." In a malpractice case, allegations must be substantiated by "a fair preponderance of the evidence."

Impeachment: the fifth pillar of malpractice.   As noted in Step 1, a malpractice action must be supported by four pillars. In brief: The duty to treat must have been undertaken; that duty must have been breached; damage must have been done; and the breach of duty must have been the immediate cause of the damage. Attacking attorneys sometimes try to construct a fifth pillar: impeachment.

To impeach a defendant in the eyes of the jury means to dishonor or discredit the person. When a practitioner is impeached, his or her testimony becomes less credible. Jurors may be led to believe the defendant is callous, incompetent, lazy, and uncaring.

Some plaintiffs' attorneys hold that convincing a jury of a health-care practitioner's guilt requires more than showing a breach of duty that led to damages. Always necessary, in their view, is to also degrade the defendant. They don't want the jurors to wonder: Why should a competent, caring, honest doctor, who simply made a mistake or judged a complex situation inaccurately, be financially burdened with a large settlement? They want to show that the accused is trying to distort the facts.

Health professionals may take such an accusation personally. Plaintiffs' attorneys usually see it as just doing their job.

A strategy may be devised to disarm and discredit you as the defendant. Don't be surprised or angered. Be prepared.

The worst thing you can do is "lose your cool" or show anger at a personal attack. An emotional outburst will only show the jury just how out of control you can be in a tense situation. That's just what the plaintiff's attorney hopes to demonstrate. The defaming attorney will be skilled and experienced enough to seem calm and innocent of malice when making damaging insinuations against you. The defamer need not be reasonable. As the defendant, you must.

Reasonable care. Health professionals have an obligation to use a reasonable degree of care in attending to their patients. "Reasonable" is defined as the degree of care a prudent practitioner would render in the same situation.

A licensed nurse may be sued for failing to use the degree of skill and care expected from nurses of similar background in similar situations. A nurse can also be sued for performing acts not permitted under the state's nurse practice act, which defines what nurses are allowed to do. Some practice acts allow a nurse, under certain restrictions, to make a diagnosis.[219]

Should a nurse do something not authorized by the state's practice act, that nurse could be held liable for injuring a patient by failing to act with the degree of skill a physician would be expected to have.[c16,119]

Negligence is based on facts that were known or knowable at the time of the treatment. This principle applies to knowledge of the patient's condition as well as knowledge of medical practice, or the "state of the art," at the time care was rendered. Negligence is not judged in light of later changes in medical practice or after additional evidence about the patient is acquired (unless it was reasonable to anticipate that information).

Malpractice is a type of negligence. Whatever the sources of charges against you, don't neglect the legal sources that may work for you. They include:

1. Decisions from state and federal courts.
2. Statutes, ordinances, and regulations.
3. Treatises on the law, including law and bar association journal articles and reports.[79]

One of the first things to do when hit with a lawsuit is examine the pillars that uphold a malpractice case to see if they apply to you.

Did you undertake the duty to treat? You acquire that duty when you begin treating the patient. That happens in various ways.

A woman comes to your office because of a cough; you listen to her lungs and give her a shot. A mother calls your office at 4:30 p.m. because her child appears to have the flu; you suggest a clear liquid diet and an examination in the morning in the office. A man calls the emergency department to ask if he should come in to have a five-day-old sore throat checked; you tell him that he should get medical attention the next day. In all these cases, a duty to treat, an implied contract, has been established.

Did you breach that duty? Look at each of the above examples. In the first case, you examined the patient and gave, let's assume, appropriate medication. No X-rays were taken. Let's say the patient had pneumonia and died that night. Whether you breached your professional duty may be for the jury to decide. They will consider the following factors:

1. Did you note the breath sounds?
2. Was the respiratory rate, a sensitive indicator of respiratory difficulty, recorded?
3. Were X-rays or arterial blood gas measurements taken? (These expensive and sometimes harmful tests would not be indicated unless the patient appeared to be ill.)

Just how ill must a person look before further tests are taken or before the patient is admitted to a hospital for therapy with oxygen? The jury will also answer that question. Their decision will be based on the standard of care that would be provided by a reasonable, careful, prudent physician. Just how a prudent physician would act in similar cases is told to the jury by expert witnesses—physicians brought to court to answer questions relevant to the case.

The jury may decide there was adequate documentation to indicate that the patient did not look dangerously ill, and it was unpredictable that the patient would die. Such a decision would be more likely if an X-ray, showing minimal pneumonia, had been taken.

Was your breach of duty the immediate cause of damage? The jury may decide that, because her respiratory rate was double the norm, you were negligent in not X-raying the patient. Even so, if the autopsy showed that she died of a stroke, there would be no causal connection between failure to take an X-ray and occurrence of the stroke. She would have died even if an X-ray had been taken and she had been hospitalized. Therefore, while there was damage (death) and negligence (no X-ray taken), there was no <u>proximate cause</u>. Your negligence did not cause her death; you cannot be held liable for the damages.

Telephone treatment.   In the second case, you told a mother on the telephone how to treat a child who supposedly had the flu, advising her to give the child a clear liquid diet and come to the office in the morning. The child was vomiting and had a slight fever.

While such symptoms are obviously characteristic of the "flu," they are equally characteristic of meningitis or appendicitis. If the child's appendix ruptures during the night, the mother may delay seeking treatment, because she was told to follow a certain treatment.

What if the child then develops peritonitis and dies? You—or a nurse you employ who gave the same advice—could be held liable. The jury will have a number of factors to consider.

A duty to treat was established when the child was accepted as a patient and treatment was given.[c56]

Does a nurse's license permit treatment of conditions such as vomiting in children? Laws vary on this. In most states, nurses are not licensed to diagnose and treat such conditions.

What if the nurse was licensed in the state to diagnose and treat children with vomiting and fever? The question would then be: Did the nurse practitioner act in a reasonably prudent, careful manner in making her diagnosis and in prescribing treatment?

Whether you or a nurse you employ prescribed the treatment, the jury will consider the adequacy of the physical examination. Certainly, vomiting indicates that the abdomen must be examined. Was it palpated for tenderness? Was a rectal examination performed to search for a retrocecal appendix? Were the standard blood count and urinalysis tests relevant to an abdominal condition taken?

In this case, the answers to all these questions would be to your detriment. You didn't even see the patient. It was telephone diagnosis and treatment.

Much of pediatric practice in this country is still done by telephone, and that usually works out quite well because most of the time children don't have appendicitis or anything else seriously wrong with them.

Now consider the third case, the patient who called about a five-day-old sore throat. While most sore throats don't warrant immediate investigation, those that cause patients to seek emergency care are worth taking a look at. It may be a mistake to tell the caller he need not seek medical attention until the next day.

While physicians in office practice may not see many life-threatening or even serious sore throats, physicians with emergency care experience do. This situation can be an emergency because many patients delay health care until they are severely ill and only then seek medical help. Often, the only place they can get attention on short notice is an emergency department.

Emergency treatment. Many patients avoid medical care as much and as long as possible. They call a doctor or come to an emergency facility only when a problem gets so bad they can't stand it anymore.

Be on the lookout for people with diseases of insidious onset who unknowingly have serious problems when they call or come to see you.

Watch out as well for patients who deny they have a problem. Terribly afraid of medicine and doctors, or of illness, they, too, will come to you only when their problem is unbearable.

A large number of people avoid medical care until severely ill because of the expense involved.

Other patients have been seen by their private physicians, but later develop complications. One example is the patient with a sore throat who develops a life-threatening peritonsillar abscess.

Thus, the emergency physician—or any health practitioner with an open office or phone—may be confronted with an appeal for help from someone who delayed medical care until severely ill. Patients wait because they are stoic, don't like medicine or physicians, are afraid to find out about their disease, want to avoid expense, have already been seen by their regular doctor and are dissatisfied, or later took a turn for the worse.

That last category of patients may have been misdiagnosed, or their condition may not have been apparent earlier. If improperly treated, they may bring malpractice actions, as might all those classes of patients introduced above.

Emergency physicians are likely to see patients whose problems are unusual and neglected to the point of uncommon severity. The need for a physician to "see" all patients who arrive for treatment in an emergency facility has been recognized by the law in some states.[43]

In Polischeck v. US, it was decided that it is malpractice for a paramedic in an emergency room to treat a patient without having the patient or the chart reviewed by a physician. In this case, the paramedic did not recognize a subarachnoid hemorrhage. It was concluded that a physician would have made the right diagnosis.[c145]

As in emergency rooms, patients in delivery rooms should be examined by physicians, not just by nurses. In Samii v. Baystate Medical Center, for example, a patient in labor was put in the delivery room. She was attended by a nurse who was to call a physician only if a medical problem existed. A resident physician was called after seven hours of labor. The resident detected fetal distress and performed an emergency cesarean section. The baby was stillborn; the hospital was found liable.[c165]

An emergency physician may get to see several peritonsillar abscesses a year and a case of Ludwig's angina every two years. Many general practitioners with ten years' experience have never seen a case of either infection. Yet patients with these life-threatening infections call or come to doctors complaining of a "sore throat."[c66]

As stated by Paul Van Pernis, you should "make it a habit to diagnose only in person."[275] Much of medicine in this country is practiced over the telephone.[41] It is successful and very cost-effective in the vast majority of cases. But if something goes wrong, your diagnosis is difficult to explain to the dozen citizens of the jury sitting in judgment.

RAISING THE STANDARD OF CARE

Health practitioners used to be held to a standard of care requiring that their degree of skill and knowledge be similar only to that of other practitioners in the same community. This principle was known as the locality rule.

That locality "rule" now is usually held to be invalid as far as errors of professional judgment are concerned. This is because all practitioners have access to books, telephones, and continuing education, no matter where they live. Instead, the locality rule today addresses the issue of availability and adequacy of health care in rural communities.[144] Under the locality rule today, a physician in a rural community generally cannot be held liable for failing to give treatment that is unavailable or impossible because of inadequate treatment facilities. However, when time permits, the physician has the legal duty to refer a patient to another hospital or area where the facilities are available.

Even when the locality rule was held as an adequate standard of care, the need for a careful physical examination was recognized; "Although a doctor of medicine practicing in the back woods of Kentucky is not required to have the same knowledge, skill, and equipment as the university professor attached to a medical center in a large city, nevertheless, no one is excused from performing a physical examination upon a patient, since this is a basic requirement in the practice of clinical medicine irrespective of specialty, locality, or equipment."[79]

In general, practitioners in all geographical locations are now expected to keep abreast of developments in medicine and practice as competently as fellow practitioners anywhere. The locality rule may still be used, however, as a defense in cases where transportation wasn't feasible or under other uncommon circumstances.

Don't confuse usual and ideal standards of care. The usual or expected standard of care is that care which would be obtained from a reasonable practitioner. The ideal standard of care is not performed in real life.

For example, it might be "ideal" to perform an exercise cardiac stress test and glaucoma screening on all patients over the age of 40. This is not usually useful and is not cost-effective. Therefore such testing is not the usual or expected standard of practice. Thus, the usual standard of care is not violated simply because a 40-year-old man with no risk factors or symptoms does not receive a glaucoma or cardiac stress test.

However, in the state of Washington, two ophthalmologists were found negligent for failure to test for glaucoma in a patient under the age of 40. "The problem with these cases is not that they have on a few occasions resulted in an unfair and probably wrong decision in favor of a plaintiff. Rather, it is that they have sent a message to the legal and judicial communities that medically established standards of care need not be applied."[1]

A recent $500,000 malpractice award involved a 40-year-old male smoker with a cholesterol level of 325 mg/dl and hypertension.

He suddenly died after requesting and receiving a physical examination. This case suggests that stress testing in *high risk* individuals of this age does constitute practical and cost-effective care. While some plaintiffs' attorneys might try to use this precedent to imply that the standard of care requires stress testing in all men 40 years of age, a careful examination of the facts of this case will show otherwise. Physicians sued for failure to perform stress tests will need to point out differences between such cases and their own.[87]

Despite these unusual cases, you can usually count on being held only to the standard of care practiced by most competent practitioners in your field.

Optimal and actual standards of care are also quite different when it comes to screening mammography, which is used to detect breast cancer. Only 10% of women who should be screened according to recommended guidelines are screened. "Clearly, the standard of care in the community is to not follow the guidelines, although optimal care would cause the community to follow the guidelines."[199]

Similarly, a study reported that many drivers involved in automobile accidents and seen in a teaching hospital were found to have blood alcohol levels well above 100 mg/dL, but none received referral to alcohol abuse teatment programs.[51]

When a supposedly standard practice is identified, it is often easy to find data to refute the standard. It is difficult to tell what this means when one is trying to deliver therapy, but when trying to defend oneself, it is definitely useful to have a variety of different acceptable treatment protocols. For example, it is no longer necessary to give sodium bicarbonate to many cardiac arrest victims.[269] And, the value of aminophylline in treating severe, acute asthma is being questioned.[160] Other well-publicized controversies and changes in recent years have included the use of steroids and calcium chloride. Many other less-well-known studies exist on almost any subject, and these may be helpful for your defense.

Research the medical literature well. Extensive literature searches can be carried out in your home (or your hospital's library) with the use of computer search services. The one which will usually be most relevant is that provided by the National Library of Medicine.[108]

If you now feel that most of the real or potential charges discussed so far don't or won't apply to you, don't feel too relieved. Keep in mind that you must face not only the charge, but also the charger. So use this last check to prepare for the charging lawyer, who is certainly preparing for you.

PREPARING FOR THE PROSECUTING ATTORNEY

Chances are that your patient's attorney, if at all competent, will learn more than you know about the medical subject relevant to your case. That lawyer will become an expert in the appropriate narrow area of medicine, surgery, psychiatry, or dentistry.

Why not? The prosecuting attorney stands to make several hundred thousand dollars for proving that the treament you gave was not proper or up to the standard of care. Besides, like you, that attorney also has a duty to the plaintiff and doesn't want to be sued for doing an inadequate job—a form of legal malpractice.

Knowing the patient. The plaintiff's attorney will first get to know primarily his or her weaknesses and strengths, and then teach the client to testify.

Not all lawyers are skilled in getting to know their clients. They're not always "streetwise" enough to see through lies, half-truths, distortions, or exaggerations. If the plaintiff's attorney can't get the truth from your former patient before the trial, your attorney may be able to do so during the trial when all the facts are carefully examined.

Getting the medical record. The plaintiff's attorney will study medical reports from the case as well as all obtainable medical data on the plaintiff. The attorney may get that history from insurance companies, hospital records, and the plaintiff. Such older records can help prove or disprove the newness of the damages.

You can use older records, too. They may reveal something about the patient's past behavior, propensity to bring lawsuits, or accident-proneness. Such information may be used to cast doubt on the testimony of the patient in pretrial negotiations, but would be difficult to place in evidence during a trial. Your attorney would therefore be wise in searching out such information early.

To document the extent of the injury or disability, the plaintiff's attorney will first obtain photographs, X-rays, and medical records. The hospital chart will be copied and may be rearranged chronologically. Even parts of the chart that physicians sometimes fail to look at, such as lengthy routine nurses' notes, will be examined to see what happened. The original chart will be scrutinized for signs of changes, such as the use of different colors of ink and crowded writing. (Writing on small office or emergency department records with several pens in your pocket can make the chart appear to have been modified.)

The prosecuting attorney will have the plaintiff examined by expert witnesses and other doctors to determine the true extent of the injury or disability. Some physicians spend most of their time evaluating people for disability—some for plaintiff's attorneys, some for insurance companies.

Records and bills pertaining to hospitalizations, treatments, drugs, and time missed from work will be obtained. The patient may be asked to keep a log of pains and problems, the number of pills taken, crutches and braces used, and other measures of suffering and expense.

Be sure to obtain and review the following sources of information about your patient:

1. *Hospital records* (often kept in separate files in various places in the hospital): the patient's medical chart; records from peer review committees, pharmacy, X-ray, nursing office, emergency department, laboratory, outpatient department; incident reports, fetal heart-monitoring strips; social service and counseling records; letters to administration; autopsy report; hospital policy and procedure manuals; staff privilege records; consent forms (sometimes on the back of pages in the emergency department chart); notes of interns and residents; medication records; vital sign sheets; fluid balance records; anesthesia and operative reports; recovery room records; discharge summaries.

2. *Your office records*: progress notes; letters to and from referral sources and consultants; letters and forms to and from insurance companies and employers concerning payment, disability, and condition.

3. *Laboratory records*: reports of all radiological examinations and laboratory tests. If you can't get original X-rays, they should be studied and copies obtained. Photographs of X-rays made with a closeup instant camera and the proper lighting will sometimes show critical features quite clearly. The useful photographs can then be enlarged.

4. *Information documenting the patient's condition before and after your treatment*: records from hospitalizations; employment; state department of motor vehicles; insurance companies; and the military.

5. *Others sources*: ambulance and police records documenting condition and degree of cooperation; pharmacy records documenting medicines taken; physical therapy records documenting condition and treatment; medical records from other

hospitals and physicians; investigation documenting employment, drug and alcohol use, criminal record, previous lawsuits, insurance claims, previous hospitalizations; coroner's report.

Knowing about you. The prosecuting attorney will also learn about you. Your professional reputation, behavior during deposition and other conversations, participation in previous legal cases, and what others, such as your patients, say about you will all be investigated.

If you have a criminal record or another problem, you might prevent that fact from being presented in court because it would prejudice the jury.

The plaintiff's attorney, in one case, was prevented from introducing the doctor's prior conviction for falsifying narcotic-type drug prescriptions for self-administration.[c192]

The plaintiff's attorney will find faults in your treatment. A good lawyer can find some fault in almost any case, and can find an expert medical witness who will explain it to the jury. Given the knowledge that something did go wrong, you can always think of another test or precaution that may have made a difference.

Current medical literature can also be used to show that your treatment was incorrect. Medical literature presents problems because it includes so many contradictions, disagreements, controversies, conflicting studies, and special case reports. Accepted standards of practice keep changing with time.

We will deal with "medical evidence" as it comes up in the steps that lead through the presentation of your defense. Before that, however, you must take the next step to get your lawyer and evidence ready.

Getting together with your lawyer

You must be thoroughly prepared before you present yourself or your evidence to a judge or jury, but you won't be unless you work as one with your lawyer. You both must become experts on all the medical and legal issues at hand. You must know the relevant medical background material, the facts of the case, and the contents of medical records and depositions of other defendants and defense witnesses. You must also learn what you can about the plaintiff, the plaintiff's attorney, and any witnesses they will call to testify.

Clearly, the all-important need to work so closely requires you to have the utmost confidence in your attorney. Ask yourself these three questions:

ASK

Is my attorney doing what needs to be done?   Even if your lawyer is working with you on all the study, research, and investigation, the answer depends on how quickly it's being done. If it's not done well in advance of a scheduled deposition or trial, you're in trouble.

Unfortunately, not all attorneys are as concerned about preparing cases as they should be. They may be busy with other cases. They may think they know the subject better than they actually do. They may simply not be interested.

An insurance company lawyer may have other disincentives to move quickly. Your insurance carrier may use a local law firm, far from its own offices, to handle your case. That makes it more difficult for the company to stay on top of the case. Also, the attorney you end up with may be working on salary rather than on a contingency-fee basis, and so be much less motivated to prepare the case than the plaintiff's attorney.

You may even find it difficult to know who is working on your case, to say nothing about how well or quickly. You may also learn that the lawyer you're working with now isn't the one who'll try your case in court. Some consider it a mistake for a defendant to work with an assistant on preparation and meet the trial lawyer only shortly before the trial.[173] Nevertheless, this switching is standard practice in many cases because of the division of labor necessary in complex malpractice suits. An attorney skilled in courtroom procedure doesn't have the time to do all the research for every case and also make all the court appearances.

Am I doing all I should to work with my attorney? Just as your lawyer should work closely with you to understand and prepare your case, you should be a vital asset and an expert assistant to your legal defender. Your counselor will do the same things the prosecutor will: Investigate the facts, learn about all of the players, and get versed in the medical or surgical background matter and particulars of the case.[16]

Try as they may, however, lawyers can never fully grasp the physiology underlying the case. No lawyer has a good comprehension of medicine or surgery, unless that lawyer is also trained as a physician. So your lawyer needs your clinical expertise.

What can I do if my attorney isn't working out? If your attorney isn't doing a good job, take action. First, state your concerns. Be specific about what you think should be done and when it should be done. If the attorney doesn't do it, ask to have another member of the law firm consult on the case. If this doesn't clear up the difficulties with your current counsel, insist that your insurance carrier obtain a new lawyer for you.

To convince your carrier to get you a new attorney, you must at each step have made your comments, suggestions, requests, and demands in writing to your assigned attorney. You can then easily document the problems. Although you may need to hire a separate attorney to consult on the case, it's far better to have your insurer provide adequate legal counsel.

Does my attorney have a conflict of interest? In one case we heard about, several physician-defendants in a case all had insurance with the same carrier and were represented by the same attorney. This attorney tried to put all the liability on the one physician with the lowest policy limits. This ploy could save the insurance carrier millions, but made problems for the physician with inadequate policy limits.

Such conflicts of interest have been recognized in the past. For example, in August 1986, the ethics committee of the Florida Bar cited these rules.[39]

> A lawyer shall not permit a person who recommends, employs or pays him to render legal services for another to direct or regulate his professional judgment in rendering such services.
>
> A lawyer may represent multiple clients (insurance carrier and physician) if it is obvious that he can adequately represent the interest of each, and each consents to the representation after full disclosure of the possible effect of the representation on the exercise of his professional judgment on behalf of each.

INVESTIGATE

The plaintiff. Your patient's medical history should be thoroughly investigated. Insurance companies have common files on claims made, amounts paid, physicians seen, and hospital admissions. The history, physical examination, or X-ray report from an old hospital chart may give evidence of a pre-existing disability.

Knowledge of previous illness or injury can be of use to your defense in at least three ways:

1. The record may show the plaintiff had similar problems in the past. If the patient has walked with a limp since an accident several years earlier, for example, that would prove the current disability was not caused entirely by your more recent care and treatment.

2. You may find an unreasonable number of injuries or unsuccessful treatments. This suggests that the plaintiff tries to become injured, doesn't cooperate with treatment, or, at the very least, isn't careful. The poor result of your treatment will be seen in a better light if six other doctors also had bad results with this patient.

While such evidence is not admissible in court, it can serve to destroy the trust the prosecuting attorney placed in the plaintiff, and thus lead to a quick and easy settlement. You can also benefit from the distrust factor by showing that the plaintiff brought several suits in the past for a variety of problems. This implies a habit of suing.

3. Your investigation of the medical past may reveal a cover-up of old injuries or illnesses. They may not be contributing much to the present disability, and the plaintiff doesn't want the jury to think they are. One way to impeach is to let the plaintiff deny having any such injury or illness in the past; then present evidence of the earlier problem. Caution: If the evidence is brought up before trial or in the opening statement, the opportunity to impeach is destroyed.

It may seem cruel or sneaky to impeach a patient in such a way. Some plaintiffs' attorneys, however, believe that winning depends on contrasting the morality and innocence of the patient with the immorality and guilt of the physician.[243,244] You must combat that tactic whenever the facts are on your side.

A plaintiff who has been severely intoxicated may have his or her testimony discredited in the eyes of the jury. The intoxication may have been due to alcohol or drugs. Try to show that the patient was intoxicated at the time the events testified about occurred. A jury wouldn't expect either the power of observation or the memory of such a patient to be accurate.

Sufficient documentation is available to show that people have inaccurate, if any, memory for events that happen when they were drunk. So if you can reveal that the plaintiff had been drinking at the time of the alleged acts of malpractice, show it.

Many other conditions, including epilepsy, head injury, hypoglycemia, drug usage, psychosis, and acute emotional stress, can also impair memory.[28,112,197,283]

Even showing that the plaintiff was irresponsibly intoxicated at any other time, for whatever reason, may be enough to cast doubt on the testimony. The implication: A "witness" who has been severely intoxicated is irresponsible.

You can use the same tactic with a repeatedly intoxicated plaintiff arguing that he or she wasn't going along with your treatment, and was therefore at least partly responsible for the bad outcome. If you can show that the plaintiff was failing to take medicine, wear a splint, watch for signs of infection, or follow other instructions, you can invoke the principle of contributory negligence. That may even put the blame for the failure of treatment totally on the plaintiff.

Medical records. The prosecuting attorney will try to prove your negligence based on the facts of the case. The facts are documented in the medical records, photographs, X-rays, and correspondence associated with the case. You and your attorney must know what those documents show.

Don't give the original charts or X-rays to anyone; too often they won't be returned. When you suspect a lawsuit, consult your lawyer before sending documentation to anyone.

Obtain copies of hospital charts and X-rays as soon as there's a hint of a problem. X-rays are easily copied, but the copies are usually not as revealing as the originals.

Previous rulings. If the patient's case has been brought up in a previous suit, the present claim may have already been decided in your favor. For example, one physician sued a patient for unpaid bills. The patient's defense was that the care was negligent, and he claimed minor damages because of the alleged malpractice. The patient lost, and the case was never appealed. The patient later developed a debilitating condition arising from the illness in question in the lawsuit. In this situation, the patient would not be able to again sue for malpractice. Under the doctrine of res judicata (the thing has been decided), a final jugment on the merits of the case has already been made. For the res judicata doctrine to apply, the parties and evidence in the two lawsuits must be the same. The same claim must be alleged, and the same findings of fact and judgment must be involved.[147]

The extent of the injury. The plaintiff's claim to having suffered some disability or harm is sometimes incontestable. If the patient loses a limb or dies, for example, the question then is: Was your negligence the cause?

But in other cases, the patient has not been injured as badly as claimed, and you must find out and show that the real injury falls short of the claim. Here are three ways to do it:

1. *Videotape the plaintiff.* Nothing will end a trial in your favor faster than visual evidence of the "disabled" plaintiff vigorously moving about. But when you show such a tape in court, be ready to hear the opposing attorney say that the plaintiff was only painfully trying to get exercise and rehabilitation.

Most lawyers know that excuse for the activity of a supposedly disabled patient. It's quoted in many books on courtroom procedure and trial tactics. To negate it, use a portable video camera with a zoom lens to tape the plaintiff on a number of occasions before the trial. And be sure to get a lot of close-up shots of his face.

Be careful if you hire private detectives to do the taping or any other investigating. They're not all equally skilled or experienced, and if they're discovered, the results can be embarrassing to you. Even if the investigator isn't discovered in the act, the evidence of spying will still be displayed in court.[72]

Since almost everyone does things that would be embarrassing if made public, few people like the idea of spies watching private citizens. And the jury may not think kindly of you when they learn that you sneaked up on the opposition.

So if you plan to reveal in court any secretly-acquired information—tapes, photos, or anything else—be sure it contains dramatic and conclusive evidence in your favor.

2. *Get the facts on the patient's past.* You may, for example, be able to prove that the plaintiff was making a smaller salary before the injury than the amount now being claimed for lost earnings due to the injury.

3. *Document the current extent of injury.* Your physical examinations recorded in the patient's chart should verify what the examiner finds the plaintiff's condition to be. In any case, a careful and complete examination of the patient by an expert witness close to the time of trial can help your defense.

If the plaintiff gives inconsistent physical evidence while being examined by an expert, the examiner should record that discrepancy. Your expert witness should not, however, make judgments about the patient's motives by saying the patient was malingering. The observer should record just what is seen. Don't settle for an incomplete examination. If the patient resists or rushes through it, have the examiner record that the patient was uncooperative.

The plaintiff's attorney may also hire expert witnesses to examine the client for the degree of disability. Some physicians do a lot of examining and little practicing of medicine. They examine those who sue for malpractice and claim to have been injured on the job or in an automobile accident. To impeach the testimony of such a witness, you can use the tactics described in Step 6. Be sure to make the jury aware that the witness practices little medicine, is highly paid for serving as a witness, and got different results examining the plaintiff than you and your expert witness.

Caution: Efforts to impeach a witness can go too far—or backfire. Insurance companies and their expert witnesses have sometimes been accused of conspiring to prove that a patient was not disabled. In one such suit, a $5.1-million award was made to the patient, a supposedly disabled truck driver; $100,000 for compensatory damages, $5,000,000 for exemplary or punitive damages.[12]

The opposing attorney. Find out as much as you can about the plaintiff's lawyer. In coming after your money, the prosecutor may come to court in cheap suits and worn-out shoes, thereby appearing to be poor and put upon. Your lawyer can deal with that during jury selection by asking prospective jurors if they're familiar with the opposition's Park Avenue office or any of its twelve secretaries.[16]

Be sure to examine other cases the plaintiff's lawyer has tried and look for the answers to these questions:

1. What were the tactics?
2. Were they honest?
3. How were witnesses questioned?
4. What methods were used to present prejudicial evidence, upset defendants on the stand, and make the jury sympathetic to the plaintiff?

The opposing expert witness. Supposedly, experts are unbiased witnesses who, for a reasonable fee, explain to the jury the facts of medicine needed to understand the case. When a case is so clear and obvious that the average person can tell right from wrong without help from an expert, you can apply the doctrine of _res ipsa loquitur_: "the thing speaks for itself." In such instances, no professional witness is needed.

A second type of case in which no expert is needed is that in which the physician essentially admits his guilt. For example, in one case a patient's vagina, cervix, and urethra were lacerated during childbirth. The physician described his delivery as a "tight mid-forceps rotation," one in which he used "excessive pressure."[c76,251]

A third type of case in which expert testimony is not needed to prove negligence involves "the common knowledge exception." The plaintiff argues that the medical practice in question can be found to be negligent by using the "common knowledge" of a lay person, such as when a patient is physically beaten in order to calm him down. This doctrine came into use when there was a "conspiracy of silence": few physicians willing to testify for plaintiffs' attorneys. In such a case expert testimony may still be required to show causation.[163]

Res ipsa loquitur does not apply in most cases. Most things are not obvious; they need to be explained. The background material and basic medical facts are hard to understand and may even be controversial. No two cases are exactly alike, and the response of the patient to the treatment may have been influenced by many outside, unusual factors. How can lay jurors understand all that? The expert witnesses will explain it to them.

Expert witnesses are supposed to be impartial, but in practice each side usually hires an expert of its own.

The expert witness should be of the same standing as the defendant. So if a general practitioner is being tried for a poor job of suturing, another GP, not a plastic surgeon, should be the expert witness. And if a nurse is being prosecuted, a nurse of similar background should advise the jury on the relevant standard of nursing care.

Be sure to investigate the expert who will testify against you. Your attorney should talk with the witness' peers and employers, and to personnel in hospitals with which he or she is associated. That must be done with care. Under no circumstance should those people be inconvenienced, nor should implication be made that the witness is doing something unethical in testifying. Impugning the ethics of a fellow professional would be a terribly unethical move on your part. You can't harass an expert witness in any way.

If the witness is a physician, check credentials in the *Directory of Medical Specialists*. Your state medical examining board can tell you about any disciplinary problems.[63] Check the *Index Medicus* to see if the witness has written any articles your should read that may relate to your case.

In cooperation with malpractice insurance companies, the Defense Research Institute lists medical witnesses and lawyers who have come up against them in the past. The Association of Trial Lawyers has a similar listing. From those sources, you should obtain copies of depositions, court testimony, and personal information about those involved in your case. Finding conflicting testimony from previous cases—or conflicting information in published articles—may enable you to discredit an expert witness who testifies against you.

Your attorney. The last person you may think needs investigating must be checked out: your own attorney. Ask the same four questions given above to check the record of the opposing attorney. Watch out too for a possible conflict of interest. A conflict exists if someone is biased for or against an issue when neutrality is supposed. One physician sued his insurance company because it settled a malpractice case without his permission. The law firm that represented the physician in this suit also represented the insurance company. A conflict of interest arose because the law firm was suing the same insurance company it was employed by.[c161]

REVIEW

In going through the preparations listed above, be sure your attorney understands the case in medical terms as well as in legal terms, and has done everything that should be done well in advance of the deposition and trial. Understand what your attorney has done, not only for your own information, but to make sure it's been done properly from a medical point of view.

Medical records. Go over the entire medical record. Personally review all papers relevant to the case. Dictate all hard-to-read medical records. Arrange the information chronologically, go over it with your lawyer, and use it as a data base in your defense.

Included in your record, and clearly identified as such, should be your own recollection of events not in the written record. Everything you remember should be compared with and added to the written record. You'll be questioned in detail about your recollections during the deposition and during the trial, so collect your thoughts ahead of time.

You and your attorney must also know the medical data relevant to your case. This background includes knowing the content of appropriate textbooks and journal articles.

Legal precedents. You must also know about court cases relevant to yours, because the courts try to rule on the basis of previous decisions—*stare decisis*. Similar circumstances may have led to a judgment establishing a precedent that affects your case.

Statutory laws are passed by legislation. But legislators can't think of everything, so courts have to decide right and wrong when no relevant statutory law exists. Such court decisions establish case law, also called common law. A decision made in another state is less binding than one made in your own, but it can still be applied.

You and your attorney should search the legal literature for cases with elements similar to yours. Look for any legal precedents, arguments used, methods of presenting evidence, means of cross-examining witnesses, and trial tactics. Computerized listings of cases make the search much easier than it used to be. (The "Case Citations" documented in this book are a good place to start.)

Standards of care.   Test all aspects of your care against recognized standards of care. Current standards can be inferred from articles, texts, recent court cases, the *PDR (Physician's Desk Reference)*, and package inserts of medications.[215]

Be prepared to defend the adequacy of your history, physical examination, and laboratory workup. Be ready to defend your use of medications, or your failure to use them. Be able to answer all the allegations in the plaintiff's complaint.

PRACTICE

You must practice your speaking, and how you'll be answering questions. Step 8 on the art of testifying should be studied carefully before you try to give a deposition or testify in court. It's not enough to be honest and know the answers to all possible questions. You must speak in such a way that the plaintiff's attorney can't distort what you say. You must please and convince the jurors. They will likely take offense, for example, if you refer to the plaintiff as "that patient" rather than "Mr. Smith."

Testimony.   Your attorney should hear you practice answering all the key questions you may be asked. Listen to your counsel's opinion on what you say and how you say it. Are you exaggerating? Are you playing down or overstating an issue?

If the jurors feel you're insincere or trying to bend the facts, your case will be weakened. Much rides on the subjective impression you make on the jury.

Your counselor is in a better position than you to judge court matters and manners. Even though we health-care professionals communicate with people every hour in our work, we're often found to be poorly equipped with the type of communication skills needed in the courtroom.

Practice giving a deposition with your lawyer before the actual deposition. Also practice going through direct testimony and cross-examination before your trial. This will help you prepare for what's coming and prevent embarrassing or damaging surprises in the courtroom.

Practice giving a deposition and testifying in front of a video tape recorder. Play it back. Let your lawyer and peers intensely question and even insult you. Questions can be drawn from Douglas Danner's *Pattern Interrogatories: Medical Malpractice.*[61]

You can learn more about the reality of testifying by reading depositions, watching real trials, and volunteering to be a defendant at a moot court in a law school.

"Have you practiced your testimony? Have you spoken to anyone about this?" You may be asked those questions to imply to the jury that you've prepared made-up, false answers. It's unfair to be asked such questions, but if you are, stay calm. And don't become argumentative.

Your answers to such questions must be strongly stated, with no show of embarrassment: "Of course I have discussed this case at length with my attorney."

Tactics. The tactics to be used during your deposition and trial must be prepared ahead of time. While virtually all the information in this book might be classified as tactics for preparing your case and going to trial, here are some of the key strategies to use in the courtroom.

In the end, the jury will decide your case, so present yourself and the facts of the case with this vital principle in mind: Presenting a complex, logical, airtight argument will only confuse the jury and make them think that you and your attorney are intellectual snobs.

Reduce complex arguments to a few main points—basic facts presented over and over again to the jury. Stating your key argument in a few brief sentences is ideal. Doing it in one longer, yet clear, sentence is even better.

That capsule of facts must be presented during your attorney's opening statement. It must be reviewed when you undergo direct questioning, recalled when expert witnesses are questioned, and restated during your attorney's closing statement.

A jury is exposed to many hours of complex testimony, and only a small fraction of what is said—only facts repeated in a variety of ways—will be remembered.

The prosecuting attorney will also hammer away at the jury with the plaintiff's own facts and accusations. So it's important to deny those charges repeatedly—and in as many ways as possible—throughout the trial.

Controlling the pace of testimony is an effective ploy. Let the conversation move slowly when points you especially want the jury to understand are being made. Let those facts sink in. Never assume that, once a logical point is made clearly, it will be remembered. The jury can't immediately separate important findings from many unimportant details. Things you want remembered will have to be restated and re-emphasized.

Try to reduce the effect of the plaintiff's friends or relatives. They may testify about what you did or said, or about the disability of the plaintiff.

On cross-examination, your attorney should make a point of asking them if they are friends or relatives. They should then be asked if they want the plaintiff to be paid for whatever happened. While this question may not totally impeach such witnesses—and the plaintiff's attorney will object—it shows the jury that they may be biased. If witnesses for the plaintiff are obviously biased, obnoxious, or irritating, keep them on the stand as long as possible to let the jurors figure it out themselves.

If there is a weak point in your case, consider bringing it out in the open yourself. This prevents the prosecutor from making a surprise exposé of it in cross-examination. If your lawyer, for example, questions you to show that your notes were written a day after you saw the patient (and after he died), the prosecutor won't be able to "reveal" later that you were trying to conceal your late charting.

When the plaintiff or another witness gives false testimony, it may be better not to challenge it then and there. Leave the inaccurate testimony as is, so your attorney can ask the witness in several ways about the information to help the jury remember it as something the witness is definite about.

Then, at the critical summing-up point—or at least after the witness has fully and irreversibly committed to the key details—contrary evidence can be presented to the jury. That's much more embarrassing to lying witnesses than immediate confrontation which cuts off the flow of inconsistent facts and gives the witnesses opportunity to change their minds.[212]

Abraham Lincoln applied that tactic when he elicited specific details from a witness who claimed he saw in moonlight a shooting from a great distance. Then Lincoln used an almanac to show that the moon had not yet risen at the time of the shooting.

If you catch a false statement, don't distract your lawyer from listening to the ongoing testimony. Give your observations later. Leaning over to confer prevents your lawyer from seeing and hearing what's going on, makes the jury think you're anxious about something, and tells the plaintiff's lawyer the points of testimony you're concerned about.

As a defendant, you probably won't be given the choice between having a jury or a judge decide your case. The initiator of a suit usually insists on a trial because juries tend to make higher awards out of sympathy for injured plaintiffs, or dislike for insurance companies.

Insurance companies, however, often insist on a jury trial. They foresee less chance of 12 citizens making an unreasonable judgment than of one judge being biased in some way.

If you get the opportunity to let a judge decide, consider both the past decisions of the judge and the rules of evidence that would apply. Evidence may be more freely admitted before a judge than a jury, because a judge is less likely to be prejudiced by it. The past criminal record of either plaintiff or defendant probably would not bias a judge as it would a jury.

This step has introduced you to the first important things you and your attorney must do to prepare your case. The next step will take you through the final preparations.

Being and beating experts

No one can be an expert on everything. But you'd better be the world's greatest expert on one thing—your own case. You'd better get together with co-defendants and expert witnesses. You'd better be ready, with your attorney, to answer all accusations and to refute the expert witnesses and evidence against you.

ON THE DEFENSE

To knock down the four pillars that support a malpractice charge (duty, negligence, damage, and cause), you'll need to set up solidly these four corners for your case: yourself, your lawyer, your co-defendants, and your expert witnesses.

Yourself. You can—and must—be your own best expert. Follow all the preparations and actions detailed in Step 5. Gather your evidence, learn it, and be ready to use it. Plan your defense and practice it. Be definite, not defensive. Decide before your deposition or trial just what you did and didn't do while treating the patient. Be definite when you speak about what you did. Be ready to fill any gaps in the medical records or your memory.

If you're being sued because of an infection that developed following a laceration, and the prosecuting attorney sees that the chart makes no indication that the wound was cleansed, you may be asked: "Did you clean the wound?" Don't answer: "I probably did because I usually do." You don't remember the case, but you do know that you always cleanse wounds before suturing. Just say: "Yes, I did clean the wound."

The prosecutor may counter: "How do you know that you did? It's not recorded on the plaintiff's chart." Simply answer: "I never suture a wound without cleaning it."

<u>Lack of evidence does not make a case</u>. <u>Facts do</u>. <u>Facts are found in testimony as well as in written evidence</u>; Testimony and evidence are often contradictory, and the jury must decide which and what to believe. The jury weighs evidence that's stated and shown, determines the "facts," decides if you are liable, and levies the amount of damages you must pay.

The jury doesn't decide questions of law; that's the function of the judge and the court. When there's no jury, the judge also decides questions of fact. Even in a jury trial, however, the judge determines such issues of "fact" as whether evidence is admissible or whether a certain witness is competent to testify as an expert.

The question of malpractice by negligence can involve issues of both fact and law. So know the facts and the law before you face the judge and the jury.

Your lawyer. The expert who can best help you put fact and law together is your lawyer. Step 5 showed you what to prepare and how. But you must decide, with your attorney, which tactics and defenses best fit your suit. (Steps 10-12 give you specific court cases and defenses you might use.) Nevertheless, it's your lawyer who must come up with and thoroughly prepare your best defense before you go into the courtroom.

Your co-defendants. If others are being sued with you, don't try to make your stand alone. Your strategy should have all defendants working together. The plaintiff's attorney hopes that each defendant will give evidence to show how the others were guilty. That's one reason why multiple parties are sued in so many cases. When one defendant gives evidence against another, the plaintiff's attorney saves much time, money, and bother in researching and presenting the case. For that same reason, parties not actually being sued are sometimes called to give depositions.

Preparation of your case involves finding definite reasons why you were not responsible for the plaintiff's damages. Proof of negligence depends on the four pillars—duty, breach of duty, damages, and proximate cause. You can prove your innocence by showing that any one of these elements was not present in your case.

You may be able to show that you had no duty to treat the patient. You may reveal that, even though you had a duty, you—or a co-defendant—did your duty. You may be able to show that the patient was not damaged. If there was damage, you may be able to prove that your actions were not the proximate—or sole—cause of that damage.

Your expert witnesses. An essential part of your defense strategy will be to have at least one expert witness who knows the subject matter well, agrees with your intrepetation of the facts, can speak well in court, and is honest. Be careful in your selection. Don't get one who totally agrees with every single thing you did, or who doesn't take a reasonably open-minded, balanced view of the case. The jury will see such an obviously one-sided witness as biased. But if the jurors see an expert who is truthful, impartial, and able to see aspects of both sides of the case, they'll likely believe the testimony.

Medical experts can provide you with many services besides testifying in depositions and in court. When you're being sued, discuss the case in detail with your expert. You'll be able to tell him more about the case than is contained in the medical records. The expert should be able to tell you which aspects of the case are of importance legally.

Be sure that you and your attorney don't withhold information or slant the facts of the case in an attempt to convince your expert that you weren't negligent. The facts will eventually come out. If the expert learns embarrassing information while being deposed by the opposition or while testifying in court, he won't have time to properly consider the information; the results could be disastrous.

Be certain that your medical expert understands and can work with the exhibits of the case. Exhibits can include physical evidence, diagrams, charts, timetables, and X-rays. The expert should not only be familiar with exhibits, he should help prepare them. If an exhibit is likely to be written on or otherwise distorted, use copies of it during the deposition. If the opposition insists on handling the actual exhibit, have your attorney make it clear the exhibit or evidence is not to be modified in any way. When possible, save the best copy of the real piece of evidence for the settlement table or courtroom.[81]

FUNCTIONS OF YOUR EXPERT WITNESS

1. Drafting of written question lists (interrogatories) to be submitted to the opposition.
2. Identifying documents in the possession of the opponent or third parties that should be inspected.

3. Preparing your attorney to depose (question) the opponent's expert.

4. Analyzing depositions that have already been taken.

5. Preparing you and others to be deposed and to testify in court.

6. Helping prepare diagrams, exhibits, and other information for deposition and the courtroom.[81]

ON THE FENCE

Here are some participants in a malpractice trial who should be impartial. But watch out: They could be influenced by prepayment, prejudice, or passion.

The expert witness. A witness called to testify as an expert on the case is supposed to give factual knowledge to the jurors, not to support one side or the other. That unbiased information should help the jury reach a fair verdict.

In fact, the expert witness is the defendant's or the plaintiff's expert witness, hired by one side or the other. In many states, the expert's identity need not be revealed prior to a trial. The expert can also give a deposition. Expect the expert called—and paid—by the opposition to be for the opposition. Even if you don't know whether they'll have an expert witness, you'd better have one of your own.

The juror. The other person whose balance and lack of bias is assumed and essential in any case is the juror, whose selection is predicated on the absence of prejudice. But don't take a juror's balance for granted. Jurors quickly fall off the fence—and often to the side of the offense—for two reasons: arrogance and compassion.

You may not expect it, but along with hidden prejudice against the "deep pocket" and arrogance of some physicians, jurors may be harboring some arrogance of their own. They can become instant experts. Most laypersons think they know much more than they really do about medicine, psychology in particular. And they expect medical professionals to know and do more than we can. They may think they know enough about your case, or want to know more than they can understand. Nevertheless, they can be taught, and should clearly and openly be given the facts in your defense. Do that, not to feed their arrogance, but to provide them with the resources they need to make a responsible decision.

Jurors can also be swayed by compassion. They sit patiently for many boring hours hearing the plaintiff's attorney repeatedly explain how and why your negligence caused the victim's injuries. They may develop a strong sympathy for the injured person, who now needs money to compensate for the damage and to make a new start in life. Because jurors are sensitive to such issues, it's important that you show no guilt concerning the plaintiff's injuries. A genuine display of compassion, however, would be appropriate.

Unfortunately, the jury's sympathy may not be carried over to you. They are often untouched by the suffering they will inflict by levying heavy damages against a supposedly rich doctor, hospital, or insurance company.

ON THE OFFENSE

Their expert witness. Jurors will learn what they need to know about medical practice, facts, and standards of care. An expert witness is supposed to educate the jurors by providing the information they need to judge right and wrong. In practice, the opposing expert witness is there to verify that what you did was wrong.

You and your attorney must refute the opposing expert's testimony. You must prove that the "expert" is unfamiliar with the subject or incorrect in interpreting it, and therefore is not qualified to claim that your treatment was negligent.

Be careful, though, when you and your counsel assert that the opposing expert's testimony is not true. You may come close to calling the witness a liar. Instead of trying to discredit the person, discredit the testimony. You're not out to show the testifier as dishonest, only to show the testimony as uninformed or mistaken.

Some doctors make court appearances a major part of their practice. They are "hired guns," paid by prosecutors to take the stand against peers accused of malpractice. It may be necessary to draw first on them and discredit their background, practice, and partiality. Expect that the expert witness is there to attack you, and is expert at breaking down your defenses. If you and your attorney don't arm and defend yourselves against the attack, you can't expect anyone else to protect you.

Here are six bullets you can use to disarm the hired gun and show that he's firing blanks:

- *Sneak up on peripheral vision.* An expert may be questioned at length about matters relevant to the case. The witness will surely have prepared for this. One way to determine if the hired gun is an expert—in the view of the jury—is to question the witness at length about subjects only peripherally related to the case. If unable to handle your flanking movement, the witness is obviously not expert in the field in general, but is armed only for the case at hand.[114]

- *Who's on the patient's side?* If the challenging expert witness has not examined the patient, your attorney should make a big point of it in the questioning. That will show the jury the expert is not familiar with the major factor in the case—the patient. Show how much more you knew and cared for the patient.

Even if the expert examined the plaintiff recently, you may gain some advantage by pointing out that the witness had not examined the plaintiff at the time of the alleged malpractice. Since the patient's history and physical examination play such a large part in diagnosis and evaluation of therapy, how can that expert witness criticize your actions in the distant past?

- *Dodge the point-blank shot.* Expect to get hit with a strong, direct accusation. If the opposing doctor comes out and says point-blank that your treatment of the patient was incorrect, your attorney should ask if the witness is absolutely certain this was malpractice. The witness may say, "Yes, as certain as one can be of anything."

Your attorney should then have the witness answer questions that show how, over the years, the diagnosis and treatment of the particular condition has changed; that what used to be accepted truth is now obsolete, false, or no longer useful. The "truths" of medicine are changing all the time. Medicines and surgical procedures not long ago thought to be helpful have been found of late to be useless, or actually harmful. Ask the expert questions that bring out those uncertainties. And try to elicit the admission that there are no absolute truths in this case.[16]

- *Put in your shoes.* By law, the training and experience of the expert must be similar to that of the defendant. The witness should have been exposed to the same kinds of patients under the same conditions. Otherwise, how can the "expert" possibly know how such cases can be or usually are handled? If you practice in a busy outpatient clinic, treat uneducated patients, and work in a hospital with limited facilities, a witness without such experience would have a difficult time understanding the problems of your practice. That inexpertise should be pointed out to the jury.

Some experts may not be allowed to testify in certain cases. In one case, an orthopedic surgeon was not permitted to testify as an expert on the standard of care expected of a chiropractor. An orthopedic surgeon will sometimes not be allowed to testify in a case involving a podiatrist.[c198]

Since the late 1980s there has been a trend toward allowing "cross-discipline" expert witness testimony. Although courts in different states rendered conflicting decisions, in some areas courts would permit an orthopedic surgeon to give an opinion concerning the surgery performed by a podiatrist.[166]

A general surgeon was judged qualified to testify in the trial of an orthopedic surgeon who had failed to detect a surgical wound infection. The court ruled that because infections were similar in all types of surgery, and because the general surgeon had assisted in many orthopedic operations, he was knowledgeable about the necessary standard of care.[c147]

An anesthesiologist was judged qualified to testify against an orthopedic surgeon concerning the necessary standard of care in taking a patient's medical history. The court ruled that the taking of a patient's history was similar in all areas of medicine.[c124]

A nurse was held qualified to testify about injury caused by an improperly administered intravenous solution. The nurse had special training in IV therapy. A doctor's degree in medicine, the court decided, was not needed to make the witness an expert in this case.[c111]

A general practitioner was allowed to testify as an expert concerning a neurosurgeon's decision on when to obtain a computerized tomography scan of the head. Though the general practitioner would not be competent to comment on surgical procedures, the ordering of CT scans was within his professional experience.[c37]

In psychotherapy, many different schools of treatment exist. An expert witness must be knowledgeable about the defendant-therapist's methods in order to testify about them.[c10]

Attorney David Harney has described a trend toward accepting as common the methods for treatment that are recognized and used by MDs. Accordingly, a chiropractor is held to the same standard of care established by the medical profession.[114] Harney cites relevant cases involving appendicitis,[c100] arterial occlusion,[c25] and diabetes.[c49]

Harney further suggests that naturopaths—and other practitioners with no acceptable standards of their own—will be judged according to regular medical standards.

In addition, allied health practitioners with acceptable, recognized standards of care may be judged by the standard expected of physicians, when they render care outside their areas of specialization. That would apply to podiatrists (chiropodists), nurses, chiropractors, respiratory therapists, physician assistants, emergency medical technicians, paramedics, midwives, dentists, optometrists, and physical therapists. In many states, the standard of care and areas of recognized competence of allied health practitioners are not clearly defined. Future case decisions will have to map that professional turf and competence more clearly.

- *The hired gun backfires.* Some hired guns have shot down their own expertise. They were shown to be untrustworthy by their own past "testimony," saying one thing in court now, but earlier having said the opposite. ("Earlier" can refer to earlier in the same court hearing, in a deposition, in previous court cases, or in publications the witness authored.)

If the expert testified in similar cases, review previous depositions and courtroom testimony for statements that might be contradicted at your trial. That's likely if the witness previously testified for the defense, but now is for the plaintiff. Files of information on expert witnesses are available from insurance companies and associations of trial lawyers.

An expert may be asked, "How much are you getting paid for your testimony?" To show impartiality, the correct answer would be, "I'm not being paid for my testimony, just for my time and expenses."

Still, if you can show that the expert's fee is excessive, the jury may be convinced that the witness is not impartial. They may, however, feel that the expert must be someone special to have commanded such a high fee. In any case, it's usually illegal for the witness fee to be dependent on the outcome of the trial.

- *The repeating hired gun.* You may be able to cast doubt on the testimony by showing that the "expert" is not a health-care provider, but a professional witness. Ask this: "In how many cases did you testify during the past year, and in how many was it for plaintiffs?" Take particular note if the witness claims to be an expert in such diverse areas as orthopedics, ophtalmology, and pediatrics.

If the witness is armed with academic credentials, ask this: "How many papers and books have you published and how many lectures have you given in the last year?" If they are few—or few in the area of testimony—you might question the level of expertise in this case. If they are extensive, you might then ask: "How have you been able to keep up clinical skills and practical judgment when so much time has gone into writing, teaching, and traveling?"

It seems reasonable to require that expert witnesses spend a certain amount of their time actually practicing medicine. For example, in Ohio expert medical witnesses must spend 75% of their professional time practicing medicine. There are a number of "experts" who make their living testifying rather than practicing medicine. While some of these experts may give valid testimony, they cannot be in touch with clinical reality for many years after they stop practicing. Under our legal system, experts are needed by defendants and plaintiffs. If legitimate physicians do not serve as experts, others will. It has been suggested that the role of the expert witness be taught in medical schools to offset the damage done by irresponsible witnesses.[10]

Doubt can be cast on the expertise of a witness who doesn't practice in the area of supposed expertise. A few pointed questions can disarm the expert: "How many cases of this specific condition have you personally taken care of in the past six months? How many times have you managed this problem under the same conditions as in this case—crowded, busy emergency room inaccurate history of a patient who is intoxicated, under stress, in shock, or unconscious?"

Two recent cases support such challenges to the objectivity and expertise of witnesses hired to shoot down practicing doctors:

An Ohio appellate court in 1978 ruled that an "expert's" opinion, based on the medical literature rather than personal experience, was insufficient evidence to substantiate a claim of malpractice.[c173] In 1981, the Michigan Supreme Court ruled that an expert witness could be cross-examined about his previous experience in testifying, the number and type of cases, and whether he was for the plaintiff in those cases.[c203]

In any case, both you and your lawyer need to become experts on the evidence for your defense, get the best experts to testify to your innocence, and get ready to meet and disarm the experts who come out against you.

When you have all your evidence, allies, and strategies together, you'll be ready to take the next steps and present your case before a judge and jury.

PRESENTING YOURSELF AND YOUR CASE

The deft deposition: "your day in court"

The deposition is sometimes called pretrial testimony or examination before trial. Whatever it's called in your case, it may be the only real chance you get to testify and present your side of the story. Don't look ahead to the trial. This deposition may be, in effect, "your day in court," because most malpractice cases don't go to trial. The majority of suits are "settled" on the basis of evidence and events presented in deposition.

The procedure may include written interrogatories (see Step 3), lists of questions you must answer in writing. You must be careful to be complete and honest in responding to all questions, while at the same time giving the opposing attorney as little evidence against you as possible. This may be the only time you're questioned.

Each attorney may also be asked to bring X-rays, documents, and other evidence to the deposition. That's all part of the process of "discovery," in which each side learns more about the case from the other. This step of discovery, however, can become the step of decision. The deposition often decides the case. If handled poorly, it can destroy your case. Handled deftly, it can fortify your case and disarm the opposition.

At this stage, you should be thoroughly prepared by having followed Steps 1-6. The deposition is where you first present what you have prepared. The next time—if there is one—will be on the witness stand during the trial. If you do go to court, your deposition is essential. Everything you say in the deposition is sworn testimony, admissible as evidence in court. Here are the ways to make the most positive deposition you can:

CROSS PURPOSES

The declared purpose of the deposition is for all the participants and attorneys to learn the facts upon which the case is based.

The undeclared purpose—for the plaintiff's attorney—is to discredit and entrap you. Your accuser's goal is to win the case and make money. The means to the goal is evidence that you damaged the plaintiff. If you forget that simple, basic fact, you may lose your case and your money.

The purpose of the deposition—for you and your attorney—is to present evidence that clears you of the claim, and to avoid giving evidence that supports the case against you.

Within your limits.   Subject matter not relevant to the lawsuit may not be covered during the deposition. It's your right to refuse to speak about material not having to do with the case. The limits of this material are defined by the complaint, the answer, and the other papers filed before the deposition.

When questioned by the plaintiff's attorney, you are an adverse witness. State laws vary as to whether an adverse witness must answer questions requiring an expression of medical or expert opinion. You may be allowed to refuse to answer questions of general medical fact and hypothetical situations.

Before the deposition starts, the plaintiff's attorney may try to engage you in friendly conversation on just about any topic, saying, "I just want to get to know you." It's just to get you to say something about yourself or your beliefs that can be used against you. Don't forget, that attorney has been spending a lot of time and money trying to find out more about you and your case. The only thing your opponent should learn from you in conversation is that you know how to appear cordial without conveying any information.

Show that you can keep your composure, think clearly, and control what you say. The plaintiff's attorney may be discouraged from pursuing the case if it seems it's going to be tough making you look bad or appear guilty on the stand.

Appear to be a good speaker who can probably make a favorable impression on a jury. That will make the plaintiff's attorney think twice. Unless the facts are favorable to the plaintiff, there may be an early, reasonable settlement.

Give as little information as possible. Answer questions briefly. Don't try to talk the plaintiff's attorney out of suing you by explaining your case. You will simply be revealing your defenses to your attacker, who'll then prepare to counter them during your trial.

What the plaintiff's attorney is after. You'll be questioned at length about your background, education, training, qualifications, experience with similar cases, and hospital affiliations. Any problem you've had with your credentials will be brought out in the questioning, because the plaintiff's attorney has probably already investigated your past. In one deposition, for example, the fact that a resident had failed his licensing boards several times was revealed.

During questioning, the plaintiff's attorney will learn if you're knowledgeable about the medical facts of the case. If you don't know certain things, that limitation will be documented and can later be presented to the jury as evidence. If you don't remember the case in question very well, that, too, will be documented.

ON DEPOSIT: HOW TO BE OPEN TO QUESTION

You must answer all questions, but you need not answer them without referring to the medical record.

Refresh your memory. It's acceptable to say, "I need to look at the patient's chart to refresh my memory."

If you 'refresh your memory" repeatedly in front of a jury, you'll create a bad impression. Yet during the deposition feel free to refer to the patient's chart as much as you please. If that makes the plaintiff's attorney impatient and disrupts the line of questioning, so much the better.

The plaintiff's attorney, however, may make you take the time to read your notes aloud from the medical record. That makes previously difficult-to-read material easier for the opposition to examine. Before the deposition, make sure you can decipher your own handwriting in all parts of the medical records.

During the deposition, the plaintiff's attorney will determine how well you speak, answer questions, and "think on your feet." Leading questions and complex arguments may be used to get you to say things you don't mean to say. Your attorney should object if the questioning becomes abusive or argumentative. Don't automatically go along with the implications of questions.

Don't admit to any author or textbook as being "authoritative." That gives the plaintiff's attorney the right to say you agree with everything the author or book says. It's better to state that much of what the author or book says, but certainly not everything, is true. Take one fact at a time. Make the plaintiff's attorney be specific when asking if what a certain source says is authoritative. If the questioner tires of this slow process, great.

Stay in control. The plaintiff's attorney will try to discover how to upset you, in order to make you raving mad and a sad spectacle in front of a jury later. The probing is designed to make you stop thinking clearly and make inaccurate or self-implicating statements.

The attorney can drag out the proceedings and get you tired. You must recognize this tactic ahead of time and be prepared to stay and fight. Don't lose patience and try to end things quickly by giving in to arguments because you want to get home in time for dinner, or get back to your office. The deposition often is a waiting game, with high stakes.

The plaintiff's attorney will also try to learn your feelings about the case, the plaintiff, and other patients. The slightest suggestion that you don't care for or about this patient—or that you were discouraged by the case even before the "accident" in which the patient was injured—will be used as an exhibit of your carelessness.

Before giving a deposition, you must decide what you really do and don't remember. You must be aware of the areas, if any, where your recollections disagree with your notes or other people's accounts. You'll be questioned at length about those facts. Your story must be consistent during both deposition and trial.

The plaintiff's attorney will ask you about the facts of the case. When did you first see the patient? Did you examine the patient carefully? If the chart doesn't show certain key elements of the physical examination, did you do the examination but not write it down? Why? Sometimes nothing is written because the examination was normal or unremarkable. If you remember that to be the case, be prepared to say so.

The plaintiff's attorney will question you about the history, physical examination, and laboratory data you obtained. These three items make the "data base" on which medical decisions can be made. You will then be asked about your differential diagnosis, treatment, and consultations.

Take your time. If the deposition last long enough, you may make statements that seem to negate others you made earlier. A sure way to impeach yourself is to make a statement you later contradict.

If your deposition grows long, don't try to cut it short. Many questions can be taken out of context, so always qualify answers that need qualification. Be precise. Don't be afraid of boring the lawyers or of wasting *their* time. It's *your* time and future that are at stake.

Your testimony is taken seriously. It's worth its weight in gold to the opposition. Attorneys study all depositions before they go to trial. Every topic covered will be marked, indexed, and referenced. Topics will be selected to question you and others about during the trial. If your answers are inconsistent with those given during the deposition, you'll be impeached as a liar.

Choose your words carefully. A physician may be a witness against himself, as when one physician described his midforceps rotation as involving "excessive pressure." Perhaps he really meant to say, "greater than usual pressure."[c76,251]

Is that all? When covering various topics, the plaintiff's attorney will ask you, after each area is explored, "Is that all?"[188]

Never answer, "Yes." If later, during the trial, you tell more about the particular topic, you can be accused of covering up or withholding evidence during the deposition.

When asked, "Is that all?" you should answer, "At this time, that is all I can remember."

Last tactics to upset your deposition. Other tactics may be used to trip you up during your deposition. If you've not been thrown by the plaintiff's attorney taking up a lot of your valuable time, getting you tired, insulting you, and asking leading or tricky questions, at least four more moves may be tried on you:

- Delaying and changing the date of the deposition or trial.
- Acting informally and seeming to be friendly.
- Telling jokes and recording your responses.
- Suing for an exhorbitant amount of money.

Any of the above tactics might induce you to prepare inadequately or to perform poorly during the deposition.

Watch out: The plaintiff's lawyer may try to lull you into not taking the case seriously by suing for a ridiculously large sum. The amount claimed may later be reduced, but will still be substantial.

Or the prosecutor may instead lull you into not fully preparing for the deposition by talking about settling for a small amount, then later withdraw the offer. You may be sued for a small amount, then later be asked for enormous punitive damages or other costs.

AFTER DEPOSITION

Record it.   A deposition is usually recorded by a certified shorthand reporter, and transcripts are available to both sides. Tape recordings may also be made. Depositions often last for hours and are very complex and detailed, so the only way to check the accuracy of the transcript is to make your own recording of the deposition, though this is rarely done.

Check it.   Before you sign the transcript of your deposition, read it carefully. Check all details. Did all the right technical words get in? Are modifying words such as "probably" or "sometimes" left out? When in doubt, check it against your taped records. When you make corrections in the deposition, you are not allowed to *change* what you said. You are allowed only to *correct* any errors that were made by the reporter and typist.

Listen to your tape both for transcript errors and for a check on your own presentation. Listening to yourself and your performance under the fire of questions from the opposing lawyer is extremely worthwhile preparation before going to trial.

Sign it.   Remember that once you sign a deposition, you thereby swear to its accuracy. It can be used to impeach you in court, so it's well worth verifying the accuracy of all statements recorded there.

Help get other depositions.   Depositions also will be taken from expert witnesses, co-defendants, and various other people involved in the case. You can help your attorney greatly by being present and telling what to ask them. Even though your lawyer is the one who decides how your case is handled, your knowledge of medicine in general and of this case in particular is invaluable.

The plaintiff and relatives are less likely to lie or exaggerate in their depositions if you are staring them in the face. If you're not there, they'll feel that no one present really knows what happened, and will be more likely to be untruthful.

Keep them in mind.   A long time often passes between the taking of depositions and the trial. Sometimes a year or more goes by. You and your attorney must carefully review all depositions just before the trial to keep the facts, tactics, and participants fresh in your minds.

Further preparations.   An entire book devoted to helping the physician prepare for depositions is *Malpractice Depositions, Avoiding the Traps.*[81]

On the stand:
the art of testifying

Testifying in court is an art. It's a form of role-playing. Your part is yourself. It's vital that you present yourself to the judge and jury in the best possible light. The deposition didn't stop the malpractice charge; your presentation in court is your last stand.

Courtroom behavior and tactics have evolved over centuries. Yet all the active ingredients, from how you dress to what you confess, remain intact today. The rules, laws, etiquette, and procedures may seen foreign to the uninitiated. You have to become familiar with them so you feel comfortable and in control when you're called to the stand. Here are directions on how to look, what to say and how to say it, what to show and what to withhold, and what to ask.

HOW TO LOOK

Your court "appearance" is more than your "arrival." How you appear can determine how your case is decided. In everyday life, clothes may—or may not—make the man or woman. In court, they can definitely break your case.

Neat and discreet. As a health-care professional, you had better dress like someone who cares about how you look. You must *appear* to be competent, sharp, self-disciplined, and careful. After all, you are claiming that the treatment you gave was performed with competence, discipline, intelligence, and care. It will be difficult to convince the jury you gave such care if you have unkempt hair, sloppy speech, raggedy clothes, or a lazy posture.

Your dress should be conservative and neat, as if you were going to an important business meeting or religious service. A suit, white shirt, tie, and polished shoes are appropriate. Avoid flashy, obviously expensive, or sporty dress. Being in court is an important and serious appearance. You should dress accordingly. So should your attorney.

Composed.   Take care to maintain your composure on the witness stand. If you get angry or lose your temper, the jury will see you as a hothead who goes out of control and is unreliable in times of stress. Such a person won't be perceived by the jury as a competent health care professional.

Things can happen, though, that would make any reasonable person lose composure. Expect it to happen, so that you don't get upset by it. Many lawyers don't try to provoke anger. But others do.

Prosecuting attorneys may try to upset you. Obviously, if you can be made to look dishonest, callous, fraudulent, irritable, or incompetent, the jury may award larger damages. Some trial lawyers see the purposes of cross-examination as discrediting the witness, laying the groundwork for impeachment, and obtaining evidence to damage the defense.

Compassionate.   If you are scared, you will think more slowly; if you are angry, your judgment will become defective.[285] Try to be neither. Instead, show courtesy to the questioning attorney and great concern for the material being discussed. True, the attorney may be trying to discredit and ruin you financially, but the judge and jury recognize that the plaintiff may have really been injured and needs compensation. Often they are correct.

So don't act holier-than-thou. Don't appear to be insulted or pompous. Too many health-care practitioners have injured too many patients for you to expect the jury to automatically assume that you are innocent.

When you leave the witness stand, retain your composure. Don't wipe your brow, smile, or wink at anyone. When sitting in court, remember that at least one juror will be watching you at all times. A courtroom fact: The plaintiff will probably win if you lose your composure.

Poised.   We all communicate by body language, even when we don't want to. The angry, aggressive person, for example, leans forward and points a finger. The nervous person sits straight on the edge of a chair and fidgets. The confident person sits in a relaxed and poised manner.

Your body language, like your tone of voice and facial expressions, can be brought under conscious control. Avoid jumping to your feet in anger, shaking your fist, nervously tapping your fingers, or sitting with poor posture. Your role is to appear honest, poised, concerned, and confident, but not arrogant.

Have your spouse or a friend watch for any flaws as you practice testifying. Consider videotaping yourself while being questioned. Watch your posture and movements in the fast-foward-playback mode (3 to 15 times normal speed). Practice looking good "in court." Attorneys have much experience with this, so you're at a disadvantage while being questioned by them in court.

Posture can convey a feeling of fear or of confidence. Sit with your lower back against the back of the chair and both feet flat on the floor. Keep your hands in your lap. Don't appear stiff. Try to avoid nervous habits, leg-crossing, and leaning—especially on the judge's bench. Relax, but don't repose. And don't slouch; that only suggests indifference and disrespect.

You may use your hands to illustrate concepts. Expressive movement is acceptable so long as it doesn't turn into histrionics. As we will see later, drawings and other illustrations can also be used to show you and your case in a positive light.

Expressive.   Keep a pleasant look on your face. Smile, if something really funny happens. But if you laugh too loudly or show too big a smile, you may be told, "Doctor, this is nothing to laugh about. We are discussing a person who will be unable to work or play for the rest of his life because of injuries sustained under your care."

Your facial expression will be noted by the jury and the plaintiff's attorney. It can inform a skilled lawyer of your dislike for the patient, your confusion about the issue at hand, or your uneasiness about the current questioning. Don't let it.

Practice feeling and looking calm and confident under cross-examination. Be conscious of your expressions and movements when sensitive issues are brought up. Train yourself to show only what you want to reveal through nonverbal means.

To the jury.   You're in court to present information to the judge and jury. They'll decide whether malpractice occurred and, if it did, how much you must pay the plaintiff.

Try to face the jury most of the time you're speaking. That's difficult if your questioner is standing in another direction, because it's natural and courteous to look in the direction of the person talking with you. Still, as much as is possible, look at and speak to the jury when you answer questions. You can look at the attorney while the questions are being asked.

HOW TO SPEAK

Truthfully. Above all, and at all times, as it was in your deposition, so too what you say in court must be truthful. Don't tell even little white lies. If you have done wrong, the patient deserves to be compensated for the resulting injuries. Don't try to obstruct justice. If you lie, chances are it will be found out. Such damaging detective work is what attorneys are trained to do. The award to the patient will be much higher if you are proven a liar.

If you unintentionally make an unclear or untrue statement, correct it as soon as possible. Bring it up yourself. Don't think that what you said has been overlooked. It's a well-known trial technique to wait until an opportune, dramatic time in the proceedings to bring out a previously made false statement. This will embarrass you far more than if you bring the issue up yourself. Raise it by having your attorney question you on the matter.

Calmly. While in court, your tone of voice should be natural and calm. Don't ever raise your voice in anger. Don't sound as if you're trying to sell something. You're on the stand to answer questions honestly and tell things as you remember them. Don't make obvious attempts to push your story onto the jury. Your story should come out in the questioning and in the natural course of the dialogue.

Your lawyer is the one who needs to arrange the questioning, statements, and objections to best present your side to the jury. Help plan this before the trial, but don't think you can control the course of events during the trial. That's your attorney's role.

Clearly. Talk loudly enough for the judge and jury to hear you at all times. Don't ramble. Speak in reasonably short, complete sentences. Limit answers to a few sentences, if possible. Let what you say sink in before you go on.

Your tone should convey confidence, credentials, and beliefs. When questioned, answer definitely, without repeating, "Most physicians would say" or "The literature says."

A defendant or witness should never memorize answers to questions or give prepared speeches. You must speak plainly and naturally. Expect a variety of questions. Know your material, but don't memorize statements word for word.

Prepared testimony will sound stilted and prepared. It will also sound ridiculous if a word or phrase is left out. The plaintiff's attorney will recognize a memorized statement and will interrupt to throw you off.

Specifically. Your attorney should object if you go beyond answering a question and give additional, unasked-for information. But you may be called an "unresponsive witness" if you fail to adequately answer the question.

Your attorney should also object if a question is too broad. "What happened when you saw the patient?" would be too open-ended a question.[129]

A non-word such as "uh-huh" will not easily be heard, may not be recorded properly by the court reporter, and may make you appear too casual. Use clear English. Say, "Yes" or "No." Avoid shaking your head: That, too, is difficult to record.

Avoid such phrases as "To tell you the truth," "You might not believe this, but," and "Actually what happened was." Such statements imply that you were lying at other times, and feel the need to let everyone know you are really going to tell the truth this time.

Don't give the impression that you were guessing or supposing. You want to show that you were giving your best consideration to the matter. It may have been faulty, but it was your best effort with the information available at the time.

If you can't recall something, it's acceptable to admit, "I don't remember that now."

Don't feel you must have an answer for everything to seem truthful. Just the opposite is true. Someone who has fabricated a story will have an answer for every question. The honest witness or defendant won't remember everything that happened or everything that was said. But if you can't remember a major item—or many minor items—your credibility will be damaged.

When asked if you recall anything else about a certain situation, answer, "I can't recall anything else right now."

The examining lawyer may counter, "What do you mean by that? Are you hiding something?"

Simply state the truth: "Further questioning or review of the recordes may remind me of something else, but right now that is all I remember."

Plain English. Many medical practitioners use technical terms when talking to patients: "You may have a pelvic abscess. Your white count is high." No wonder patients don't understand or remember what doctors tell them.

When speaking to patients during treatment and to a jury in court, define your terms. To do otherwise is to annoy and insult your listeners.

Explain: "You may have a collection of pus near your womb—in other words, a pelvic abscess. Your blood count showed a lot of white blood cells. That's a sign of infection."

When you must use a technical term, define it in plain English. That will keep the possibly already tired, suspicious, or bored juror from being annoyed by your use of unintelligible words.

A good example of how to explain technical terms comes from the opening statement in the famous Darling case: "Pat remained at the hospital for two weeks. During that period of time the soft tissue, as they call the flesh around the bone, started to swell from the damage to the tissue. Because of the constriction of the cast, the foot swelled and turned a sort of dusky color, sort of a gray-blue."[53]

Note that the attorney didn't expect the jury to know the meaning of the terms "soft tissue" and "dusky."

In addition to not knowing the meaning of medical terms, jurors are often ignorant of medical facts. You must explain things as if you are talking to someone with less than a high school education, which is often the situation.

Assume no prior knowledge on the part of the jurors. Even worse, any knowledge they have may be from old wives' tales, the lay press, or the plaintiff's attorney. Your explanation of what happened, and why it was not your fault, must come across simply, in easily understood terms.

Modestly.   You shouldn't need to brag. The jury already knows you are a health professional. They'll notice if you try proving yourself by correcting others' definitions of terms or pronunciations. They will notice and be embarrassed themselves if you "speak down" to the plaintiff's attorney in explaining what happened, or if you seem bored at having to explain technical matters.

Your attorney will question you in a way to make your explanations clear to the jurors, in words they understand, with key points repeated enough to be remembered. So don't look bored or talk down to your own attorney when asked redundant, apparently simple-minded questions.

If the plaintiff's attorney appears to be ignorant, that may just be a sign of not understanding something. More likely, though, it means being up to something, throwing you off your guard. The intent may be to get you to go along with inexact statements, say things which can later be disproved, or look like an arrogant tyrant who tires at explaining the facts of the case to someone not so quick at understanding. Beware.

You may be up against an expert witness with whom you disagree. Don't speak harshly of the person or criticize the testimony. Simply say, "I do not agree with what was said about that."

Into the mike.   Speak into the microphone, if there is one. It may be hidden, built into the desk in front of you. If so, you can't adjust its position. If the witness chair is bolted to the floor, you can't move closer to the mike. That's why it's wise to visit the courtroom ahead of time to look into the acoustics.

Microphone or not, be sure your voice is projected so the judge and jury can hear it. If there is a mike, but you can't adjust it, you must adjust the loudness of your voice so all can hear.

The questioning attorneys should know not to stand in a direction opposite from the jury. If they do, be sure the jury can always hear you. Look at the jury, at least occasionally. If you find it impossible to let them see your face or hear you well because of where the attorney is standing, ask, "Would you mind standing on this side, please, so the jury can hear my answers also?"

In the courtroom.   Keep your testimony in court. During recesses, stay away from and don't communicate with jurors. You could be accused of trying to influence them.

Don't be late to court. Be there early and don't look bored or upset. If possible, have your spouse sit near you in court during the trial. This shows how much the case means to you and gives you a personal, family-oriented image.

WHAT TO SAY

To an insult.   If insulted, don't show anger. Keep calm. Don't shout back nasty comments. If you're cool enough to turn the tables after being insulted, you may be tempted to do so. But remember that you're fighting in enemy territory.

The charging attorney may say, "You've bungled several cases like this before, haven't you?"

In response, you can turn the accusing finger by saying, "It seems that your sources of information are inaccurate."

Insults should be handled in a composed and clinical way, exchanging positive facts for negative feelings. Accept the fact that the plaintiff's attorney is trying to get you mad, lose your train of thought, and make a spectacle of yourself. If you're asked an insulting question, refute it honestly and pointedly.

The attorney may say, "Were you playing golf when you refused to come see your patient?"

If that was the case, answer, "I instructed the patient to go to the emergency department so that proper evaluation of her condition could be performed."

That you were playing golf is immaterial. No matter where you were, the emergency department physician would have taken care of the patient or called you if admission or advice was needed.

Coming up with a witty retort to a nasty insult can win you sympathy with the jury. Nothing is better than making the jury laugh at the plaintiff's attorney. But remember, the plaintiff's attorney is a specialist in the area of verbal sparring, and you are in unfamiliar territory. You're better off letting your integrity show through as you bravely handle terrible insults.

Unprivileged information. In most situations, a doctor would not be allowed to openly state information given by a patient or client. This is the principle of privileged information. Things a patient tells a doctor, or a client tells an attorney, are secret. Once a patient sues you, however, there's no more privilege. You can reveal anything and everything in court.

Your "secrets." If the suing patient has no secrets, neither do you. Know that sharp attorneys know what you are going to say. They only ask a question when they already know what the answer will be. Moreover, an excellent attorney will have so skillfully presented the plaintiff's story that the jury will also know what your answers will be before you give them—and they will fit persuasively into the plaintiff's version of the dispute.

So try to give answers that support your defense of what happened. Try not to give answers that support the plaintiff's charges.

If the plaintiff's attorney tries to discredit you personally, give your testimony in a way that destroys your negative image. Many attorneys frown on underhanded, personality-smearing techniques. Still, some lawyers will attempt to make you appear to be negligent, greedy, dishonest, impulsive, incompetent, lazy, and callous. Some see this personal discrediting of the defendant as an essential element in winning a malpractice case.[243,244] A jury won't hesitate to find against such a defendant—and to award a large sum to the victimized plaintiff.

Testifying in court is like playing a game of chess: Each player plans a series of moves designed to defeat the other. By the time you get to trial, most of the facts—the chess pieces—are on the board. The trial is your chance to play with and move those pieces. Be prepared to discover that the other side knows some things about your case that even you don't know.

So why so much questioning in court? Two reasons: The challenger wants the jury to hear you say things that support the plaintiff's version, and to hear you lie or contradict yourself. If you've been covering up, the questions will work to uncover it. In short, the other side moves to make you make a wrong move.

Even if you're perfectly innocent and honest, however, you can still be set up to give apparently contradictory testimony. An adroit attorney can make you look wrong or dishonest with several moves: by asking complex, hypothetical questions, taking things out of context, twisting the facts, bringing up exceptions to general rules of practice, and ignoring any special circumstances.

Look for the hidden meaning in every question. Ask yourself what the questioner is leading up to:

- "Is the question applicable to my case?" If not, you'd better tell how your case differs.
- "Is the attorney trying to imply that because my associate was on call, I was indifferent to the needs of my patient?"
- "Am I being accused of neglecting my patient because I was busy elsewhere?" If so, be sure to say and show how well your patient was covered.

Reasonable certainties. Watch out for a particularly tricky move that can be used against you. Legally, you're required only to know and practice "a reasonable degree of medical certainty." That's your standard of accuracy. Keep in mind when the plaintiff's attorney asks, "Medicine is an inexact science, isn't it, Doctor?"

Don't simply say, "Yes." That will only open you to further questioning designed to show that you're not sure about your testimony—and that you can't be sure your treatment was right.

So answer such a leading question with a positive, confident statement, such as, "Much of what is known about medicine today is known with a high degree of certainty because of the tremendous advances in scientific research."

Contradictions. Any contradictions in your defensive evidence will lose the case for you. Everything you say must be consistent. If it isn't, you'll be accused of lying. The plaintiff's attorney will remember everything you said in your deposition and everything you say in court. If you change your understanding of some point in the case from one time to another, you must honestly explain why. Let your lawyer frame it in the best light as a positive discovery or revelation. It's all right to admit you don't know everything.

Put your "but" first. One of the most frustrating things about testifying is the impossibility of giving complete answers. You'll be required to answer narrow questions. You won't be allowed to ramble on with explanations. So if you're about to answer, "Yes, but," don't. The safe way to begin is, "No, unless certain conditions are met."

Some attorneys will start questioning slowly and easily, gradually building up to critical questions, or more suddenly slipping in a trick question.

Other attorneys start their questioning on only one of the points they're trying to impress on the jury. A small number of such points add up to make the plaintiff's case, so the attorney will make sure the jury hears those points repeatedly. Don't get caught off guard.

Don't help the plaintiff's attorney by answering questions in the expected manner. Recognize what the plaintiff's attorney is trying to prove. Calmly discredit each point, or at least cast doubt on it at every opportunity. If you're asked, for example, to comment on a certain set of circumstances similar to but not exactly those of your case, you're being set up. Any answer you give will be applied to your case. The way out of the trap is to say, "I am here to discuss the case of this plaintiff, not other cases which are different."

Don't be limited to "yes" or "no" answers. Court testimony need not be limited to "yes" or "no" answers. "If you can't reply YES or NO honestly without qualification, you can turn to the judge and let this be known. Say you'd like to answer truthfully and fully, but the lawyer is making it difficult for you."[133]

Hesitate before answering. Your natural-appearing style of speaking on the stand should include a brief pause before each answer. If done properly and consistently, you'll have time to think, and the jury will see you giving due consideration to each question. Your pause also gives your attorney time to think and time to object to the question. Drawing from a broad legal background, your attorney will spot problems you can't see, and will often object when you don't expect it.

Hesitation also breaks the speed and momentum of the opposing attorney's train of thought. In fact, a slight pause calls attention to what you're going to say and away from the examiner's ideas and insinuations. Be mindful, too, that attorneys are alerted to an uncomfortable topic when the witness hesitates before answering. A pattern of always pausing denies them that advantage.

Caution: Don't hesitate and pause so much that you delay the proceedings. You'll be seen as obstructing justice, slowing things down, or being passive-aggressive. That could turn both judge and jury against you.

Correct the question. Sometimes a question is an answer. The attorney may ask a question that includes a damaging statement: "When you saw Mrs. Smith, you briefly spoke to her and then prescribed penicillin, isn't that right?"

Forget the penicillin! The accusing lawyer is telling the jury that you didn't care enough to spend much time with this poor, unfortunate victim.

Your correct answer: "Your statement is incorrect. I spoke to her at length about a, b, c, and d. I then carefully examined her."

Don't be modest about the amount of time and effort you put into working up your patient. Yet you can never claim to have done a complete examination. If you say you did a complete neurological examination, for example, you'll be discredited when asked about the snout reflex and two-point discrimination on the inner thigh. You never do a complete examination; you can only do what seems to be indicated and needed at the time.

Among the most difficult questions is one that forces you to admit a damaging fact, or else appear dishonest if you don't: "Isn't it true that Mr. Jones died just one-half hour after he left your office?"

Don't simply say, "Yes." That implies that you could and should have done something to prevent the death. And don't say, "No." That would be lying.

What can you say? Just answer: "Yes, it's true that the patient died a half hour after leaving my office." Say it loud and clear. Show no guilt or shame. And don't burst into tears.

If you're not ruffled by the admission, the jury may get the idea that there's nothing you need be ashamed of, and perhaps there's an explanation. Your attorney will have to find a way to fit the explanation into the opening and closing statements, and several places in between. That must be a part of your overall defense strategy.

Say as little as you can. Questions should be answered as briefly as possible. To say more than was asked for is to give more ammunition to the opposition. If points must be made by you let your attorney ask the questions to bring them out. To ramble on is to give the potentially damaging impression that you're anxious to prove something to the jury.

Testifying in a child abuse trial.   Your strategies and purposes are different when you are a *witness* to the effects of child abuse (rather than a *defendant* being sued). Still, you can expect to come under attack.

When you are cross-examined in a child abuse trial, three areas are likely to be attacked: your credibility as a physician, the validity of your evidence, and the logic of your conclusions.[93] Trick questions may ask about theoretical possibilities or the minimum number of certain kinds of blows required to cause certain injuries.

The defense attorney may question your ability to recognize child abuse because you are not board certified, have not written papers on the subject, and have not testified about it before. These arguments are meant to make you lose your composure and become defensive or arrogant. The best response is to take the high ground with a common sense argument: "The child had three separate burn imprints on her buttocks. It doesn't take much expertise to realize that a 6-month-old child doesn't get this kind of injury in a normal home environment."

Describe injuries and physical findings. Do not relate details about who reportedly did what, how, when, and where. Tell what you saw. Let the detectives figure out who did the battering. If your history differs in some detail from that of the detectives, the defense attorney will point out the inconsistency. The person who beat the child will go free because the inconsistency raises doubts.

Your conclusion that injuries were caused by abuse may be challenged by asking you if each of a series of injuries could have been caused by falling down stairs or other accidents. It is important to respond that abuse was suggested by the pattern of injuries, and they are not consistent with an accidental cause.

Watch for questions which ask for possibilities: "Is it possible these bruises could have been caused by being hit by the open hand...a spanking?" Don't just say "yes." Say, "It would have taken many hard blows."

If asked to estimate the *minimum* number of blows it would have taken, realize you are being asked a trick question. Explain what you are thinking about in making your estimate: "Twenty well-placed, extremely forceful blows by a strong man could have caused such bruising." To just say "Twenty blows could have caused the bruising" would be misleading.

Explain your answers fully, or the abuser's attorney will explain what you meant later after you have left the courtroom.

Ask for clarification.   In spite of adequate preparation, the pace of questioning may get too fast. You may feel rushed or get confused. That's likely to happen because most trial lawyers are practiced speakers and communicators. In contrast, most health professionals have no training and little skill in oral communication.

Too often we've asked patients what consulting or previous physicians thought about an illness or injury, only to be told, "I don't know what they thought or said," or, "I don't know what they found was wrong with me when I was in the hospital."

Many health practitioners don't practice good communication skills. So, when they get on the stand and face an expert lawyer, it doesn't go well for them.

How can you slow down that Mack truck of a malpractice lawyer who is about to run over you? By asking questions yourself:

If you're confused, ask for clarification. Ask that the question be repeated or restated.

If you're not sure a term is being used properly, ask the attorney to explain what it means in the present context.

Admit damaging evidence.   Uncomfortable as it may be, admitting facts that damage your case is much better than covering up or denying them. You must present your case in an honest, positive way. Dishonesty and cover-ups will be discovered by a skillful attorney— and will lead to larger-than-reasonable settlements and punitive damages that your insurance may not pay. If you really were negligent, decide with your attorney before the trial how best to handle it.

When asked if a damaging but accurate statement is true, just say, "Yes," clearly and calmly. If you stay composed, the negative effect on the jury will be lessened. But if you turn red and whisper, or give an evasive answer, you'll lose their respect. If your admission actually damages your case, the opposing attorney will call attention to the fact. Don't add drama and emotion to it.

Correct misconceptions on redirect examination.   After the plaintiff's attorney questions you, your attorney can re-question you. After the initial (direct) examination, your attorney has the right to perform a redirect examination. The purpose of the redirect examination is to allow you and your attorney to addresss all of the opposition's misleading questions, as well as any inaccurate or confusing answers you may have given.[133] Speak to your attorney before redirect examination to be sure that all the problem areas recognized by either of you will be covered.

WHAT TO SHOW

As noted earlier, how you look and what you say isn't all that counts in the courtroom. What you show will also have a negative or positive effect on the jury. First look at what not to show:

No notes. Don't take the stand with written notes in hand. They'll show you as unprepared, leaving the impression that you don't really know what you're talking about or what you really did to the patient. Even more important: Once you use notes, the opposing attorney can have them entered as evidence. They may contain information you don't want brought before the jury.

Have all relevant information in your head. If asked about some details you can't remember, there's no shame in saying, "I need to refer to the hospital chart to refresh my memory on that point." You should, however, know the main points of your case before entering the courtroom.

Exhibits. An exhibit can be the key evidence in your defense. In cases involving fractures, for example, you'll have a tough time trying to make a point if you can't show X-rays taken before and after your treatment. Biopsy or tissue specimens and photographs also provide impressive evidence of the original extent of damage, or the nature of the underlying disease.

Models. Anatomical models or parts of a skeleton can be useful in revealing the three-dimensional relationship of body parts. And the procedures you performed can be demonstrated on the model.

Illustrations. Prepared figures or drawings on a blackboard can also help to present your case. Some medical procedures or series of events and consequences are often too complex to explain in words alone. Illustrations help clarify material and make it easier to recall and refer to.[16]

Without models or illustrations, for example, it would be nearly impossible to explain to a jury a football-related knee injury consisting of tears of the medial collateral ligament, medical meniscus, and anterior cruciate ligament.

Listing events in chronological order on a blackboard can also prove useful. This is especially true when numerous events occurred

96

during medical care and hospitalization. Your detailed case history, for example, can illustrate how long and well you took care of the patient. Such a listing will show that you fulfilled the doctor-patient contract that binds you to continue care until the patient gets well, dies, or is turned over to another physician. It doesn't matter if the patient didn't pay bills, take medicine, or keep appointments. Yes, it's strictly a one-sided contract; but it's recognized in law. Refusing to continue treatment leaves you open to a charge of abandonment—a form of malpractice.

Just what does it take to establish a binding practitioner-patient relationship? Not much. If you see a patient lying on the ground and walk by, there is no relationship—and you are not much of a practitioner, either. But if you stop to check the person, call an ambulance, get the person into the ambulance, and then leave, you have abandoned the patient.

You must stay with the injured person until another doctor—with abilities that are at least equal to yours—assumes the continuing care of the patient.

If you are sued, you must show how you met your one-sided responsibilities in the doctor-patient relationship. It will also help to some degree if you can show the patient's failures to keep appointments, take medicine, and follow your orders. You can document the results of those failures with the exhibits and other evidence you bring in.

WATCH WORDS

What you say on the stand can either help your case or destroy it. Some things speak clearly. But few things speak for themselves. Certain terms are particularly critical. Here are some that can speak for or against you:

"The thing speaks." The accusing attorney may try at the deposition or in court to close the case and convict you by claiming *res ipsa loquitur*—"the thing speaks for itself." This seldom happens, and it should not apply to you.

For example: A patient goes to surgery for a hangnail and suffers brain death for some unknown reason. Obviously, negligence of some kind must be involved. An expert witness isn't needed to explain things to the jury.

To apply *res ipsa loquitur*, the issue must be within the scope of a layman's knowledge. For example, a clamp or sponge left in an abdomen is an error a layperson can understand.

In the past it was necessary to use *res ipsa loquitur* rather than medical testimony to explain or "prove" issues to juries because medical experts were difficult to find. Today more physicians are willing to serve as expert witnesses and explain issues to juries.

Three conditions must be met if *res ipsa loquitur* is to apply:

1. The event must not ordinarily occur without negligence.
2. The event that apparently caused the damage must have been within the exclusive control of the defendant.
3. The plaintiff must not have contributed to the negligence or to the damage, [209,243]

"Hypothetical." A "hypothetical" case is more than hypothetical. As explained in Step 6 on how to prepare for your trial, expert witnesses are used to help the jury decide the verdict.

If the expert witness is told about the case and says, "Obviously, the defendant is negligent," jurors have no choice but to agree. So the "hypothetical" case is used to give the jury freedom of choice.

In presenting the hypothetical case, the attorney presents all undisputed facts in a storylike fashion to the witness, who may ask questions. The expert then is asked for an opinion about what should have been done in the imaginary case, but not in your actual case. The jury retains the ability to decide your case based on whatever factors they consider to be relevant.

The hypothetical case can be long and tricky. It can deviate from the real case in important ways. As a defendant, you may be asked questions about the hypothetical case. If an important point is omitted or changed, bring this out.

Let's say you failed to detect a pneumothorax in a semi-conscious patient, and are asked in court, "Doctor, does a pneumothorax cause pain?"

Your answer should reflect the actual circumstances: "Not if the patient is so intoxicated that the sensation of pain is dulled."

"Possible, probable, likely, usual." We all use these words to mean different things at different times. But they have definite meanings in court. Their definitions vary, yet you can avoid tripping over them by keeping the following in mind:

1. Anything is *possible.*
2. It is *probable* or *likely* if it occurs more than half of the time.
3. It is *usual* if it occurs half of the time.

To see how the confusion surrounding these terms can be used to distort the truth, consider this hypothetical case:

A 26-year-old, seemingly healthy male comes to your office with a dull, mild, midsternal pain. You take a cardiogram. It's normal. You tell the patient, "You *probably* have heartburn, *possibly* an ulcer. Take antacids and come see me again in a week, or sooner if your condition gets worse." He goes home and an hour later dies of a myocardial infarction.

You're in court. The opposing attorney asks, "Is it *possible* for a 26-year-old male feeling dull chest pain to have a heart attack?"

Don't say, "Yes." Your correct answer should be: "It would be extremely *unlikely*."

You're then asked: "Is it not well known that patients with myocardial infarctions *often* have normal electrocardiograms?" The fact is that only one cardiogram in ten is normal during early infarctions. So your truthful answer should be: "No, people with myocardial infarctions usually have electrocardiograms that show the problem." If the plaintiff's attorney wants to get into the statistics of the matter, that won't hurt you.

"Hearsay."   Hearsay is evidence you don't personally witness. For example, someone tells you that Mr. Smith was drunk, but you didn't see him yourself. Such hearsay evidence usually isn't admissible in court. But there are exceptions. Answer questions from your lawyer, assuming that your counsel knows the exceptions to the rule.

If asked by the plaintiff's attorney about something you know only by hearsay, answer: "I have no direct knowledge of the subject; I have only heard rumors about it."

"Authoritative."   Beware when asked if a certain author or paper is "authoritative" or "well-accepted." The plaintiff's attorney is trying to establish that you admit a reference is correct. If you fall into the trap and say, "Yes," the attorney will submit something in the reference that conflicts with your treatment or with something you said.

Many authors have written numerous papers, some of which are out of date. Therefore, when asked about an author's credibility, your answer should be along this line: "Much of what Dr. Jones has written is accurate, but I can't vouch for everything."

Similarly, when asked if a certain book is authoritative, answer: "Most of what the book says is accurate, but not everything is."

Another way to explain why it is impossible to agree that a text is authoritative is to say, "I have not read this text in preparation for this trial. There are many texts on this topic." If asked about quotes taken out of the book, realize that they are being taken out of context. Therefore you should insist on an examination of the entire section of the text being considered. The opposition may find this too boring or time-consuming.

Conflicting data can be found in every area of medicine. Even a new book has taken a year to get to press, and in that time there have been new discoveries, new drugs, and new surgical techniques.

It is often best to claim that your clinical experience and your discussions with other physicians are your sources of knowledge. If the plaintiff's attorney pushes you to accept published material as being authoritative, tell him that there is excellent evidence in the medical literature that proves the medical literature is inaccurate: In 1987 a group of biostaticians at The Royal Free Hospital in London found many flaws in articles in the *New England Journal of Medicine, The Lancet,* and *The British Medical Journal.*[190] In 1977 similar results were published by professors of statistics at the University of Florida.[148]

Make it clear that you're willing to comment on particular points: "I would be willing to comment on certain theories of the author or on the accuracy of specific statements in the book." If you refuse to comment at all, you'll be telling the jury that you don't recognize any book or author as "authoritative."

All of your testimony should show that you are cooperative, consistent, clear, right, and defensible.

Anatomy of a trial

Before examining the anatomy of your trial, be sure you and your lawyer have already dissected all depositions, and the original complaint and bill of particulars entered by the plaintiff. Inconsistencies and conflicts should be identified and plans developed to correct or expose them. Missing parts should be spotted and filled, and defenses prepared against all particulars of evidence against you.

Chapters 10-12 give specific defenses. This chapter brings you into the body of the courtroom, where you must enter and apply your defenses. It examines the participants, movements, and results of the trial. To what purpose?

The common purpose of a trial is to serve justice. Representing society, the jury's responsibility is to punish or remove disabling agents from the body politic—and to exonerate the innocent. The plaintiff and the defendant, however, enter at opposite sides of that common purpose.

For the plaintiff, the purpose of the trial is to be compensated for damages.

For you, the purpose is to defend your actions and absolve yourself of the charges.

For the jury, it is to weigh all the agents, actions, evidence, and effects from both sides of the case to make a just decision. It begins with the participants who can tip or balance the body of evidence.

PARTICIPANTS

Judge. The judge calls the trial to order, and keeps it in order, in balance, and moving to an informed and just conclusion. Along the way, the judge grants or denies motions from both sides, and directs the jury on issues of law as they emerge.

Sometimes, a judge's bias influences a jury. When that happens, the case may be appealed. Many defendants seek a jury trial in order to avoid the possibility of getting a biased or unreasonable judge. You're less likely to get twelve biased or unreasonable jurors than to get one such judge.[173] Unfortunately, juries, too, often have a kind of bias—a tendency to give a large award to a plaintiff who was badly damaged, even if the defendant wasn't responsible.

Abusing the privilege of argument. There is no "right" to present an argument to a jury. Making an argument to the jury is a "privilege" and is subject to abuse. One type of abuse of privilege involves making statements that would unduly prejudice a jury.

Judges can rule that certain actions in court would unduly prejudice the jury, and your attorney should ask the judge to so rule when it would help your case. The types of actions you should object to are illustrated by one successful plaintiff's attorney who had eight verdicts and settlements above a million dollars in 1986 alone. This attorney's view of doctors is, "I enjoy suing the bastards."[257]

> A woman who lost a leg stripped down to her shorts: with that leg hanging there, he argued her case. The jury went for $3.4 million.
>
> A young beautician who set herself on fire was badly burned over her upper body. She sued her psychiatrist, arguing that she had already tried suicide once and he should have hospitalized her to protect her. In court she stripped down to her bra and panties, showing ugly scars. The jury awarded $2.1 million.
>
> When a plaintiff dies, the widow is put on the stand.
>
> A seven-year-old read a poem she had written about how much she missed her dead sister.

Object to such ploys before and during trial. Such prejudicial actions may serve as the basis for an appeal to a higher court if the case is decided against you.

Jurors. A jury usually consists of twelve men and women (the size differs in a few states). They're chosen after being questioned by both the plaintiff's and the defendant's attorneys.

Many legal texts devote extensive, detailed discussions to the process of picking jurors (called *voir dire*). These considerations are beyond the scope of this book, but be aware that your lawyer will devote considerable time and effort to the vital function of selecting jurors. After all, they'll decide whether you're liable for the patient's damages, and how much you must pay.

Witnesses. The key agents in moving a jury to a decision are the witnesses. They include you. They may be your health-care peers. Some may be professional medical witnesses. Be ready to listen—and to support or refute them. You were introduced to some of them in Step 6. You'll meet more in the next four steps.

Lawyers. The attorneys for the plaintiff and defendant direct the courtroom drama, framing the facts to fit their opposite purposes. Each sets a scenario to sway the jury to his or her client's side. And like you and the plaintiff, the lawyers are leading performers in the unfolding drama.

MOVEMENTS

Opening statements. The judge opens the trial and charges the jury. The plaintiff's attorney then makes an opening statement, and your lawyer follows with the defense's opening statement. Those statements are not used to present evidence or specific details; they are outlines of what each side intends to demonstrate later.

The importance of your attorney making a strong and concise opening statement can't be overemphasized. One study shows that jurors in 65 percent of cases had their minds made up by the time the opening statements ended.[16] The same statistic may also apply to judges. Why?

A primary cause of quick decisions is the strong and lasting influence of initial impressions. Attorneys who briefly portray their sides more understandably and convincingly than their opponents are way ahead right from the start. At that point, the jurors aren't yet confused or bored, and remember most of what they've just heard.

Surprisingly, not all courtroom lawyers appreciate what a key opportunity the opening statement gives them.[188] For one thing, it's the best time to explain to the jury how the evidence to be presented later fits into the overall picture. That's critical, because to a jury of layfolk, a medical malpractice case is complex—full of clinical terms, procedures, and diagnostic or therapeutic evaluations and therapies that are difficult to grasp. The opening statement can be the most effective vehicle for simplifying the case and explaining why what you did or didn't do was correct.

Keep in mind also the need to repeat your side of the story again and again throughout the trial. That should be done in different ways at appropriate times. But it must always be done simply and coherently. The opening statement is the first chance your attorney will have to do that. Don't waste it.

Though evidence is not presented in the opening arguments, they can be used to cast doubt on or destroy opposing evidence, even before it's introduced. Consider the case of a plaintiff who goes back to work after a "disabling" injury, then engages in sports:

In his opening statement, his lawyer may say, "The plaintiff has heroically—and with great pain—tried to go back to work and return to normal life by making a supreme and courageous effort to engage in exercise." Your reports or films showing the plaintiff comfortably engaged in strenuous activity would make that statement lose much—if not all—of its impact.

If the plaintiff's injury predates your treatment, your attorney can tell the jury. "The plaintiff will try to prove that he has been disabled since he was treated by the defendant. That is true. It is also true that the plaintiff had been hospitalized for similar conditions before he was treated by the defendant." That makes the jurors aware of a pre-existing disability, and lets them see your alleged act of malpractice had little to do with making the condition worse.

The plaintiff's case.   The opening statements are followed by presentation of the plaintiff's case. That may include calling the plaintiff and other prosecution witnesses to the stand.

Your case.   Next, your attorney presents your case. That will include calling you and other defense witnesses to the stand. When your attorney questions you, you're under what's called direct examination. Normally, this will be the first time you're on the stand. Later, you'll be cross-examined by the plaintiff's attorney.

You may, however, be called as a witness during presentation of the plaintiff's case, before direct examination by your attorney. That tactic is designed to make you say things out of context, because you haven't yet had a chance to put the events and your actions into the right perspective. So be careful how you answer questions if that happens.

Motions.   A motion is a request made by either lawyer to the "court"—the judge.

1. An *objection* is a motion asking the court not to allow a question and its answer to be entered in the proceedings.
2. A motion to *dismiss* the case may be based on a technical consideration: invoking the statute of limitations, for example.
3. A motion for a *mistrial* may be made if the plaintiff's attorney asks you a question that presents inadmissible evidence to—or prejudices—the jury. That motion would be in order if you're asked, for example, how many times you've been sued for malpractice. Even if your attorney objects to the question, and you don't answer, the jury will likely believe that, since you didn't answer, you must have been sued quite a few times.
4. Your attorney may make a motion for a _directed verdict_. It's made on the basis of insufficient grounds to uphold a lawsuit—not enough evidence for a jury to consider. In effect, you claim that even if all the accusations are true, there's not enough proof to convict you. The judge isn't being asked to evaluate the evidence, just to judge it inadequate.

A directed verdict may be requested at the beginning of the trial, even if there seem to be few if any grounds for getting it. That's an important tactic if you later want the appellate court to review your case.[129] In general, appellate courts won't consider any questions the trial judge had no opportunity to consider.

A motion for a directed verdict should be made with the jurors out of the room. If it's denied, they'd get the impression that the court has found against you. You certainly don't want the positive move of requesting a directed verdict to influence the jury negatively.

Questions. Questioning can be difficult, especially when you're cross-examined. Many questions will be leading and narrow. You will be interrupted and frustrated in your attempt to speak. Interruptions are intentional, aimed to upset and get you excited and throw you out of control. Anger in any form, including arrogance, destroys the image of a competent practitioner who stays in control under pressure. So don't let the manner of questioning get to you.

Interruptions can also make you feel that you're not able to tell the "whole truth"—that what you say will be misinterpreted. Your lawyer should give you the opportunity to clarify your statements later in the trial.

If you feel it important to make a point immediately, tell the judge that you're being forced into committing perjury, and therefore would like a chance to speak. If possible, discuss this tactic with your attorney before you do it. And don't overdo it. Judges won't always let witnesses address them, and the jury may get the impression that you won't answer questions simply and honestly.

Direct examination. In direct examination, the attorneys question their own witnesses, thereby presenting their cases, their sides of the story. When a lawyer questions someone from the opposition during direct examination, that person is termed a "hostile witness."

During direct examination, your attorney is limited in how much he can lead or help you. Your counsel's questions may not put words into your mouth. State your observations, but don't give conclusions that require long proofs and are open to argument.

"What was the condition of the patient when she came to you?" your attorney may ask.

You'd be unwise to say, "She was drunk." That's a conclusion open to question and debate.

You'd do much better to answer, "The patient was unable to sit unassisted. She had the odor of alcohol. Speech was slurred. There also was rapid eye movement, termed nystagmus, which is often seen when someone has been drinking alcohol."

Those words paints a clear picture of someone whose memory of what happened at the time your care was rendered is probably inaccurate. That information suggests that the patient may not have felt the pain which would have led you to a correct diagnosis. It also suggests that the instructions for care that you so carefully explained to her were likely forgotten.

Cross-examination. The more the cross-examination becomes hard, nasty, and belligerent, the more calm and courteous you should be. That will earn you the respect and sympathy of the jury for your ability to think and respond calmly and responsibly under such adverse conditions.

An attorney cross-examines a witness for one of two reasons: to impeach or otherwise weaken the direct testimony, or to elicit testimony that supports the cross-examiner's side of the case.[50] Remember, most attorneys ask a question only when they already know what the answer will be.

Be careful not to let words be put into your mouth by leading, pointed, suggestive questions. Don't automatically agree to anything. And don't be afraid to qualify an answer.

If asked, for example, whether a patient with a broken arm would usually have signs or symptoms that a reasonably competent doctor would be able to recognize, don't give a "yes" or "no" answer. Say that it depends on the situation.

If asked to explain your answer, confidently state that many patients with broken arms show little or no signs or symptoms because of insensitivity to pain. This insensitivity can be caused by pains elsewhere, low blood sugar or oxygen, sensory nerve damage, cerebral concussion, or dulling of the senses due to alcohol or other drugs. If the break is undisplaced or incomplete, there may not be much functional impairment. If the patient is uncooperative, physical examination also may prove to be as unrewarding as it is difficult to carry out.

Such answers nullify the point of view the plaintiff's attorney is trying to implant in the jurors' minds. They also give them an understanding of the difficulty involved in making a diagnosis, especially if you mention points relevant to your case.

Such informed answers take preparation and thought. That's why you need to know both the medical literature and cases similar to yours—and be able to apply that background material to your case. (Steps 10-12 provide specific legal aids that can help you disarm your accusers.)

Cross-examination is a difficult experience for many witnesses. Your reputation and money are at stake. If they weren't, the witness might view the cross-examination experience as a matching of wits, nothing more than an intellectual parlor game. It isn't a game, by any stretch of the imagination.

The plaintiff's attorney will pound away at your story, trying to uncover lies and inconsistencies. The manner of questioning may be friendly and reassuring—or antagonistic and insulting. Either way, the purpose is to discredit you and your defense.

During cross-examination, you're expected just to answer questions. Don't argue or give uninvited explanations. Answer with short, simple statements that support your side of the controversy.

Other witnesses also will be cross-examined. Expert witnesses, for example, can be examined in a way that casts doubt on the adequacy of their experience or shows them as biased. Expert witnesses are supposed to be neutral, credentialed sources of information—not easily swayed or discredited.

Witnesses can be cross-examined to discredit their testimony. Inaccuracy can be demonstrated by showing that the witness:

- Was not in a position to see or hear what was claimed.
- Is confused or has forgotten what was seen.
- Has given previous contrary testimony.[39]

Other pointers on impeaching expert witnesses were given in Step 6.

Redirect examination. Only material discussed during the cross-examination can be subject to further examination. Redirect examination is a means your attorney can use to undo any impeachment that occurred on cross-examination. In short, the purpose of redirect examination is to correct harm done to you or your witnesses during cross-examination. Although it's technically improper, redirect examination can also be used to bring up items you and your attorney forgot to discuss earlier. If the plaintiff's lawyer objects, your lawyer should move to "reopen direct examination."

Re-cross-examination. Only material discussed on redirect examination can be re-cross-examined. To discuss material not covered during cross-examination, your attorney asks for cross-examination to be reopened.

Rebuttal. New or unexpected evidence introduced by your attorney after the prosecution has rested its case constitutes rebuttal. In response, the plaintiff can exercise the right of surrebuttal.[53]

Objections. Your attorney should object to any question that leads you toward trouble, stating the reason you shouldn't be asked that question: "It's unreasonable to ask the witness to recall exactly what was said in a conversation that occurred a year ago, because no one's memory is that good."[188]

The rules governing testimony are complex. An objection is a means of controlling testimony by pointing out that a rule is being violated. But don't always be a stickler for the rules. If testimony is technically improper but is helping your side, don't object.

When your attorney raises an objection, see it as a signal to you that the item in question is dangerous. Always remember to pause before answering any question. That gives you time to think and your attorney time to object.

You may also object to the "form of the question." That objection may refer to questions that are leading, argumentative, confusing, or immaterial. An argumentative question states or assumes a "fact" that's not already known to be true,[1] a fact not in evidence.[188]

An objection may lead to a question or statement being stricken from the record. The jury will be instructed to disregard it. But it may still have an effect on the jury. In fact, strenuous objection will probably call attention to the statement and make the jury more aware of it than they otherwise might have been.[285]

Your attorney can object to questions that bring up information not material or relevant. Information is _immaterial_ if it has no logical connection to the case. It's _irrelevant_ if it doesn't support the conclusion the questioner is attempting to prove.

The jury may be prejudiced by questions that give negative implications about your character. If that happens, your attorney will move for a mistrial. If granted, the motion would invalidate the trial, ending it then and there. The reason: Introducing such evidence is a prejudicial error that can't be corrected at trial.

Even if evidence brought into court stands the tests of materiality and relevancy, a mistrial can still be declared because of its nature—if, for example, the prejudice generated by the evidence outweighs its legitimate value.

Videotapes shown in court. A common ploy is to present a videotape to the jury showing the disabled plaintiff trying to function. After watching a graphic "Day in the Life of the Injured Plaintiff" show, many juries are moved to compensate the victim, no matter where the blame may lie. In some cases, the defense has had the judge view the show and rule that it would unduly prejudice the jury.

In other cases defendants have made their own videotapes. For example, in one case a child had been born prematurely and weighed one pound at birth. The child had many problems and these were blamed on poor care. The defense made a videotape that showed how immediate life and death decisions are made in an intensive care nursery. It showed the loving care given to the delicate, severely premature infants, and it demonstrated the miracle of neonatal intensive care. The jury decided in favor of all defendants, just three hours after the plaintiffs turned down a settlement offer of $2.2 million.[57]

Videotapes must be prepared with input from physicians and defense attorneys. The videotape must be produced in accordance with rules of evidence in order to be admissible in court. Evidence requirements are summarized in table 9-1.

Closing arguments. Summations are made by the plaintiff's and defendant's attorneys at the end of the testimony. New evidence isn't supposed to be presented during the closing argument. Important areas, especially those in conflict, will be reviewed. The statements by each attorney remind the jury of items favorable to their respective clients. If a witness, for example, was biased or didn't seem competent to testify on the subject, that will be emphasized. Relevant and favorable legal precedents will be cited.

TABLE 9–1. REQUIREMENTS FOR COURTROOM VIDEOTAPES[57]

Videotapes must be:

- Relevant to establishing material (pertinent) issues in the case.
- Authenticated as true reproductions of conditions existing at the time of the incident.

Videotapes must not contain material that is:

- Hearsay evidence.
- Imflammatory, biased, or prejudicial.
- Opinion. This is the subject of expert testimony.

FACTORS AFFECTING PAYMENT AMOUNTS AND CONDITIONS

Jury instructions and attention to state laws and other sources of compensation can greatly affect the final settlement and how it is made.

A $19.9 million award resulted when the court and jury ignored the significance of future interest on money awarded and the ability to pay out damages periodically (at $100,000 a year). The "present value" of a verdict takes into account the earning power of the money awarded.[230] The laws relating to these issues vary greatly from one state to another.

In a federal case an Army hospital was ordered to pay for failure to diagnose and treat a patient for cancer. It was determined that CHAMPUS (Civilian Health and Medical Program of the Uniformed Services) benefits received by the patient should be deducted from the payment.[113]

A 1986 Illinois law allows collateral sources for medical benefits over $25,000 to be offset as long as the offset does not reduce the judgment by more than 50%. Also, the law prevents plaintiffs from asking for punitive damages in their original complaint, though subsequent motions to add punitive claims can be made if it is shown there is a reasonable chance the plaintiff will win.[106]

RESULTS

Jury decides.   At the end of the trial, the jury discusses and votes on the defendant's guilt or innocence. In some states, a unanimous verdict is required. If the jurors can't reach a unanimous verdict, it's a "hung jury." When that happens, the judge instructs them to deliberate further for agreement, or declares a mistrial.

Judge overrules. If the jury decides a case contrary to the evidence, the judge can set aside that verdict and order a new trial. As with dismissing a case before going to trial, the judge will dismiss a verdict only when there's no clear evidence to support the jury's finding. If the money damages awarded by the jury to the plaintiff are grossly excessive, the judge may, as a matter of law, order the plaintiff to remit only a portion of the award. The procedural process that diminishes a jury's award is called *remittur.*

For example, a jury awarded $1.1 million to a patient for birth defects that occurred after the mother took Bendectin. The court ruled, however, that no reasonable jury could find that Bendectin had caused the birth defects because there was universal scientific consensus that Bendectin was not a teratogen.[156] Despite this, there have been over a thousand Bendectin claims filed.[174]

Bendectin was effective and safe but was finally removed from the market because of lawsuits alleging it caused birth defects. On the other hand, prematurity is the most common cause of infant mortality in this country, and smoking in pregnancy can cause prematurity.[63] Also, 34,000 American women will die this year of lung cancer. Yet, the tobacco companies are still making billions and are not held liable for the damages they cause. State and Federal governments permit the sale of tobacco products, and stores of all kinds sell them. Yet, if a physician or drug company were to sell something that might be harmful, lawsuits result.

Mistrial. A mistrial may be declared because of an event, mistake, or blockage that makes a responsible conclusion impossible. *Black's Law Dictionary* notes that a mistrial may be the result of an extraordinary, disruptive event, such as death of one of the attorneys, a prejudicial error that can't be corrected at trial, or a deadlocked jury.[30]

Appeals. Either party in a civil suit may appeal a decision. Even though a case is appealed, damages awarded by the trial court are still owed to the plaintiff by the defendant. One way to get around or delay paying the award until your appeal is heard is to have your lawyer file a *"supersedeas bond."* Take this action if a large amount of money is involved.

The decision of the jury can be overruled by appellate courts, or even by the trial judge in the instances we've cited. An appellate court will overrule a jury decision if it believes that the jury wasn't property instructed in the law, wasn't allowed to hear important evidence, or heard unfair, prejudicial evidence. If a principle of legal procedure wasn't followed, the appellate court can overturn a decision made in the lower court.

If you appeal a decision made against you, you must prove that errors made in the trial caused the case to be decided wrongly. Primarily, the appellate court will be interested in the legal issues of the case: Was the jury properly instructed in the law? Was evidence withheld from the jury for invalid reasons? Was prejudicial evidence presented?

The appellate court won't concern itself deciding the facts of the case, unless you claim that there was insufficient evidence to justify the verdict. The decision of a trial judge or of a jury won't be overturned unless the court record shows the decision to be "clearly wrong."

To preserve your opportunity for later consideration by the appellate court, you must raise any questionable legal issues while your case is being tried in the lower court. That's why many objections and other motions are made during the course of a trial, even though it's fairly obvious the judge won't go along with them.

Appeal of a judgment must be made within a given time. The limit varies from state to state, but is usually about a month. Fees must be paid, and specific forms must be filed for the appeal.

A brief must be presented to the appellate court. The specific requirements for such briefs differ between states. Usually, they include a description of the facts, a discussion of the contested issues, and a review of the relevant law. In effect, the brief is a data bank on which the appellate court bases its decision.

In addition to reviewing the written brief, the appellate court will sometimes ask the attorneys to make oral presentations. This request may be made when there is confusion on certain issues, or when the case is difficult to decide. The court will also consider what expert witnesses said. If more information is needed, the appellate judge may send the case back to the trial court.

Appellate court work is extensive and expensive. To prepare an appeal, your attorney must study the trial record, determine the legal issues involved, research the law, and present convincing briefs and oral arguments.

Rather than worry about having to appeal a bad decision, work to prevent that decision by making sure that you and your attorney effectively prepare and carry out your defense in the lower court.

Understanding the art of testifying and the anatomy of a trial, you can apply the already tried resources in the following chapters to shape, animate, and present your case in any court.

Defenses involving the patient

This and the next two chapters deal with various defenses you can use against charges of malpractice. Chapter 11 gives defenses to specific charges, and 12 offers defenses that involve other defendants and other sources of responsibility or payment. This chapter presents defenses to be used when the plaintiff may have played a part in the act of negligence.

Examine each defense in all three chapters to see if they apply to your case. And then be sure to research recent court cases similar to yours for potential defenses not presented here.

CONTRIBUTORY NEGLIGENCE

Simply put, contributory negligence means that the plaintiff has caused part of his injuries through his own actions or inaction. In such a case, what he did or didn't do as a patient can be compared with or shown as contributing to your acts as the practicing physician. Consider the following kinds of contributory negligence:

Comparative negligence. The doctor accused of malpractice need not be held accountable for all injuries and damages in evidence. Comparative negligence is measured in terms of percentage. Accordingly, a patient may have had a million dollars' worth of damages, but be considered 30 percent responsible for causing them. In that case, the defendant would have to pay $700,000.

Applications of the doctrine of negligence varies from state to state. The Illinois Supreme Court, for example, adopted comparative negligence in 1981.[c6]

Noncompliance. Contributory negligence may be claimed when a patient doesn't follow your recommended treatment or fails to return for requested office visits. It's common for patients to ignore instructions. One team of doctors, for example, found that far fewer than half the patients who came for emergency treatment followed recommendations for follow-up visits.[276]

Many patients refuse treatment or hospital admission because of job or family responsibilities, the expense, or just the fear of being hospitalized.

Whatever the reasons, noncompliance should be documented. The medicine not taken would have helped. You can show how. The return office or emergency department visit or hospital admission would have given you the opportunity to re-examine and diagnose the problem as it became more advanced, severe, and easy to detect.

Your records may be incomplete in the recommendations for treatments, hospitalization, or appointments that the patient refused. If they are, don't try to modify them. Just write down your recollections, with the current date. Such documents can be used in court. If they're written six months after your encounter with that patient, a jury could reasonably believe you really did remember such things. If you go to trial three years after the encounter, however, the jury would be far less likely to believe your memory is that good.

For practical purposes, write down all your recollections of the case as soon as you learn of a lawsuit. Such documentation is often required by insurance companies. Your memory is fresher than it will be by the time you give a deposition or go to court.

There may be a disagreement about what happened when you treated the patient. Demonstrating to the jury that the patient didn't follow your instructions may become a necessary part of proving contributory or comparative negligence.

In determining the reliability of the plaintiff's testimony, the jury will consider the patient's character. Is the plaintiff honest and conscientious? The jury will likely decide that a patient who falsely claimed to have followed treatment recommendations probably won't give accurate testimony about what happened.

On many issues, it's your word against the patient's. If the issue isn't clearly documented in the medical record—and sometimes even if it is—it's your memory and testimony against the plaintiff's. The jury will tend to believe the one who appears to be more honest, reliable, and respectable.

Many patients are unrealiable in complying with treatment. One study of outpatients found that only 22 percent took their prescriptions properly, while 31 percent took them in a dangerous manner. A review of 50 studies revealed total noncompliance in 25 to 50 percent of outpatients.[3]

Although you can use many measures to increase patient compliance,[200] they're not of concern here. The applicable fact is that non-compliance is more the rule than the exception. So if the rule applies in your case, use it.

You may be able to find indirect evidence of your patient's noncompliance. If you record when prescriptions are refilled, you may be able to show that the patient must have run out of medication at certain times. Pharmacy records or the patient's income tax records showing medical expenses may prove that medication wasn't being taken. If levels of a drug in blood tests are low, you have evidence that the drug wasn't being taken regularly. That happens frequently with patients who have seizures.

A patient of yours may be injured because of a seizure, but blame you for it. If you warned the patient of the need to take the medicine regularly, and documented your instructions, you're in a strong position. If you also warned the patient that consumption of alcohol can induce seizure, and can document that the plaintiff had been drinking at the time of the seizure and injury, then you should escape blame for the damages.

If a patient arrives at your office not using the crutches you gave or the splint you had put on, or wearing dirty and wet bandages, you have evidence pointing to negligence on the part of the patient. It's to your advantage to show that such neglect caused the damages.

Denial of symptoms.   Evidence is sometimes withheld in a court-room; it's also withheld in an emergency room. Many patients don't describe their symptoms and problems fully. They give an in-complete or inadequate medical history and picture. That makes proper diagnosis and treatment difficult or even impossible.

Failure to give an adequate history can be due to forgetfulness, drugs, denial, or senility. Certainly, remembering a half dozen symptoms and other problems can be difficult for anyone, especially when in pain. If the patient has been taking medication or alcohol to lessen the discomfort, or for any other reason, the story will likely be inaccurate and incomplete. Sometimes the patient's condition itself will cloud mental abilities, as in cases of head injury, and distur-bances in blood sugar, electrolytes, or oxygen.

Denial often causes patients to minimize their symptoms. It's common for patients with myocardial infarction to admit only vague, minimal discomfort. Speaking to the patient's spouse often brings out an entirely different story. When patients deny the severity of the condition, they impede—even damagingly delay—diagnosis and treatment.

The effects of such negligence by a plaintiff were verified in one case when the court was shown that self-denial of her terminal condition (she died during the trial) kept her from continuing treatment for recurrence of cancer. She claimed to have been told her X-rays were normal, but well-kept records refuted that assertion.[94] Cancer patients, as well as those with acute myocardial infarctions, often deny the existence of their problems.

Misleading the physician. It is well established that in making a diagnosis and choosing treatment physicians rely on what a patient says (the medical history). If a patient lies, it should be claimed that the physician was prevented from making proper choices. For example, a woman with late menses denied being sexually active. She was given a hormone shot but soon found out she was pregnant. She had a miscarriage a few weeks later. She sued for mental anguish, and the physician was found to be not liable.[c172]

Contributory negligence. A patient's contribution to his own injury was judged relevant in a California Court of Appeals ruling. An obese, diabetic patient developed a foot infection. It evolved into gangrene, and he eventually needed a below-the-knee amputation. He sued his doctors. They presented evidence showing that he had neither controlled his weight, followed the recommended diet, nor taken prescribed medications. The lower court refused to instruct the jury on contributory negligence, but the appellate court ruled that the patient's actions were a relevant consideration.[168]

In an Illinois appeal, a doctor properly diagnosed a myocardial infarction. He wanted to call an ambulance to take the patient to the hospital, but the patient insisted on driving his truck back to his employer and arranging for a later ride to the hospital. The patient died soon after leaving the doctor. The doctor was sued, but was found not negligent. The patient died because of his own negligence.[c75]

Ignoring danger can also be an indication of negligence. Persons near oxygen sources can be burned by flash fires. If a patient is warned about the danger of smoking near oxygen, yet does so, the hospital and the doctor won't be held liable for resulting damages, provided the patient is mentally competent.[c61] But if the patient is shown to be mentally incompetent because of senility, intoxication, or disorientation, the doctor and hospital can be held liable.[126]

Limits to contributory counterclaims. The last case illustrates that legal limits have been placed on the use of contributory negligence as a defense. The possibility of negligence, for example, is certainly relevant in a case of suicide. One can argue that the patient was somewhat responsible for what happened, having, after all, performed the act. But that argument would not be valid if the person should have been recognized as disturbed enough to be not responsible for the act. Nor can the doctrine of contributory negligence be applied in cases involving children, the mentally retarded, or those who have been declared legally incompetent.[209]

Take the case of a psychiatric patient who jumped through a hospital window. The hospital was held liable because the condition of the patient was judged sufficiently volatile to indicate that she might try to hurt herself. The patient had been restrained and had broken loose. She then jumped out a window that didn't have the safeguards required by law.[c107] There have been many such cases in which medical treatment facilities were held liable for patient self-injury, including suicide.[56] Foreseeability of the event is a key issue in such cases.

Similarly, patients who take overdoses and intend to kill themselves cannot be permitted to leave the hospital "Against Medical Advice"—to sign out "AMA." When patients take an overdose or try to kill themselves, they lose the legal right to refuse treatment from the attending physician.[103]

If a patient of yours who has tried to commit suicide is released from the hospital and commits suicide, your defense would have to be that the patient didn't appear suicidal during your examination. You judged that the patient had only made a gesture to get attention, or had performed the act on a transient impulse because of alcoholic intoxication or some event that caused temporary emotional upset.

The defense that a patient caused or contributed to the damages isn't valid when the patient's noncompliance takes place after your negligent act.[c84]

STATUTE OF LIMITATIONS

An injured patient can wait just so long before deciding to sue for malpractice. This period—usually one to four years—varies from state to state and is called the statute of limitations.

The time limit also varies for different offenses. A patient or a relative may decide to sue after the statute of limitations for malpractice has run out. In such cases, health-care defendants find themselves being sued for offenses that have longer limits. Those offenses include breach of contract, wrongful death, and assault and battery.

In many states the statute starts to run from the time the allegedly negligent treatment was given. Thus, if the statute of limitations is two years, a patient could not file a suit more than two years after the treatment.

Many states, however, specify that the statute begins to run when the injury is recognized, or when a reasonably diligent patient should have been able to notice the injury.[c41,c68,c133] This standard is referred to as the discovery rule.

A case in point: A Tennessee dentist cut his own finger and the lip of a patient on a dental bridge. As a result, the patient developed serum hepatitis. The patient was unable to figure out that the hepatitis had developed as a result of his dental visit until sometime later. The state had a one-year statute of limitations at the time, and the patient didn't file suit within a year of his visit to the dentist. The Tennessee Supreme Court found that the statute did not begin to run until the patient had discovered the cause of his illness. So the statute of limitations was not a useful defense for the dentist.[c70]

In another case a woman was told by a foot specialist that a surgeon had incorrectly operated on her feet, but she did not have a "suable" case. Five years later the woman did sue. The court ruled that the statue of limitations had not run out because she had discovered the elements of her damages initially, even though she did not understand that she had a legal cause of action.[c132]

Most states allow extension of the statute of limitations in some situations. For minors, the time often doesn't begin to run until the child reaches majority. The statute often can be extended if you continue to treat or resume treatment of someone you allegedly injured many years ago. It can also be extended if you fraudulently concealed the harm done: failed to inform the patient of the problem, denied it, or said it was only temporary.[c22,243]

A plaintiff failed to extend the statute of limitations by counting the time spent with a physician the defendant had sent him to for interpretation of radiological tests.[c51] In another case an emergency department physician provided emergency care and instructed the patient to seek specialized treatment in event his condition did not improve within three days. He was treated by other doctors on the same day. The continuous treatment doctrine was judged to be inapplicable when the malpractice action was brought two and a half years later. It was felt that the patient terminated his relationship with the emergency physician when he sought care by other doctors on the same day.[c20]

Some states also have a foreign object rule that extends the statute deadline until the time the object is discovered. Thus, if a surgical instrument is found many years after it was left in a patient, the patient can still sue, even though the usual statute of limitations had long since run out.

The foreign object rule was applied when a prosthetic heart valve was found to be defective when the patient died four years after it was implanted. The valve was judged to be a foreign body; therefore the statute was extended beyond the usual three-year limit.[c112] A contraceptive IUD (Intra-Uterine Device) was also ruled a foreign body to extend the statute of limitations.[c136]

GOOD SAMARITAN LAWS

Various laws have been enacted to encourage physicians to care for patients in emergency situations. These statutes provide that, in providing emergency treatment, the health practitioner is held to a lesser standard of care.

A Good Samaritan won't be held responsible if an act involves only ordinary negligence. Accordingly, a doctor giving emergency care won't be held accountable for some mistakes that would usually lead to liability. Under most Good Samaritan statutes the provider of care is liable only for gross negligence or willful and wanton acts.

Good Samaritan laws usually don't apply if you're dealing with a patient in a hospital, emergency clinic, or medical office, or if you bill a patient for services rendered. And they don't apply just because a patient fails to pay the bill.

A broader interpretation of the Good Samaritan Law has been adopted in several states.[175] In Illinois the law has protected physicians acting in a hospital.

Search for other statutes that grant you immunity. The Washington (State) Paramedic Civil Immunity Act, for example, guarantees immunity to paramedics while treating patients in immediate danger of dying. This act includes patients with cardiac arrest, as well as those with such other injuries as neck fractures.[c110]

Good Samaritan rules are sometimes applied liberally. Take the case of a surgeon who operated on an automobile accident victim. The surgeon was not "on call." The patient remained in critical condition until he eventually died. The court found the surgeon to be protected under Michigan's Good Samaritan statute.[c112]

In California, a hospital resident responded to an emergency call to help a patient having a seizure and cardiac arrest. The resident was not on emergency call, nor was he the patient's regular doctor. He was therefore not responsible.[c117]

In another California case an obstetrician requested a pediatrician STAT when an infant suffered severe intrauterine hypoxia due to the umbilical cord being entangled about his neck and feet. A pediatrician did respond within a minute and cared for the child. The child developed cerebral palsy and permanent neurological damage, and at age 6 the obstetrician and pediatrician were sued for malpractice. The court noted that the child was the patient of the obstetrician, who did not customarily refer patients to the pediatrician.

The court ruled that the applicable sections of the Good Samaritan laws applied to emergencies both "within and without a hospital." The court felt the Good Samaritan laws applied to hospital-designated team members, such as a cardiopulmonary resuscitation team.[c30]

Similarly, a vascular surgeon called in the middle of emergency surgery obtained a summary judgment in his favor because he was a "rescuing surgeon." In California, statutory law provides Good Samaritan protection for such defendants.[226]

In New York, a physician was asked to look at a neighbor who was ill. The physician took the man's pulse, told the wife that hospitalization was needed, called for an ambulance and left. After the man died, the wife sued, but the court found that the Good Samaritan Law applied in this emergency situation.

EMERGENCY CASES

A health practitioner can't be expected to act with the same skill and completeness in an emergency as in a normal case. Not only is there little time to think about the problem, there's often too little time to perform all desired acts or to be as careful as in a noncritical situation. Thus, in emergency cases, practitioners have not been held liable for letting intravenous lines infiltrate,[c39] for leaving foreign objects in the body,[c187] and for other acts usually considered to be negligent.[126]

RELEASE OF DOCTOR BY PATIENT

A patient may release an attending physician from liability. If the doctor pays a settlement and secures a written release from further liability, the patient can't file suit later for additional damages from the same occurrence. Depending on the wording, all defendants may be simultaneously released through the agreement with the one practitioner.[60]

Settlements with people other than health-care professionals may also release the accused practitioner from liability. In an appeals case in Georgia, a patient who suffered a broken arm in an automobile accident settled a claim against the driver of the other vehicle. As worded, the release applied to all other persons who might be liable for any future injuries that developed. The patient had undergone two operations to repair his arm. During the second, the radial nerve was injured, causing disability and pain. The appellate court held the second surgery to be an aggravation of the original injury. The doctor, therefore, was protected from liability for any negligence by having been previously released by the patient.[c33]

REFUSAL OF TREATMENT

You may also be released from legal responsibility if a patient refuses your treatment. Refusal may be perfectly rational. Let's say you've recommended surgery to relieve pain, but the patient decides the suffering isn't bad enough to justify the risks of surgery. Maybe you're about to suture a laceration, but the patient chooses to let it heal on its own. Or perhaps it's because the treatment regimen you suggest is similar to one that didn't help the patient in the past.

When a patient refuses treatment, always explain why you think it's needed. Then discuss the alternatives. Document in the medical record the efforts you made to convince the patient of the importance of your workup or treatment. In one case, a California doctor was successfully sued following the death of a patient who had repeatedly refused pap smears. The doctor hadn't documented informing her of the risks of not having the smears done.[c193]

When treatment is refused, and the patient later sues, documentation of what you told that patient about the need for treatment is vital to your defense. If you can show that the patient refused treatment and later had a poor result, you can argue that, had the patient allowed treatment, the result would have been different.

Against Medical Advice. Every hospital has standard AMA forms patients may sign to refuse treatment. This doesn't stand for the American Medical Association; it means "Against Medical Advice." Is signing such a form proof that the patient refused treatment? That's for the jury to decide.

A signed AMA form might not release a doctor from responsibility because most patients don't understand what they're signing.[48] Studies show that 20 percent of adults in the United States are functionally illiterate or incompetent, and an additional 34 percent are barely functionally literate.[183,193] So what does signing a form mean for most people? Not much. More than half your patients may not be able to read it.

Some studies have suggested that consent forms be worded at a seventh-grade level. Others have found that many patients are not able to understand material even that simple.[184]

At times, even well-educated people will sign the wrong form because of the urgency and stress of the situation. One such patient, for example, signed a permit for a certain type of X-ray instead of a permission form for a blood transfusion.

Research has also shown that addiction to alcohol or drugs is a factor in more than half the cases of patients signing out AMA.[141] Most patients who leave AMA, however, do maintain some contact with the hospital afterward.[238] Failure to communicate information or feelings is involved in many cases.[102]

As already noted, a charge of negligence can be made against a practitioner who allows a patient to sign out of the hospital against medical advice. That's most likely to happen when harm befalls the patient because of premature departure from the hospital. The best defense to such a charge would include as many as possible of the following elements:

1. A description of the efforts made to discover and respond to the patient's feelings and fears, and to communicate the possible consequences of leaving the hospital and of not following recommended treatment.

2. Signs indicating that the patient understood the consequences of leaving.

3. Indications that the patient intended to seek further medical care elsewhere.

4. Evidence that the patient was leaving to pursue a drinking or drug habit, even though help was offered for coping with the problem.

5. Documentation that you recommended further medical care be sought elsewhere, even though the patient was rejecting your treatment.

Always exercise caution in consciously providing less than complete treatment to a patient leaving the hospital AMA. The patient could later claim that your continuing care was evidence that you agreed with his leaving. A case in point:

A patient needing intravenous antibiotics insists on leaving the hospital against your advice. You prescribe less-effective antibiotic pills, hoping the inferior treatment will be adequate. It isn't, and the patient becomes a plaintiff. He charges you with providing inferior treatment. Your defense would have to include documentation that you tried to convince him to stay, that he insisted on leaving, and that he assumed the risk of the inferior treatment. Further details of the assumption of risk defense are discussed below.

Document your advice.   Remember—or better yet, document in the chart—just how you explained the situation to the patient, and how he communicated his understanding back to you. Equally important: Document that the patient was mentally, physically, and legally competent to make a decision.

If patients' mental abilities are dulled, doctors or nurses must sometimes make decisions for them. This requirement applies when you treat drunk patients who refuse limb- or lifesaving procedures, asthma or coronary sufferers who rip off oxygen masks, diabetics whose blood sugar is so low that thinking is impaired, psychotics who are out of control, the head-injured or drugged who are out of touch with reality, the suicidal who are bent on self-destruction, and many others who need, but resist, care and restraint. When such a patient signs out AMA, you'll have little or no excuse for giving inadequate treatment.

The broken crystal ball defense.   Many patients who refuse medical workup and treatment later develop complications of their condition. The physician might explain some of the possible consequences of refusing treatment. However, the physician cannot be expected to foresee all complications, especially when a *workup and observation have been refused*. In your defense, explain to the jury that continued observation and workup are needed to understand a patient's condition.

For example, one woman who refused the hospitalization suggested by her physician died a week later. Her physician had performed intestinal bypass surgery a year earlier, and the patient had lost weight. Hospitalization was recommended when the patient developed abdominal pains and appeared quite weak. The patient had substantial debts and was separated from her husband. She did not want more debts, and refused to go to a charity hospital. She went to live with her parents, received no further care, and died a week after admission had been recommended. An autopsy showed that she had died of peritonitis which resulted from perforation of the blind loop of intestinal bypass. The claimants argued that the standard of care required that the physician tell the patient's mother of the need for hospitalization but produced no expert witness to support this argument. The defense held that the standard of care did not require notification of relatives. The defense also argued that intestinal perforation was usually fatal within 48 hours, so when the physician last saw the patient, a week before her death, she did not have the condition that proved to be fatal.[194]

EUTHANASIA

Several physicians have been unsuccessfully prosecuted for mercy killings:[233]

In 1950, a doctor was acquitted of murder for injecting air into a patient's veins after the patient asked to die.[235]

In 1974, a doctor was found not guilty in the death of a terminal cancer patient he allegedly injected with potassium chloride.[186]

In 1980, a mentally competent but terminal patient asked and was allowed to be taken off a respirator. The court decided that the right to privacy includes the right to refuse medical care, and that the right is more important than the state's interest in preserving life.[c167]

In 1982, another doctor was acquitted of attempted murder by injecting air into the veins of a patient who had been shot in the head in a barroom brawl.[11]

Most of us don't like to face critical health problems. Yet we must think about what should be done to help people with such problems when they become our patients.

Consider the common practice of nursing homes transferring a patient about to die to a hospital emergency department:

The patient may have been unconscious for several years, and the family had never decided or told the nursing home to let the patient die if a terminal illness developed. So when the patient appears ready to die, the nursing home quickly transfers the patient to the hospital.

Emergency physicians are thus often faced with moribund patients whose histories they know little about. Seldom is there time to contact relatives or friends to see how aggressively to treat. One thing is clear: Unless something is done within a few minutes, the patient will die.

A good emergency physician can keep almost anyone alive, and greatly improve the vital functions of moribund patients. But that improvement often comes at great expense and discomfort to patients and their families.[46]

Medical considerations play only a part in determining the proper course of care for patients who are brain dead, suffering intractable pain, or slowly dying of cancer. There are religious, economic, and social considerations as well. And if you end up in court because of treatment you did or didn't give such a patient, you'll quickly see there are also legal implications that can take precedence over all others, including common sense, and can put you in court if you're not careful.

Take the case of John Storar. He was 52 years old; mental age, 18 months. Condition: inoperable terminal bladder cancer with many metastases. His family wanted the state facility where he lived to stop the blood transfusions that were keeping him alive, but causing him great pain and distress. A lower court so ordered, but the New York Court of Appeals reversed that decision.[269]

So even when the family and physician agree that the situation is hopeless, the courts may not allow painful, expensive treatments to be discontinued.

Quite often, a patient's family doesn't understand the concept of brain death, or has religious convictions that prohibit allowing the loved one to die.

The laws that apply to withholding life support are changing rapidly. More and more states are recognizing brain death. In many areas, it's common practice to write a "Do not resuscitate" order in a patient's chart.[267]

DO NOT RESUSCITATE POLICIES

It is becoming acceptable and more common to not resuscitate certain patients. The first DNR (do not resuscitate) policy was written in 1976. In 1986 only 59% of the institutions studied by the JCAH (Joint Commission on Accreditation of Hospitals) had formal or informal policies on resuscitation.[66] Many hospitals have had unwritten, unstated policies. Some physicians have been reluctant to write DNR orders for fear of being sued. The acceptance of (and sometimes the requirement to have) such policies make it defensible to not resuscitate certain patients.

A 1988 JCAH standard requires hospitals to formulate guidelines for DNR orders. The JCAH credentials 5,100 acute care hospitals in the United States. Hospitals will not be directed on the content of their policies, and these policies will vary considerably.

New York State has a DNR law of its own, article 29–B of the Public Health Law. Under this article, the decision to write a DNR order is formalized and documented on special forms requiring certain types of witnesses.[140]

Many cases in several states have questioned whether feeding tubes, life support systems, and other treatments should be withdrawn given the presence or absence of DNR orders and living wills.

HANDICAPPED INFANTS AND BABY DOE

Common practice in this country has been to withhold surgery and medical care from severely retarded infants with Down's syndrome (mongolism) in order to bring death sooner. These infants usually have several congenital defects. A nationwide survey of pediatricians found that two-thirds would agree with a parental request not to treat duodenal atresia, which prevents the passage of food.[245]

Yet when a newborn with Down's syndrome was allowed to die rather than undergo corrective surgery in 1982, there was a public outcry, fueled by the news media. The US Department of Health and Human Services notified hospitals they could lose federal funds if nutritional, medical, or surgical support required to correct a life-threatening condition were withheld from a handicapped infant.[67] As a result of this and similar cases, failure to feed and care for handicapped infants "seemed for a while to be prohibited by federal law."

These laws have become known as "Baby Doe" regulations. In 1986 the obstetrician who delivered Baby Doe testified that the decision to not perform life saving surgery was based on the fact that the child had Down's syndrome. Disability rights activists protested that such decisions discriminate against the handicapped, and President Reagan ordered the U.S. Department of Health and Human Services to notify health care providers that newborns with disabilities were protected under Section 504 of the 1973 Rehabilitation Act, which prohibits discrimination against the handicapped by recipients of federal funds.[99] Hospitals were told to post notices of this regulation in wards, and a 24-hour hot line was staffed for callers to report allegations of abuse.

The American Medical Association and other groups protested that such regulations could lead to unwarranted government intrusion into medical decision-making. They filed the 1986 case, *Brown v American Hospital Association et al.* As a result of this case, the U.S. Supreme Court effectively overturned the regulations, saying it was the (non-federally funded) parents who made decisions in such cases. Therefore the anti-discrimination law did not apply.

Disability rights advocates (and a late-1988 report of the U.S. Civil Rights Commission) then argued that parents make decisions under the influence of medical personnel, so the law should apply.

The issue of what care should legally be given to various types of handicapped infants is unsettled. Also, there will be further advances in the technology that keeps alive infants who in years past could not have survived. No doubt the law will continue to change in this area.

What the physician can do is to, first, be aware of current practices. Second, if a lawsuit arises, research the references given in this section and later information. Court decisions, laws, and commission reports give credibility to many alternative courses of action.

Be careful when dealing with a patient who is severely retarded and deformed at birth, brain dead, or in intractable pain and wishing to die. As in the situations described, the legally proper course of action is not necessarily one that follows the wishes of relatives, or even the wishes of the patient.

The best course is not to make the decisions yourself. Always consult with other practitioners before you decide. And once you've decided, always get a court order before you act.

In discussing the withholding of life-sustaining treatment from the terminally-ill, incompetent patient, Daniel Suber and William Tabor state: "Court orders permitting the withdrawal of life supports contain provisions purporting to exonerate the attending physicians, the hospital, and persons acting under their direction from potential civil and criminal liability." They go on to state that while such guarantees are helpful, they are not complete protection from civil liability. As further protection, they also suggest getting committee review of the actions to be carried out under court order.[265]

ASSUMPTION OF RISK

This defense is difficult to apply. You must show that the injured patient clearly understood the risk of a particular treatment, yet insisted on it, and convinced you to give it.

Medical researchers Alan Rosenberg and Lee Goldsmith cite two cases in which the assumption or risk defense was successful. In one case a plaintiff with a badly healed broken arm insisted it be rebroken and reset. When the reluctant physician finally agreed, the results were worse than before. In the second case, a patient allowed himself to be treated by a doctor who was grossly intoxicated. The court decided that the average layman should have known better.[215]

Assumption of risk is a type of contributory negligence. To claim it, you must prove that the patient insisted on an inferior course of treatment, and you went along—that both of you understood and assumed the risk taken at the patient's insistence. That's hard to prove because the doctor is usually expected to have a better understanding of the medicine than the patient.

Yet a risk-sharing situation arises more often than most doctors realize. Patients often refuse X-rays when they're recommended, or insist on them when they're not needed. Many insist on antibiotics for colds, even though taking any drug involves risk, and cold viruses are not affected by antibiotics. Many patients don't take important medicines because of minor side effects, or refuse needed surgery. Nevertheless, when doctors go along with inferior treatment, they, rather than the patients, may be blamed for the damaging results.

One of us spoke to the angry daughter of a 70-year-old woman who was brought to the emergency department badly dehydrated and with blood sugar over 800, more than five times normal. The patient had poorly controlled diabetes, but her physician was still treating her with pills rather than with the more effective insulin shots. The daughter complained that the doctor had seen her mother in his office recently, but had done nothing about the diabetes.

Such lack of proper care was difficult to understand, since the doctor was one of the most competent general practitioners in the area. The answers came from looking at hospital records and calling the doctor. The chart from a previous admission revealed that the patient refused to take insulin injections, though the doctor told her she needed them. He said he tried several times recently to convince her to enter the hospital to control her diabetes, but she refused.

That's a clear case of assumption of risk by the patient. Her regular physician continued to prescribe pills, even though it was clear that insulin shots would be much more effective. It was hard to predict if or when the patient would get into serious trouble because of the inferior treatment.

The case also illustrates a potentially dangerous situation for doctors. Without first examining the medical records, it would be easy for anyone—including a juror—to jump to the conclusion that the attending physician was practicing incompetently. The patient's family knew nothing of the patient's refusal to go along with the recommended treatment. If the patient had died—a common result when someone has so much sugar in the blood—the family might well have sued the physician. Assumption of risk would have been the valid defense.

Risk-taking is a way of life for all of us who are responsible for patient care. There are risks of treatment, and risks of nontreatment. We weigh those risks and suggest a course of action for the patient. The patient may not agree for reasons of cost, discomfort, inconvenience, denial of the problem, disagreement over treatment, or even willingness to assume the risk of not being treated at all.

That people are willing to assume risks can be seen in these contrasting data gathered by Bertran Dinman: The risk of a person dying in one year from taking contraceptive pills is 1 in 50,000; from smoking a pack of cigarettes a day, 1 in 200; from motorcycling, 1 in 50. In contrast, the involuntarily-assumed risk of being struck by lightning, which so many of us worry about, is only 1 in 10 million.[65]

UNCOOPERATIVE PATIENTS

Patients don't cooperate with diagnostic procedures and treatment for a variety of reasons, some already discussed under assumption of risk and euthanasia. Transfusions, for example, are sometimes refused because of religious beliefs. Parents who aren't patients themselves sometimes refuse treatment for their children.

Although there are exceptions, courts usually allow rational, mentally competent adults, who are not responsible for minor children, to refuse lifesaving treatment for themselves. Parents, pregnant women, and children will not be allowed by the courts to go without treatment. The parents of a New Jerey child needing blood, for example, refused to permit transfusion. So the court appointed a guardian through whom consent was obtained. Even though the child died, no damages were found. The court ruled that adults without dependent children had the right to be martyrs, but no one had the right to make children martyrs.[c183]

Similarly, in a 1981 Georgia case, the right of a pregnant woman to refuse transfusions was denied. Reason: She would be harming the unborn child.[c92]

A competent adult with no minor children might well be judged able to refuse the transfusion that could save his or her life. But refusal in a life-or-death choice could cast doubt on the person's ability to think clearly. That interpretation by the jury would hurt your defense. In that event, you'll need prior evidence or testimony showing that the patient did not want transfusion.

UNDER THE INFLUENCE

What is your duty to an injured or ill person who is intoxicated? No one answer can apply to every case. For one thing, signs and symptoms can be masked by alcohol or drugs. What's more, the person will often refuse examination, workup, and extended periods of observation.

How much a patient's judgment, competency, sensitivity to pain, and psychological and physical conditions are influenced by drugs or alcohol is difficult to estimate. Yet this is critically important when someone has occult, difficult-to-detect injuries.[170,201,208]

Suppose you're reasonably certain there's no injury, but just want to keep the patient from self-injury while he sobers up. Would you do what a well-meaning Illinois doctor did? He admitted the patient and put him in restraints, intending only to let the man recover from the effects of alcohol. The patient had a different idea. He freed himself, found some matches, and started a fire. He later sued the hospital for failing to adequately care for him.

In Illinois, the law states that when a physician is aware of a patient's intoxication and incapacity, he has a greater duty toward that patient. In such circumstances, the patient is excused from contributory negligence. In reviewing the case, the appellate court did not agree unanimously that the hospital be held liable.[c24]

Decisions in similar cases in other states will certainly vary. Treating intoxicated patients is risky: You can be sued for harm that befalls an intoxicated person after he is seen by you and admitted to the hospital.

You might also be sued if the person is not admitted. In that event, your defense would be strengthened by notes in the chart, or by remembering events indicating that the patient didn't appear to be drunk: "Patient oriented and able to walk and talk normally." Past charts and data, especially on emergency visits, may show that the patient is often intoxicated. Properly presented, such information can prove that the patient is accustomed to handling that condition. Your defense will be bolstered by showing that the patient was sent home with a responsible relative or friend.

Consider the common case of a person who has been drinking and smashes his car. In the emergency room, he is awake and says he has no pain. Should he be admitted and observed overnight? Should he have $300 worth of X-rays and $400 worth of hospitalization?

Those of us who frequently see such people know that they can have fractures in any part of the body, lacerated livers, or ruptured spleens, yet feel no pain. Fracture of the jaw should be suspected in an intoxicated person if he doesn't open his mouth widely when speaking; don't expect to see signs of pain.

An intoxicated patient may have fractures of the leg with the ends of the bones trying to stick through the skin, yet feel no pain. One such patient seemed to be alert, spoke clearly, and even forgot that her leg was broken soon after being told about it and shown the X-rays and leg deformity.

If an intoxicated patient is sent home with a less-than-obvious injury that later leads to a complication, you may be sued for not detecting and treating the injury. Or if a person noticeably under the influence of alcohol is discharged and then suffers another injury, you may be sued for allowing him to leave the hospital while intoxicated. He may even claim that the new injury was present before he left the hospital. In any case, be aware that people who drink often can't remember much about what happens when they are drunk.[11]

Individuals vary widely in how they are affected by alcohol. How any individual is affected also varies at different times and in different circumstances. Some, with blood alcohol measuring under 200 mg/deciliter, may be unconscious and be sutured without anesthesia. Others, with levels over 400, look normal and alert. That wide a range makes judging how well a patient can describe pain and other symptoms a difficult, if not impossible, task.

IMPROPER JUDGMENT

Making an improper diagnosis or choosing the wrong treatment is not an automatic indication of malpractice. Legally, you're required only to possess a reasonable degree of skill, and to exercise care in using it. You can defend an improper judgment by arguing that, given the facts known at the time, your decisions and actions seemed to be correct.

The patient's history, physical examination, and laboratory tests constitute your data base. It should permit you to make a skillful, competent judgment about the patient's condition.[16] True, armed with those data, you can usually make an accurate diagnosis. But not being accurate is not proof of negligence. If you use your best judgment, that's all that can be expected.

"Failure-to-diagnose" cases are difficult to prove. If there is a detailed, recorded physical examination that supports your diagnosis, the plaintiff probably won't win the claim against you.

UNAVOIDABLE COMPLICATIONS

Patients sue for complications from a medical or surgical procedure. Your line of defense should be that complications occur in a significant percentage of cases, no matter how skilled the doctor.

That defense can be weakened, however, if the procedure was unnecessary, due care was not exercised, or informed consent was not obtained.

Let's say a patient dies from an unpredictable allergic reaction to a penicillin shot. If the patient had a strep throat, you could argue that the small risk of such a major reaction is usually outweighed by the benefit of the medication. But if you gave the fatal shot for a migraine headache, you'd have no defense, because—as the plaintiff's attorney would then surely tell the jury—penicillin has no value in treating migraine.

In a case involving complications, a patient developed a staphylococcal infection shortly after back surgery, and sued the hospital for failing to meet the required standards of care and not diagnosing and treating him properly once the infection developed. He tried to apply the doctrine of res ipsa loquitur—"the thing speaks for itself." In other words, he had no infection before the operation; he developed one shortly afterward. Thus, anyone can see—without the aid of expert witnesses to explain things—that negligence on the part of the surgeon must have occurred.

Both the trial and appellate courts, however, held that res ipsa loquitur did not apply; there was no proof that infection would not ordinarily occur without fault on the part of the hospital. Moreover, the courts found that an acceptable standard of care—surgical scrubs and other precautions—had been exercised.[c158]

It's impossible to discuss every known complication of a procedure. Nevertheless, the common and the serious—even though uncommon—complications should be explained to the patient and family. Your discussion must be done with an understanding of what they want to know and can tolerate hearing at the time.

UNUSUAL ANATOMY

Complications sometimes arise because of an unusual anatomy. They commonly occur in obese patients. When a patient is overweight, it's difficult to determine where an area of tenderness is, feel masses, reach structures on pelvic or rectal examination, hear heart and lung sounds or interpret X-rays. Surgery and other procedures also are more difficult. As a defense, you could reasonably say that you would have made the proper diagnosis or been more successful with treatment if the plaintiff hadn't been so obese.

Some of the abnormalities that can cause problems are well known. Many people, for example, have only one working kidney. You'd have no defense if you removed a traumatized kidney without making sure the other was present and functioning.

Other anatomical abnormalities might not be anticipated—the bile duct unusually close to the gallbladder, for example. That's what led one surgeon to damage the duct during a cholecystectomy. And because of the abnormal anatomy, the court ruled that the doctrine of *res ipsa loquitur* could not be applied.[c186]

Unusual anatomy due to cancer may make surgery more difficult than usual. That fact has been effectively used as a defense when complications occurred during surgery.[c27]

UNKNOWN CONDITIONS

Patients sometimes don't tell the whole truth about their past medical history, current medications, emotional problems, or other important personal items. If you're sued because such an omission contributed to a bad result, be sure to make the fact known in court.

If a young woman denies having had sexual relations, you won't worry about an ectopic pregnancy being the cause of her pain. Of course, you must be careful about how you ask the question; don't ask in front of her mother.

Be careful, too, about prescribing. Many patients take medications from several physicians. But polypharmacy can lead to many dangerous drug interactions and side effects. So be sure to ask what medications the patient is taking before you prescribe. Problems are especially likely to occur with medications for controlling hypertension, heart rhythm, and serum potassium levels.

BEST TREATMENT

In retrospect, it may become clear that your treatment didn't work well, and that another would have done much better. Nevertheless, you're not automatically liable for resultant damages. As part of your defense you will need to show that your treatment was then recognized by a "respectable minority" of your peers practicing in the field, and that your actions were similar to those of many competent, respected practitioners.

The medical literature is full of alternative treatments, debates, and disagreements. The variety of possible treatments for any given case is usually large.

INACCURATE HISTORY

The patient, or relatives, may give you an inaccurate or incomplete history. They'll do it for a variety of reasons, including fear, embarassment, unawareness of important details, or even just plain forgetfulness.

In many instances, you won't be held liable for damages if you believed and depended on the patient's faulty or hidden history. One doctor, for example, was found not liable for failing to diagnose a poisoning when a father didn't reveal that his child might have ingested aspirin.[c93] An incomplete history also served as a successful defense when a doctor was sued for underestimating the seriousness of a patient's heart condition, because the patient had failed to mention earlier attacks.[c7]

When a patient's history doesn't agree with your physical examination, you might be held liable for not suspecting a condition suggested by the physical signs.[126] So you can be held responsible for *not taking* a complete enough history, or for *not suspecting* that the patient was giving an incomplete or untruthful account.

ABSENCE OF DUTY

Absence of doctor-patient relationship. A specialist giving a lecture to a hospital medical staff was asked how he would handle a certain case. His advice was followed, and the patient died. The specialist was included in a malpractice suit against the attending doctors and the hospital. The plaintiff's attorney claimed that the specialist formed a relationship with the patient by giving an opinion on the case. The judge ruled for the specialist, stating that he had been asked for an opinion by the medical staff in general, not the patient or the attending doctors. The expert had qualified his opinion by saying that he was basing his opinion on what he had heard; he had not examined the patient.

Another physician, a surgeon, *did* examine a patient at the request of a hospital nurse. He told the nurse, "It's not my case. Let that other fellow cover his own practice." The surgeon lost the malpractice suit which resulted when the patient continued to do poorly.[62]

The sections of this book on workers' compensation examinations and peer review proctoring discuss other examples in which no physician-patient relationship exists.

When examination is requested. Three similar cases occurring in a short period of time in one town raised a number of questions concerning the rights and responsibilities of minors, parents, and physicians. In each case a mother brought her daughter to an emergency department to have evidence of sexual intercourse collected. The daughters were 13 to 16 years old. In each case it was suspected that the daughter had had a voluntary long-standing sexual relationship with a man. In each case the daughter did not want evidence collected because she did not want to get her partner in trouble.

In these situations the patients' mothers were asking for examinations to be forced upon their daughters. The mothers felt that their requests gave the physicians the right and responsibility to force pelvic examinations upon the unwilling teens. One mother told the physician that she would sue him because the physician was not willing to force her daughter into being examined.

Commenting on these cases, Dr. James George said,

A legal duty to treat a patient arises out of the establishment of a physician-patient relationship. Except for a medical emergency in which the patient is unable to provide consent, a physician-patient relationship generally is established when the patient agrees to be treated by the physician and the physician agrees to treat the patient.
It is unlikely that a court would conclude that a ... relationship was established when a minor female was brought to the hospital against her will by a parent for the sole purpose of obtaining medical proof of the minor's voluntary sexual activity. Many states have enacted laws that permit minors to give legal consent to medical treatment for pregnancy or sexually transmitted diseases. Consequently, the minor who enjoys the legal right to consent also would enjoy the legal right to refuse treatment or examination.

The United States Supreme Court also has held that the female minors have a constitutionally protected right to obtain a legal abortion and that their parents have no legal right to prevent it. A minor patient who is forced to undergo a pelvic examination against her will has a valid cause of action for assault and battery against the physician who performs the examination.[96]

If you are among the health professionals who examine patients for employment or insurance, you are, in effect, employed by the patient's prospective employer or insurer. A number of cases indicate that a practitioner in that position does not have a duty to the patient, and so is not liable for failure to diagnose a disease or injury. What's more, the practitioner is expected to divulge to the employer or the insurer information that would usually be held confidential.

In addition to, or instead of, the defenses we have seen that shield you from or draw the patient in on the liability, you can try to apply the defenses to specific changes in the step ahead.

Defenses to specific charges

When it comes to malpractice, nothing could be truer than the saying, "There are more ways than one to skin a cat." And plaintiffs' lawyers know them all.

Virtually all health-care professionals—physicians, nurses, dentists, psychotherapists, and pharmacists—can be sued on one or more of a wide variety of specific charges. The most common charges include: guaranteed results, libel and slander, breach of confidentiality, improper blood transfusion, fraud, wrongful birth, pain and suffering, abandonment, lack of informed consent, improper psychiatric commitment, misusing drugs, and failure to treat or control a problem patient.

Let's examine those charges to see how you can defend yourself against them.

GUARANTEED RESULT

As a professional whose job is to help people, you probably have a strong desire to assure patients that all will be well. But until medicine becomes an exact science, guaranteeing the outcome of your treatment is improper, dishonest, and dangerous. A common cold may turn into meningitis; a patient can take a medicine for years, then suddenly develop an allergy and die. So don't give a guarantee. Ever. To guarantee a result may only guarantee you a lawsuit.

Reassurance. Fear of guaranteeing a result should by no means stop you from reassuring patients. But just remember that the line between the two is thin.

Have you ever said this to a patient? "Don't worry; everything will be fine." That kind of offhand remark, intended only as reassurance, could be considered a guarantee. Even coming from your nurse, those well-meaning words can be taken as a binding guarantee of your work. So be very careful—and caution your employees—about such comments.

You can reassure patients without making any guarantees. But you'll have to experiment and rehearse, perhaps with your office staff standing in as patients. Practice answering questions about the prognosis for various conditions in ways that calm and reassure the patient and family.

Often all it takes is something along this line: "I really think you'll be better in a few days. But if you do have any problems, let me know right away. It is possible that your condition could get worse, and hospitalization may become necessary. Now don't be alarmed. That's only a possibility. With the treatment I'm prescribing, patients almost always get better."

Said properly, that kind of statement will be reassuring to most patients. Some, however, may challenge it: "You really don't know if I'll get better, do you?"

All you can do when that happens is to be perfectly honest: "It's true that we can never be certain of a result, but I know that we're doing the best we can, and that this treatment usually does work."

Breach of contract. A charge based on guaranteed results can hurt you in several ways. Even if the plaintiff can't prove negligence, he can still collect for breach of contract. His award would include his medical expenses.[136] But he could not be awarded damages for pain and suffering.[117] Nevertheless, you could still end up paying much more than just basic breach of contract damages. Reason:

The plaintiff's attorney will be sure to elaborate on the simple fact that in any medical case, no matter how careful and competent the treatment, some fault can almost always be found. More tests could have been ordered. An alternative treatment would have been better. A consultant should have been called. Juries tend to reward plaintiffs for such ex post facto sins of omission, even in the absence of negligence or injury.

A promise to cure is a contract. If your state statutes require that contracts be made in writing, then a patient may not be able to successfully sue you for breach of an oral contract. More than half the states have enacted medical malpractice statutes, and some of these statutes contain "statutes of frauds" provisions that require a contract between physician and patient be made in writing.[274]

Implied result. Guaranteed results can't be implied. Planning to perform a procedure doesn't, in itself, constitute a guarantee of its success. The purpose of a vasectomy or a tubal litigation, for example, may be to render a patient sterile. But just because you perform the procedure doesn't mean that you guarantee the result. No surgeon can perform such common procedures without having the operation fail in some cases.

Some lawsuits, nevertheless, are based on a premise of implied guarantee. One such case involved a periodontist who performed several procedures to straighten a patient's teeth. The patient ended up with a worse malocculusion than he started with. No evidence of wrongdoing on the part of the dentist was presented, and expert witnesses couldn't agree on why the treatment didn't work. The dentist was found not liable for the damages.[c195]

In defending yourself against a charge of breach of contract, or failure to obtain a guaranteed result, you'll need hard evidence. So ask yourself these questions:

- Does the medical record clearly show what I told the patient concerning prognosis?
- Do I remember all the details of conversations concerning the possible outcomes of the case?
- Were there witnesses to those conversations?
- Did I give the patient written instructions that directed him to inform me immediately if certain complications arose?
- Did the consent form clearly state that a successful result was not guaranteed?

FAILURE TO FOLLOW GUIDELINES

Thousands of guidelines and protocols for treating medical conditions have been published over the years. Perhaps the best-known and most widely accepted are the ACLS (advanced cardiac life support) guidelines. The American Heart Association (AHA) recommends that certain procedures be followed in treating conditions associated with myocardial infarction and cardiac arrest. Fortunately, the AHA guidelines specifically state that the protocols should be modified by physicians who feel that their experience runs counter to the teachings. As stated in the published standards: "Cardiopulmonary resuscitation [CPR] and ECC (emergency cardiac care) are dynamic disciplines that continue to develop through ongoing experience and research.... Deviations from these standards and guidelines may occur when a trained physician proficient in CPR and ECC recognizes that such is in the best interests of the patients."[187]

At least one physician has successfully argued in court that the AHA–ACLS guidelines need not be followed in treating cardiac arrest.[c108,247]

When you are sued for a case in which you did not follow established guidelines, do the following:

1. Search the guidelines for disclaimers saying that deviations from the guidelines are allowed or even desirable.

2. Establish through the testimony of numerous practitioners in your area that the guidelines are not always followed (the guidelines are not the standard of practice).

3. Explain what circumstances in your case made the guidelines unsuitable.

4. Search the medical literature for articles (old and new) that suggest alternative methods of treatment (possibly similar to yours).

5. Question the plaintiff's experts concerning the "proper" guidelines 5 and 10 years earlier. Why did the standards change? Will the standards be different 5 and 10 years in the future? If so, why is one standard the only right one? Establish the experts' answers to these questions during deposition. If the case goes to trial, question the plaintiff's experts in such a way as to show that standards change, and no one knows what is really the best treatment.

UNFORESEEABLE CONSEQUENCES

Physicians are not generally held liable for unpredictable consequences of their negligence. For example, a physician negligently misdiagnosed syphilis in a woman. The woman's husband was so upset that he struck her in the jaw, fracturing it in two places. When the woman learned that the diagnosis had been incorrect, she sued the physician for mental distress and battery. The Supreme Court of South Carolina held that there was a cause of action for mental distress, but not for the battery. The physician was not liable for battery because the husband's violence was an unforeseeable intervening cause of her injuries.[c87,249]

LIBEL AND SLANDER

You have access to private information about your patients. Sometimes it's true; sometimes not. As we saw in Step 10, people give false information about themselves and others for a variety of reasons. True or false, such material becomes part of the record and your "information" about the patient.

Circumstances may make certain "facts" seem true when they are not. Take caution in these kind of cases:

- A mother brings an obviously battered child in for care; don't assume that she did the battering.
- A patient seems to be intoxicated; don't assume that he or she is habitually so.
- A patient has ingested an illicit drug; don't assume that it was taken intentionally or knowingly.

Even when potentially damaging information is true, it's not proper to publicize it. It may even be improper to give it to a relative of the patient. Giving information about a patient can easily result in a libel or slander charge.

Libel is defamation by written means. Slander is defamation by means of oral expressions or transitory gestures. Speaking about a patient within earshot of other patients can be taken as slander.

You can defend yourself against a charge of libel or slander by showing that the alleged statement, written or oral, wasn't really made, or that it was made in a way that didn't identify the plaintiff specifically. If those defenses aren't possible, your case will consist of determining how much damage the statement actually did.

A physician was sued for libel and intentional infliction of emotional distress after stating on a state labor department form that a previous employee was released from employment for unsatisfactory performance, fraud, and lying.[141] The courts found for the physician. Still, in today's legal climate, few persons feel safe giving a candid evaluation of unsatisfactory employees or associates.

Laetrile distributors brought a libel action against *US News & World Report* for an allegedly defamatory article. Because there were more than 1,000 laetrile distributors across the country, the suit was successfully defended on grounds that the class of plaintiffs was too large and too geographically spread out to permit recovery for statements made in general terms about the class.[c170]

Libel and slander can also involve a breach of confidentiality between doctor and patient.

The conditional-occasional privilege defense. Physicians sometimes sue each other for defamation. The defamatory communication may be defensible if it was performed for a recognized purpose (occasion). An anesthesiologist improperly intubated two patients, causing the death of one. The surgeon made written and oral complaints to the chief of the hospital anesthesia service, other surgeons, and the chairman of the hospital executive committee. A jury awarded $400,000 in compensatory and $200,000 in punitive damages to the anesthesiologist in a defamation suit. The appellate court reversed the verdict, saying the communications were protected by the conditional-occasional privilege. A new trial on the question of abuse of the privilege by the surgeon was ordered. The court also stated that the public interest was served by physicians being able to express themselves when matters affecting the quality of care were involved.[c14]

EXPERT WITNESS IMMUNITY

In most cases, plaintiffs and defendants must both have experts. The expert who testifies just for defendants (or just for plaintiffs) will have his bias brought out in court: "Doctor, you are supposed to be an impartial witness. Why do you always just defend physicians?" Therefore, physicians who wish to testify in court will sometimes find themselves working for plaintiffs' attorneys.

One might worry about being sued for expert testimony. For example, one physician-expert witness who criticized the work of another physician was sued for misrepresentation, defamation, and intentional infliction of emotional distress. The court held that statements made in reports and depositions, even though not made under oath, were protected by "witness immunity privilege."[98] The court reasoned that if immunity was not recognized, the judicial process would be impeded by physicians fearing suits for their testimony. If experts cannot testify freely, courts will not have access to relevant facts and issues in medical malpractice cases.[145] This U.S. District Court decision would be binding only in the area in which it was made but would carry influence elsewhere.

In various ways, virtually every state has recognized the immunity from civil liability for statements made by witnesses at depositions and trials. This immunity has been reviewed and approved by the United States Supreme Court.[c23,145] Still, expert immunity is not absolute. If the witness abuses it by malicious utterances or unfairly denigrative statements, the "immunity" might not protect him.

Liability insurance for expert witnesses is available. The Harbor Insurance Company (4201 Wilshire Blvd, Los Angeles, CA 90010) provides insurance for expert witness testimony, litigation consulting, and some related activities. Information can be obtained from the John Sargeant Insurance Agency; P.O. Box 29044; Glendale, California 91209–9044 (phone (800) 666–4638).

BREACH OF CONFIDENTIALITY

Health practitioners, as well as lawyers and clergy, have a fiduciary relationship with their clients. So information given to you by a patient is confidential. This means that you are in a position of trust. In most cases, it's wrong to tell anyone but the patient the results of a lab test or physical examination, or what was said in a conversation.

Child abuse. In many instances, you are not only permitted, but required by law, to inform third parties about a patient's condition. Child abuse is an example. In most states, health professionals are required to report even suspected child abuse cases. Laws in most states protect practitioners who might mistakenly report child abuse. Of course, the information must be given to the proper social agencies, not to friends or relatives of the parties involved.

You can be held liable if you don't report a case of child abuse and further battering of the child occurs.[c104] Even if further injury doesn't befall the child, failure to report an already known or suspected case of abuse can result in a jail sentence and fine. The child abuse reporting statutes apply in many states to dentists, nurses, teachers, social workers, chiropractors, mental-health professionals, and "any other person."[164]

Three physicians and a hospital were sued for reporting suspected child abuse. When the abuse case was investigated and the charges dropped, the parents of the child sued. The judge stated, "Reporters are required to report child abuse promptly and they are subject to criminal prosecution if they fail to report as required. Accordingly, absolute immunity from liability for all reports is consistent with that scheme."[8]

Parents have sued after being reported for suspected child abuse on the grounds that the report caused them humiliation, abuse, damage to their reputation, and emotional and mental stress.[c77] Parents have also sued, claiming that the physicians involved were guilty of slander, unlawful restraint, false imprisonment, and battery.[c105] Such cases have been almost universally decided in favor of the physicians.

Consider a countersuit if you are sued for reporting child abuse. It will be important to your case that you reported your findings to only the proper agencies and that you stuck to the medical issues (e.g., the child was abused).

Dangerous patient.　You can also break confidentiality when one of your patients is dangerous. In the much publicized case of *Tarasoff* v. *the Regents of the University of California,* a patient told a therapist of his intention to hurt Ms. Tarasoff. The therapist and two psychiatrists arranged, according to California law, for the police to detain the patient as the first step of a commitment procedure. The police, feeling that the patient was lucid, let him go. He never returned for treatment. Several months later, he killed Ms. Tarasoff. The court found that confidentiality should not have been respected when someone's life was in danger. Tarasoff should have been warned.[c188]

The New Jersey Supreme Court has also ruled that a psychotherapist has a duty to warn anyone who may get hurt by a patient.[c116]

Not all states have determined that therapists have a duty to warn endangered persons, but the precedents set in the California and New Jersey cases would be a strong defense against breach of confidentiality charges in other states. Nevertheless, it would be wise to strengthen your defense by taking certain steps:

- Get the patient's consent to tell potential victims of the danger.
- Hospitalize the patient because of the danger.
- Change medications and give more frequent counseling.

Another twist to the problem: Warning the potential victim might lead to emotional or physical duress, which could then lead to damages charged against you.[240]

Defendants have been successful in arguing that reporting a medical condition to the patient's spouse is not a breach of confidentiality.[127] The appropriateness of doing so, however, would be questioned in cases of psychiatric problems.[113] Even so, when a patient is severely disturbed, the spouse or other relatives will need to be told because they'll have to take part in treatment decisions.

State laws often require that you report the discovery of various communicable diseases. Your public health department will try to contact and treat others who have been exposed. During such mandated disclosures, expect confidential information to leak out of your or the authorities' control.

Whether parents of minor patients can, should, or must be told of their children's venereal diseases, abortions, and birth control pills is the subject of changing legislation.[281]

State laws vary considerably on the requirements for—or the legality of—reporting alcoholism, seizure disorders, and other conditions that cause lapses of consciousness, and thus lead to automobile or other accidents.

Duty to third party. The disclosure of confidential information may be legally supported when the patient is examined for a third party. Thus, when a physician examines a patient for an employer, results of the examination should be made known to the employer. The patient should be made aware of this arrangement.

Similarly, when an examination is done for a court, results can be disclosed to the court. The case of *Pierce v. the State of Georgia* involved a psychiatrist who had been under court order to examine the defendant in a murder trial. The court decided that a physician-patient relationship did not exist, and the psychiatrist was free to relate what the patient had told him about the killing.[c103] In another case, a Texas psychiatrist was found to be free of any duty to notify the patient that information about him might be revealed.[c32] That is not the situation in some states.

Accordingly, court-appointed examiners can freely reveal what they find out about a patient. In addition, they usually won't be held liable for negligent judgments made while dealing with the case. That's called "absolute immunity due to judicial status."

In one case of immunity, court-appointed psychiatrists were named to serve on a sanity commission. They were entrusted with judging the safety of allowing particular patients to return to society rather than be hospitalized. The commission released one patient who had been charged with rape, sodomy, and kidnapping. Within a year, he killed a woman. The psychiatrists on the commission were found not liable because they were entitled to the absolute immunity customarily accorded to judges and other judicial officers.[c125]

Communications between patient and doctor are privileged. Privilege does not exist, however, unless the communication was necessary for treatment. If a plaintiff testifies that no treatment was rendered, then privilege would not exist.

Privilege is also lost when information is revealed in the presence of a third person who is not part of the confidential practitioner-patient relationship. One of the authors testified in court on the condition of a patient who had been examined in the presence of a police officer. The information revealed in that testimony was held to be not confidential.

Similarly, other doctors can't be held to privilege when they are present during treatment, but have not been consulted by the patient or the patient's doctor.

In some states, communication concerning intent to commit a crime is not privileged. Nor are statements concerning commission of a crime, or communications by victims of a crime.[79]

BLOOD TRANSFUSION

Lawsuits involving blood transfusions stem from many causes. Transfusions can be given too late, too quickly, when not needed, or against the patient's wishes, and they can transmit various diseases and cause a variety of "transfusion reactions." You can be sued for giving a transfusion, not giving it, or giving it improperly.

If sued for not giving one, point up the risks of transfusion and the absence of indications for giving it. You may also be able to argue that giving one would not in this case have made any difference.

Trauma, for example, can cause large holes in blood vessels, so transfusion might be ineffective without immediate surgery. And even that might prove ineffective. For example, patients with blunt abdominal trauma who suffer cardiac arrest due to bleeding in the abdomen seem to have no chance of survival.[85]

Of course, if you're sued for the results of transfusion, you'll want to emphasize the indications that justified your decision to give it. Consider the following reactions that could lead to a suit:

1. *Hemolysis* resulting from an immune reaction can occur during or after a transfusion when either the patient's own or the transfused red blood cells break down. Incompatibility of the donor blood is the most frequent cause. Such reactions vary in severity depending on degree of blood incompatibility, amount of blood given, rate of infusion, and other factors. They can damage the kidneys, suddenly lower blood pressure, cause bleeding, and sometimes even death.[289]

2. *Febrile transfusion reactions* may mimic hemolytic reactions, but are rarely as serious. Febrile reactions produce fever and

chills, and sometimes headache, rapid heartbeat, and raised blood pressure.

3. *Allergic transfusion reactions* caused by a patient's hypersensitivity to an unknown component in the donor blood, can produce skin rashes, itching, and difficulty with breathing. Those allergic reactions are usually mild, but occasionally involve potentially fatal anaphylactic shock. Other life-threatening effects are post-transfusion purpura and graft-versus-host disease.

Clearly, transfusion reactions are a quagmire of potential lawsuits. But there's one reaction you don't have to worry about: Physicians, hospitals, and blood banks have been judged not responsible in most cases of transfusion-transmitted hepatitis, because there's no reliable way to test blood for hepatitis. Yet the hospital and attending medics can be held liable if the wrong type of blood is given.

Statutes in some states further protect the hospital and other defendants in cases involving transfusion reactions. Your attorney should research the relevant laws of your state.

AIDS

The previous sections on confidentiality and blood transfusion are relevant to AIDS. However, the statutory and case laws on AIDS are changing rapidly.

When treating AIDS patients, many opposing forces, interests, and considerations become apparent: it is not possible to warn third parties (sexual partners) while maintaining confidentiality; it may not be possible to properly treat without testing for AIDS in the person who does not wish to be tested; the financial or medical welfare of the patient may not be best served by following state reporting or testing statutes. Statutes concerning confidentiality, treatment, and insurance are often in direct opposition to the usual practice of medicine. This situation has led one attorney to say that "good doctors must start breaking bad laws."[19]

The confusion and contradictions surrounding the management of AIDS patients will be the cause of many malpractice suits. It is only proper that defenses to such suits include an explanation of the factors that caused the physician to act as he or she did. In such instances, it should be easy to find articles and experts who can honestly say that the course taken by the physician was reasonable, commonly done, and in the best interests of not everyone, but possibly the patient, the state, or other third parties.

FRAUD

Legally defined, fraud is "an intentional perversion of truth for the purpose of inducing another in reliance upon it to part with some valuable thing belonging to him or to surrender a legal right. Elements of a cause of action for fraud include: false representation of a present or past fact made by defendant; action in reliance thereupon by plaintiff, and damage resulting from such misrepresentation."[12]

Fraud can involve criminal as well as civil actions and liabilities. So in a suit claiming fraud, criminal charges can be added to the civil malpractice claims. Criminal charges can lead to jail sentences as well as financial liability. And payment of awards in criminal cases usually is not covered by malpractice insurance policies.

Instances of genuine fraud are difficult to defend. These would include, among others, telling a patient that everything is all right after a known complication occurs, telling a patient a condition needs treatment when the condition doesn't exist, and knowingly treating a patient with ineffective methods.

Such deliberately fraudulent actions rarely occur. But one kind of fraud is common—hesitating to tell a patient that a complication has developed. If you're sued for withholding some bad news, a good defense, if true, would be: Knowing of the complication would have harmed the patient more than the complication itself.

Suppose a structure is accidentally cut during surgery, but is immediately repaired and doesn't cause any problems. The patient learns about it later when an X-ray shows the staples used to repair the damage.

You could say that telling the patient about the damage would have caused anxiety, whereas not telling did no harm. You would thus be arguing that the elements of a cause of action for fraud—damages resulting from the misrepresentation of fact—do not exist.

Misrepresenting facts or lying to a patient is sometimes done in the interest of the patient. Often it's better that a patient not know the truth, if, in your best judgment, the patient is unable to accept or deal with it. If so, your defense should be fashioned to show:

1. Your action seemed in the best interests of the patient.
2. No harm was caused by the misrepresentation of fact.
3. The action fell within the realm of acceptable practice.

Fraud may be claimed if you give ineffective or placebo treatment. In that case, you could argue that no treatment was necessary, yet you felt that the patient would feel better if a sugar pill, vitamin, or some other such mentally soothing agent were prescribed. And in certain situations you can take this tack: Since placebos do "work" psychologically for a significant number of patients, they can be the best treatments for someone in danger of addiction to medication.

WRONGFUL BIRTH

This charge—also called wrongful life—holds that a physician was negligently responsible for the birth of a child. It usually results from an unsuccessful sterilization procedure, failure to detect or to inform parents of a defect in a fetus, or failure to give them genetic counseling. In the latter two instances, it is assumed that the parents would have avoided the birth of the child had they been given adequate information.

Laws and case precedents are evolving in this area. To defend such a suit, you must research the latest laws and court decisions. Examples are provided here to give you a sense of the issues involved, the types of damages often claimed and the variety of conflicting rulings on the books.

An unsuccessful sterilization led to a 1981 lawsuit in which the plaintiff parents asked for, but were not awarded, damages for childrearing costs and for interference with established family relationships. The court, however, concurred that there were causes of action for negligent medical procedures, with those damages limited to pregnancy and birth-related costs. The husband, for example, could recover for loss of consortium due to the pregnancy.[c197]

In a case involving a rubella syndrome child, the parents were awarded all costs of rearing the child. There was no deduction for the cost of rearing a normal child. The woman's physician was found negligent for not informing the mother of her rubella and its probable consequences. The jury agreed that, had that information been given, an abortion would have been done.[c159]

In some cases of wrongful birth, the courts have allowed only unusual expenses caused by the abnormality.[c169]

The Illinois appellate court held, in one case, that the parents of a healthy child born after unsuccessful sterilization were entitled to child-rearing costs, but reduced those costs by the value of the potential benefits of having the child.[c102] Another Illinois appellate decision awarded complete recovery for child-rearing costs without any deductions.[c45] And in a third case, another Illinois appellate court, in a conflicting ruling, denied any child-rearing costs as a matter of public policy.[c199]

In 1983, the Illinois Supreme Court ruled that a physician is not liable for the costs of raising an unwanted child born because of an improperly performed sterilization procedure.[6]

Wrongful birth following sexual assault. The "morning after pill" does not always work. Explaining to the patient that the pill may not work can be traumatic to the patient, and giving the pill may be dangerous because the patient may already be pregnant. These facts can be used in one's defense in a wrongful birth case.

For example, Dr. Julio C. Novoa was a Maryland obstetrician-gynecologist who treated rape victims as a public service, on a voluntary basis. He prescribed a pregnancy-preventing drug with a 1% to 2% failure rate to a woman who had been raped. The woman became pregnant, refused to have an abortion, and gave birth to a child. She filed wrongful birth and wrongful life suits.

A state arbitration board, which reviews all Maryland medical malpractice cases, awarded the mother $250,000 for emotional suffering and child care expenses, but the woman turned down the award as inadequate. She sued for $2 million.

At trial the jury returned a unanimous verdict in favor of the physician.[5]

There are actually several dangers when one prescribes a pregnancy-preventing pill: the pill may not work, or the patient may already be pregnant. In either situation, the physician can be sued just as Dr. Novoa was: the precedent of the Maryland case may not provide full protection in all apparently similar cases. Also, if the baby is not normal, it can be claimed that the hormonal medication caused the abnormality.

PAIN AND SUFFERING

Pain, suffering, and posttraumatic stress disorder are defined and discussed in Step 4 of this book as well as in several other publications.[64,152,169,279,286] Keep in mind that pain and suffering as legal terms are taken to mean all unpleasant intangibles. These include the medical problems discussed below and possibly other items as well. Here are some defenses against such claims.

Noncompliance. If your records show that the patient did not go along with treatment during the period of allegedly insufferable pain, you can argue that the pain and suffering could not have been that bad. Also, the issue of contributory negligence could be raised. Document missed office appointments, failure to obtain prescribed pain medication, and any lack of participation in recommended physical therapy or psychotherapy sessions.

If a person refused to use collars, crutches, or braces—or asked for them when they were obviously not needed—those facts will throw light on the dubious claim. Look for such events in hospital charts, therapists' records, and your own memory.

Medical records.   If the patient was hospitalized, look for notes in the record indicating that the patient was not undergoing significant pain or suffering, such as:

- "Resting comfortably."
- "Ambulated normally and frequently."
- "Did not seem to be in pain during activity."
- "Did not ask for pain medication."

Examine your office records and those of physical therapists to determine just how much pain the patient exhibited.

The plaintiff's attorney might tell jurors they wouldn't accept $20 an hour to endure the amount of pain and suffering the patient endured. There are 8,760 hours in a year. Therefore, the attorney would argue, each year of the patient's pain and suffering should be rewarded with $20 $\times$ 8,760, or $175,200.

Your defense must counter such an argument by saying that the patient did get some sleep and did not seem to be suffering when observed. You must then bring in the documentation noted above to support your contention.

Many patients do have significant pain and suffering, and most have at least some amount of discomfort with any illness or injury. For that reason, never belittle the patient's suffering in front of the jury. Don't deny there is pain. And don't give the impression of being callous or indifferent to the feelings of the patient. Just give what documentation you have to show that the patient didn't seem to be suffering to the degree or extent claimed.

Nature of the misconduct.   Examine your state's legal definition of the charges brought against you, and see if the allegation really fits. For example, a radiologist was unsuccessfully sued for intentional infliction of emotional distress. He had used the phrase "determine extent of malignancy" on insurance papers related to a cancer workup. The patient was found not to have cancer, but she was upset by the wording, despite reassurances from several of her physicians. The court ruled that a cause of action for intentional infliction of emotional distress must be based on misconduct of an outrageous or egregious nature that is so terrifying or insulting as to humiliate, embarrass, or frighten. The actions of the radiologist did not fit this definition.[c65]

ABANDONMENT

A relationship exists between the health practitioner and the patient. Abandonment is the inappropriate breaking of that relationship. The doctor-patient bond is the most commonly cited of such relationships. But a similar tie and responsibilities exist to some extent for all health-care professionals, most notably dentists[189] and psychotherapists.[89]

You may be held liable for abandonment if you don't see the patient through to the end of the illness. And the inability of the patient to pay for your services is no excuse for terminating care.

Consent. Abandonment does not exist when your doctor-patient relationship is terminated by mutual consent.[160]

Notice and referral. Abandonment can be defended when you gave adequate notice of intention to end the relationship. But some cases point up the importance of making a reasonable attempt to find someone else to treat the patient. Just what constitutes adequate notice and reasonable attempt may be issues for the jury to decide. In any event, you must have documentation showing that arrangements were made for another doctor to care for your patient when you terminated treatment, or went on vacation.

Look for evidence that you (1) provided your patient with a competent substitute; (2) provided adequate notice of this substitution; and (3) gave the patient a reasonable opportunity to choose a different practitioner. Liability for abandonment should be avoided if you can show you satisfied these conditions.[172]

Evidence of these conditions being satisfied may be found in medical records or in the fact that the patient actually did obtain care from other practitioners. Evidence that a letter was sent to the patient explaining the notice and referral is often considered adequate. Such evidence is more difficult to refute if the letter was sent via the five R's: "restricted registered, return receipt requested." This type of registered letter provides a receipt from the named addressee only.[121]

152

Without such evidence, you can still defend yourself by arguing that the plaintiff wasn't harmed by the abandonment,[201] or that the patient terminated the relationship.

Failure to refer a patient to a specialist can be considered to be a form of abandonment. A tooth extraction, for example, resulted in a communication between the mouth and the maxillary sinus. This led to infection. The dentist was judged negligent in waiting four months to refer the patient to a specialist who could repair the problem.[c74]

Denial of treatment.   Too often referrals are made, but the patient doesn't get past the front desk when trying to make an appointment or when arriving for treatment. This denial of services is frequently the result of the patient's inability to pay. In many such instances, especially in group practices, doctors have no idea that patients are being turned away. When a receptionist at the front desk prevents the doctor from seeing the patient, that employee is liable to legal prosecution, but so is the employer-doctor, who is ultimately responsible.

One family claimed damages when their child died after a hospital refused admission. The hospital's policy stated that, except in definite emergencies, proof of insurance is required for admission. Although the doctors involved realized that the boy was sick enough to be admitted, they didn't know he would get so much worse. The hospital paid a large settlement and changed its policies.[22]

Discharge or transfer.   Practitioners and the hospitals they work in can be sued if a patient is negligently discharged or transferred. In such situations, negligence means that the discharge or transfer was avoidable and caused harm to the patient. In one suit, a child was sent home with osteomyelitis of both legs. His discharge was judged unreasonable since he clearly needed to receive further inpatient treatment.[c120] In another instance, a patient with impending gangrene of a toe was transferred to a convalescent home. This, too, was judged a negligent act.[c168]

In a suit against a hospital association, it was found proper to transfer a psychiatric patient to a psychiatric facility because no harm was done to the patient by the transfer.[c202] But liability was imposed on a hospital for *not* transferring a patient. The hospital was unable to care properly for a patient with severe burns who needed treatment in a special facility.[c36]

Transferring a patient can be defended by demonstrating that it was in the interests of proper patient care.

COBRA. If sued for transferring a patient, look for evidence that your transfer satisfied COBRA regulations. The COBRA (Consolidated Omnibus Budget Reconciliation Act of 1985) became effective on August 6, 1986. It requires that a medical screening examination be provided to all patients who present to a hospital emergency department. COBRA sets forth conditions that must be met before patients may be transferred to another hospital. Patients cannot be unstable or in active labor.

The hospital is a co-defendant under COBRA. In the past hospitals have sometimes successfully defended malpractice suits on the theory that they were not liable for the negligence of physicians. COBRA makes the hospital responsible for emergency treatment and transfer decisions made by physicians. Physicians, however, can also receive stiff punishment under COBRA regulations for improper transfers. COBRA also requires the transferring hospital to assume liability for assuring the medical integrity and adequacy of the receiving hospital.[86]

Refusing to provide drugs of abuse. Statutes in most states provide a defense to the charge of abandonment for failing to prescribe medications to patients who are addicted to them. State statutes usually *prohibit* prescribing of controlled substances to drug abusers except under unusual circumstances such as terminal cancer. A physician could be sued for contributing to drug abuse for continuing to prescribe medication after addiction was recognized. Medications are often given on a tapered basis or until a patient can enter a treatment program, but physicians should not feel they are legally bound to provide drugs under such circumstances.[124]

Unfilled prescription. If a pharmacist were sued for not filling a prescription, the charge probably would be based on the theory of abandonment.[263] For the most part, pharmacists have a duty to fill all prescriptions. But they need not fill certain prescriptions if they believe them to be illegal or not in the best interests of the patients. A number of valid defenses for not filing prescriptions were listed in *Jones v. The Walgreen Company,* a case that justified the defending pharmacist for:

1. Believing the physician made a mistake.
2. Not having the medication.
3. Feeling the prescription was forged.
4. Not feeling competent to prepare the prescription.
5. Judging that it was unlawful to fill the prescription.[c96]

LACK OF INFORMED CONSENT

In most situations, informed consent must be obtained before a procedure may be performed. This requires that the patient or the patient's guardian give permission to have it done.

To defend against the claim of lack of informed consent, look for evidence that you explained the following to your patient:

1. Recommended treatment
2. Alternative treatments
3. Chance of success of various treatments
4. Common complications of various treatments
5. Severe (even if rare) complications of various treatments
6. Likely results if no treatment is undertaken
7. Answers to any questions the patient or guardian has

One surgeon was sued for not warning a woman undergoing a hysterectomy of a possible complication—vesicovaginal fistula. She claimed she hadn't given informed consent. But the trial court found, and the appellate court agreed, that she had received adequate information and had given informed consent; the fistula complication was both uncommon and of less than major importance.[c103]

Drugs. Patients can't "give" informed consent if they've been given drugs, such as narcotics, that affect the functioning of the mind. In order to be sure that valid consent is being obtained, emergency physicians are often reluctant to give needed pain medication until consulting surgeons arrive.

In one extreme case, a patient was referred by one dentist to another. The patient carried a card directing the second dentist to remove all upper and two lower teeth. The patient was given a shot that made her very sleepy, and then was told to sign a paper, as "a formality." Her glasses were not on, so she was unable to read the paper. But she signed. When she woke up, she found that her upper teeth and ten lower teeth had been removed. Although the consent form she signed "gave permission" for any operation that might seem advisable, the court found the consent not valid. The judgment was against the second dentist.[c125]

Alcohol is a drug that affects the functioning of the mind. Just how drunk a person can be and still give consent has not yet been clearly defined.

Minors. Minors need consent by their legal guardians, usually their parents. Men and women reach majority between the ages of 18 and 21, depending on the state. In some states, minors may give consent for treatment if they are married, divorced, pregnant, have venereal disease, suffer from drug dependency, manage their financial affairs, have been raped, or are giving consent for their own child.[c12,c95]

Handling the simultaneous issues of confidentiality and permission for treatment in some situations can be difficult. The minor patient may not want parents told of the problem. Still, it may seem in the patient's best interest to let the parents know. The patient, for example, may be too immature or drunk to understand or remember instructions for treatment and follow-up. The proper course of action in such situations is often unclear.

When parents refuse treatment for minors. Many states have laws that allow for children in need of medical care to be reported as "dependent" rather than abused or neglected. The dependency designation implies no culpability on the part of the parents. The dependent child is said to have a condition or environment that requires the intervention of state authorities to determine proper care. Thus the focus is on the child rather than the parents. If a child is declared "dependent," a guardian is appointed to make decisions concerning care.[162] If this option is not available in one's state or does not bring the necessary results, the child can then be reported to be neglected.

No warning. A patient may suffer a complication for which you gave no warning. Yet you can defend yourself by showing that the patient would have undergone the operation even if he or she had been informed of the danger.

In a 1982 suit against the president and doctors of Georgetown College, a plaintiff named Flannery failed to convince a jury that she would have forgone breast-enlargement surgery. Ms. Flannery sued because she developed a hemopneumothorax, apparently as a result of a local anesthetic procedure, claiming she had not been warned of that possible complication. The court said proof of an undisclosed risk was not sufficient to establish malpractice. Proof would also have to show that failure to inform of the risk was the proximate cause of the injury. In other words, she would have to prove that general anesthesia—or no operation at all—would have been chosen, had the risk been disclosed.[c67]

Repeat treatment. If a patient continues to return for further similar treatments after a complication develops, you shouldn't run into much trouble fending off a charge of failure to inform. In one case, a patient suffered temporary paresthesia after removal of an impacted wisdom tooth by a dental surgeon. Nevertheless, he returned two weeks later for another extraction. The court decided the patient could not recover damages on the claim that he was not warned of the risks of temporary paresthesia. That he returned for more of the same treatment showed he was willing to undergo it after knowing about the possible complication.[c86]

Emergency treatment. In an emergency, consent is usually implied if the patient is unable to give it. Often, life or limb may be lost if examinations, tests, and procedures are not performed within a short period of time. If a patient is unable to think clearly and refuses to consent to needed emergency treatment, it should be given anyway. Try—and be sure to document your efforts—to get permission from next of kin, but don't let the patient deteriorate while trying. Minors may be treated in an emergency without parental consent.[c109]

Reduced need to obtain informed consent was pointed up in a case involving a patient who was bitten by a rattlesnake, and developed gangrene after injection of antivenin. The court ruled that the doctor did not have a duty to discuss the risks of treatment because of the time limit in the emergency situation.[c50]

There is no duty to obtain informed consent when immediate treatment is necessary to protect the patient from a serious health threat if the patient's health would be jeopardized by the delay entailed in obtaining informed consent. This concept is explained by Alan Meisel in the *Wisconsin Law Review*. This type of explanation would be helpful in the defense of a charge of failing to obtain informed consent:

> If informed consent is to be suspended in an emergency, it should be either because the patient is incapable of giving consent, or of receiving information, or both; or because the time it would take to make disclosure and obtain the patient's decision would work to the disadvantage of some compelling interest of the patient, the profession, or society. If the patient is incapable of giving consent or of receiving information, such as when he is unconscious or in such pain that he is unable to focus his attention on a conversation, none of the interests promoted by the informed consent doctrine are served. To insist upon disclosure and consent under these circumstances is self-defeating and an extreme example of honoring form over substance. The consequence of insisting upon informed

consent where is it patently impossible to obtain it is that the patient will go untreated.... To permit treatment without informed consent in such cases allows the patient's health to be restored or his life to be saved, and in so doing, the societal interest in health is promoted at little expense to the interest in individualism....

The urgency of the need for medical care is a prime deterrent of whether a particular situation should be classified as an emergency. How urgent a situation is depends primarily upon the consequences to the patient of a delay in the rendition of treatment, or indeed upon the consequences of a failure to render any treatment at all.[c180,179]

Right to consent waived. It is recognized in law that some patients understand their rights to be informed and decide on treatment, but *waive their right to informed consent.*[33] These patients prefer that the physician make the decisions, regardless of the risks involved. If your patient made it clear to you that you were to make the decisions, find evidence to document this fact for your defense. This area of the law is especially variable and unclear in many states, so documentation and reasoning must be especially clear on your part.

Therapeutic privilege. In some cases disclosure to a patient of information is likely to cause harm or distress sufficient to interfere with his or her ability to exercise an informed choice. In a situation in which information would cause significant harm to the patient, the physician need not disclose the information to the patient.[33] This exception is called the *therapeutic privilege.* For example, patients with acute myocardial infarction are given extremely strong, potentially harmful medications but are best spared hearing about the drugs' possible side effects. If you believed that informing the patient of a relatively unlikely complication of treatment would have resulted in harm, you can strengthen your defense by explaining this concept to the jury.

Clouded consciousness. Doctors can be charged with assault and battery for treating patients against their will. If applicable, your defense should focus on showing that you thought the patient refused treatment because of a clouded state of consciousness. Patients may be judged to be unable to think clearly for reasons of alocholic intoxication, drugs, hypoxia, hypoglycemia, head injury, or shock.

You could also be charged with forcefully treating, or detaining for observation, an uncooperative patient. A valid defense would be to say that—before you could deem it safe to let the patient leave—it seemed necessary to have him worked up for any or all of the above conditions. This situation occurs commonly with intoxicated patients found lying in the street, and with patients involved in automobile accidents. They may have serious injuries. But either their inability to describe the nature and intensity of their pain or their lack of cooperation makes those injuries difficult to detect.

Some patients are mentally incompetent because of insanity or retardation. They usually have guardians who should give consent for needed treatment. When a guardian can't be found, you can get a court order, if time permits. In an emergency, permission won't be necessary.[217]

Religious consciousness. Some people refuse treatment for religious reasons. They may be Jehovah's Witnesses, who refuse transfusion because they see it as violation of the biblical injunction not to "drink blood." Even so, a court order to treat can often be obtained if the patient is pregnant or has minor children, or if the patient is a minor and the parents refuse to consent. Such an order appoints a legal guardian who can give permission for treatment.

Similarly, when religious beliefs caused parents to refuse to let doctors remove a malignant tumor from their child, the court ordered the child have the operation under the doctrine of *parens patriae*.

Patient upset. Some patients simply don't want to know all the possible complications of a procedure.[c44] They just want you to do what seems best. In some instances, you may judge the patient to be in such an emotional state that an explanation of complications would be too upsetting, and would undercut approval for the treatment most likely to help. If you go ahead and treat, and are then sued for failure to obtain informed consent, your best defense is to tell why consent was not obtained. But you'll have to explain it to the jury in a way that shows your primary consideration was the welfare of the patient. You took the course of action you thought was most likely to benefit the patient, while also trying to avoid potentially damaging emotional trauma.

Pre-consent to malpractice. Many consent forms contain clauses absolving the practitioner from liability for negligence. Such forms would be considered invalid.[c21] In all areas of law, contracts that seem unreasonable are generally held to be invalid. For example, a lease for an apartment stating that the landlord is not responsible for safe electrical wiring would be considered invalid.

Prepare for these claims. Situations in which it is sometimes claimed informed consent was not valid are listed in table 11–1. While we do not agree that these conditions would necessarily negate informed consent, it is good to find documentation in your case records that would refute the claim that any of these situations existed. If a situation did exist, think ahead about why, and be ready to explain it, as: "The patient really would have died without surgery."

TABLE 11–1 CONDITIONS SOMETIMES CLAIMED TO INVALIDATE CONSENT[35]

When a patient
> is rushed, "sign up and let's go!"
> is distraught, "You'll die if you don't."
> is sedated.
> does not understand due to language or illiteracy.

When the doctor
> goes beyond the scope of consent, as during surgery.

When the consent is not truly voluntary because of
> intimidation
> coercion
> misrepresentation

X-RAY DAMAGE

The newest X-ray equipment delivers much less radiation than older machinery. Modern film and fluoroscopy equipment are very sensitive to X-rays, making large doses of radiation unnecessary.[178]

Unchecked equipment. Recent articles in the press and television interviews have claimed that most X-ray machines in the country are out of calibration and deliver many times more radiation than is needed. By knowing the type of film used in any specific case, and seeing how the picture actually looks, you can disprove the claim that a malfunction of equipment caused a grossly large radiation dose. Film that has received excessive radiation looks overexposed.

Records verifying periodic calibration of equipment, before and after the alleged radiation overdose, can also be a defense.

Malformation. Granted that any radiation to the fetus is undesirable, we must ask: At what point can it be considered likely that a congenital malformation has been caused by radiation exposure? (Remember that the legal definition of *likely* or probable is "more than 50 percent.") The answer depends on knowing the dose of radiation required to double the incidence of congenital malformations. If a pregnant woman at the effective time of her pregnancy receives that amount of radiation, and then has a child with a congenital malformation, it would be likely—50 percent probable—that the malformation was caused by the radiation.

The dose of radiation delivered to the fetus needed to double malformations is estimated to be from 25 to 80 rads. That dose would be needed to double the incidence of genetic mutations. If you gave a pregnant patient upper and lower gastrointestinal tract series, an intravenous pyelogram (IVP), and a lower pelvis study, the fetus would receive less than 3 rads.[266] So a woman in the first trimester of her pregnancy would have to receive 10 of each of the above-mentioned studies to make it probable that any fetal malformation was caused by radiation.

A plaintiff's attorney is sure to ask if it's possible that the malformation was caused by the radiation. Of course, it's scientifically and statistically a remote possibility. But be careful how you answer. Don't simply say, "Yes."

Your answer should be: "It's 30 times likely that the malformation was caused by natural occurrences than by the X-ray exposure during the pelvis X-ray. The answer to your question is yes; it is remotely possible, but very unlikely, that the damage was caused by the X-ray exposure."[185] And don't forget to emphasize that the fetus received more radiation from natural sources, such as cosmic rays, than from the X-rays.

Cancer. The situation for causing cancer by X-rays is less favorable. A dose of 0.2 rads anytime in pregnancy appears to increase by 50 percent the chance of a child developing cancer.[266]

Data concerning risks of X-ray exposure similar to that noted in the last few paragraphs are also given by the Mayo Clinic.[100] Those data, plus the previously cited references, would be useful for your defense if you are charged with causing a fetal malformation by means of X-ray exposure.

PSYCHIATRIC COMMITMENT

Physicians and psychotherapists are sometimes put in the difficult position of having to decide whether it's appropriate to commit a patient to a psychiatric facility. Emergency medicine physicians are often faced with patients who have cut their wrists, taken overdoses, or threatened suicide. In many cases, these patients feel they don't want help, but claim they were only trying to get attention. They may really want to go home and have another try at self-destruction. The physician on emergency duty must choose immediately between committing such patients or letting them go home.

Patients released from protective watching may go on to kill themselves because they are indeed suicidal—or because they are under the influence of drugs such as alcohol or phencyclidine (PCP).

Danger signs. In most states, the criteria for involuntary admission are based upon the dangerous consequences of not committing the person. Specifically, you must decide whether the person is:

- Dangerous to himself or herself.
- Dangerous to others.
- Capable of obtaining basic needs such as food and shelter.

Accordingly, you could be sued for failure to admit someone who later commits suicide. Or you could be sued *for* committing.

If sued for committing a patient unnecessarily, your defense should be that your best judgment at the time dictated that it was necessary for the welfare of the patient. If the patient seemed depressed, point out that 15 to 20 percent of patients with depression die from suicide.[69]

Suicide signs. The most recognized characteristics of the suicidal person are:

1. Old man or young woman.
2. Previous suicide attempts.
3. Completed suicides in the family.
4. Detailed suicide plans, described by the patient.
5. Unresolved and stressful precipitating events.
6. Statements about how he or she will be missed.
7. Abrupt lessening of the depth of depression, often associated with a feeling of relief that comes when the decision is made to go through with the suicide.

8. Hearing voices that give self-destructive orders.

9. A severe or chronic medical problem that is exhausting the patient or is believed to be fatal.[159]

A solid defense to inappropriate commitment of a patient thought to be suicidal would be any of those signs or symptoms.

Physicians are usually not found liable for assault and other charges if they can document why they felt restraint or hospitalization was needed for psychiatric reasons. Protective measures that are against the patient's immediate wishes are the standard of care.[c137,c154,74]

But suppose you failed to admit someone who later committed suicide or hurt someone else. Your defense would be that you used your best judgment, given the apparent facts at the time. For example, you should not be held responsible for a patient's suicide when the patient has withheld his or her intentions despite a complete examination.[241] And point out how difficult it is to judge if a patient is indeed dangerous. Many patients judged to be dangerous by classical psychiatric criteria have turned out not to be so.

In 1966, the US Supreme Court ruled that the proper judicial procedures had not been followed in the psychiatric commitment of Johnnie K. Baxstrom and others.[c17] As a result, 969 mental patients were released or transferred to less restrictive hospitals. Most of them had been judged dangerous in psychiatric or psychological examinations. But a follow-up study revealed that only seven of the released patients were subsequently recommitted to a security hospital.[136]

Stanley Brodsky's later study reveals that the overprediction of dangerousness by mental-health professionals has inappropriately restricted the liberty of many other persons.[38]

Whether or not to commit a patient to a psychiatric facility can be a tough decision. But if you can prove that your action was taken in good faith, using the best professional judgment, liability will be unlikely. For example: When a patient who had been commited sued, claiming loss of constitutional rights, the psychiatrist was judged to have acted in good faith because that patient had made repeated threats of violence.[c152]

Be sure to point out that a patient's behavior can change drastically, especially if alcohol is involved. For example, a patient drank a bottle of wine and then threatened suicide. She refused admission, and a psychiatrist involuntarily committed her. Several days later a court-appointed psychiatrist found her to not be suicidal, and she was sent home. When the patient sued the first psychiatrist, the court found that an emergency condition warranting commitment under the emergency detention statute had initially existed.[c154]

A patient's behavior can also change unpredictably if the patient is psychotic. Hallucinations can come and go, leading to changes in affect and ideation that would not be evident on careful examination.[26]

Before committing a patient, be sure to perform an examination to rule out physical conditions that might have caused the abnormal behavior.[c26,196] Before deciding there is no organic cause for the behavior, you may also need a neurological examination, and blood and urine levels of drugs, alcohol, and glucose.

Expose third party pressures. Psychiatric admissions are often difficult because of uncooperative psychiatrists, decreased funding from federal, state, and Medicaid sources, and pressures from third-party reimbursers. A growing number of mental health facilities have been hit with high six-figure verficts for failing to admit schizo-phrenic outpatients whose symptoms later worsened.[287] If you are sued for delivering less-than-optimum care that was selected because of such third party pressures, let that be known. For example, if you chose outpatient therapy over admission because of lack of coopera-tion of the inpatient facility, let that be known to the jury. Long before the trial, file a third-party complaint (impleader) to bring the facility into the case. Even if a governmental immunity is granted to the facility, the jury may come to understand that you tried to do what was right.

If your community mental health facility has drafted restrictive guidelines for admitting patients, bring those standards into the case. They will show you followed the community standard and were not in a position to do much else.

Therapeutic restraints. If a patient's mental status is such that he cannot properly give informed consent, a physician has not only the right but also the duty to suspend the patient's civil liberties and hold him against his expressed will until such time as he is able to competently give (or refuse to give) consent. In addition, if a patient's condition is such that if let out on the street he may harm himself or others, the physician should restrain the patient against his will.[118]

Even when a patient is *not* ill or injured, some authorities believe restraint is justified to prevent harm. Paul Blaylock, MD, JD, FCLM, states,

> It is the physician's responsibility to ensure that no person
> who is believed to be dangerous leaves the department to

jeopardize others. A drunk who leaves the ED, gets into his car, and drives into another car, killing or injuring its occupants, will be partially your responsibility; it is far better to restrain him."[32]

The psychiatric and emergency literature will back you up if you restrain a potentially violent patient. Just recall your reasons, which are hopefully documented in your notes associated with the case. Recognition of the psychiatrically dangerous and potentially violent patient involves many subtle and subjective signs. The physician must take into account restless and abusive behavior, body language, and other factors.[76]

Restraining the patient physically may not be enough. Especially in the presence of suspected spinal fractures, it is sometimes necessary to use intravenous diazepam or other medication to prevent further self-injury. Chemical restraints also allow X-rays, peritoneal lavage, and other procedures to be performed.

Consider a video system. Videotaping an intoxicated patient's behavior would provide a jury evidence showing the difficulty of evaluating injuries and the need for restraints. Now that video equipment is inexpensive ($1,000), juries may be provided the experience of seeing what really happened. Clinics and emergency departments that care for many intoxicated patients would do well to install a camera that monitors the bed used for most intoxicated patients. A TV in the nurses' station would allow for improved patient monitoring.

A video recorder would allow an objective record of patient-staff interactions to be made.[29] Such equipment has been used for years in residency training programs to assist in evaluating resident performance. Practitioners outside the ivory towers can receive similar benefits.

It is perfectly proper for the medical record to contain intimate details of history and physical examination. Still, some laws consider it an invasion of privacy to photograph a person, even if the image is just part of a medical record.[166] This obstacle to recording reality might be dealt with by having the standard consent form include a clause about photographing and videotaping. However, the most unruly patients often will not sign anything.

A large sign informing the patient of the videotaping, in plain view of the patient and of the camera, would further document the fact that the patient knew the recording was being done. Check with your attorney about local laws before videotaping.

Videotapes for consent. A plastic surgeon, Dr. Bart Mazeika of Dallas/Fort Worth, has founded a company (M.A.P.S., Medical Assurance Protection Services) that leases video equipment to doctors who wish to record patient interviews, informed consent explanations, medical notes, and even surgical procedures. He feels this is a logical extension of the trend toward videotaping depositions and other court testimony. Dr. Mazeika was sued by a patient who claimed that she cried out in pain during surgery, while Dr. Mazeika claims that patient was under sedation. The patient was awarded $28,000 for her alleged pain. A videotape would have shown the truth.[117]

TIGHT CASTS

Many legal claims result from tight casts. Because an injured body part can swell, tissues can be compressed. That can lead to impaired circulation, lack of blood supply, and further swelling. One defense is that the initial injury was the cause of the damage. In a case charging a Utah doctor with damages resulting from misapplying a cast, the defense successfully argued that the limb at issue would have been lost regardless of what treatment was given.[c55] Another defense in a cast injury case is contributory negligence. In such cases, your defense should show that the plaintiff caused the problem by not heeding warning signs, failing to return for needed care, or "adjusting" the cast.[c179]

For example, a patient missed her scheduled 24-hour cast check. She fell three days later, causing greatly increased pain in her casted leg. She did not seek care until the next day when impaired circulation was found. An amputation was required, but the treating physician and hospital were not found to be negligent.[c97]

MISSING A MALIGNANCY

Suppose you examine a patient and fail to detect a malignancy. One defense of your oversight, if true, might be that the patient did not complain of symptoms in the cancerous body part. Other defenses can be based on the behavior of the tumor, specifically how quickly that type of tumor grows and spreads. That would include knowing the doubling time of the tumor. With such data, you can contend that the tumor would not have been detectable when the patient was examined.[c153] or that, when the patient was seen, it was already too late to render effective treatment.[c129]

FAILING TO PERFORM AN ADEQUATE WORKUP

When a diagnosis is missed, plaintiffs frequently claim that the diagnosis would have been made had further history, physical examination, laboratory tests, or X-rays been done. When deciding how much of a workup to perform, physicians often (consciously or unconciously) perform a cost/benefit analysis. Costly workup will be avoided for minor ailments and for major but very unlikely conditions. As stated by Dr. David Bergman,[24] "A physician...may order many needless, expensive diagnostic tests (the small losses) to avoid missing an important diagnosis (the big loss)."

Use the plaintiff's expert.   It will probably not help your case to tell the jury you did not take tests because you wanted to save money. It may help, however, if your attorney can (through questioning) have the plaintiff's expert state that the patient's condition was unlikely, given the initial presentation. The expert could be asked if he *always* performs the supposedly necessary workup on patients like the one in your case, and when he last cared for such a patient.

Review the literature.   The medical literature contains many articles written by cost-conscious physicians who claim that workups are not needed in various situations.[242] For example, the many articles denouncing the taking of skull X-rays following trauma would provide an answer to the plaintiff's attorney who asked, "Doctor, why didn't you X-ray this patient's head after it was injured?"[115]

PROTECTING A PATIENT

When an inpatient is not adequately protected—from falling, for example—the institution and medical staff may be held liable.

Bedrails.   Confused, sedated patients may climb over bedrails and fall to the floor. Bedrails have also cut off fingers when coming down, and fallen suddenly when leaned on for support. Nevertheless, it is generally accepted that confused and sedated patients should have bedrails up to provide protection from falling.

When charged with not ordering bedrails raised, an effective defense is to claim that the general hospital policy is that they be raised. In other words, it isn't necessary to specify actions that are already part of the hospital's standard operating procedure.

In one such case, a physician had not ordered siderails because he wanted to encourage an obese patient's mobility. Neither had he directed the removal of the rails. The sedated patient became disoriented and fell from bed.

The teaching manual used in the hospital's nursing school called for raising rails for patients who are restless, obese, or under deep sedation. The jury held for the patient and against the hospital. The Supreme Court upheld the decision that the hospital had failed to follow its own rules.[c31]

In another incident, a patient climbed over full-length bedrails and fell. The court found the hospital staff not liable, because they had done what was reasonably expected to protect the patient.[c101]

Most patients who have been injured getting out of bed had their bedrails elevated. They were trying to climb over the rails, usually in an attempt to go to the bathroom. Sedation, time of day, disorientation, and age have not been significant factors in most of these occurrences. Bedrails are frequently elevated not because they are medically indicated, but because of fear of a lawsuit. Therefore, *fear of lawsuits causes patient injuries.* Perhaps the best defense to the claim of not keeping bedrails up is to present the data that proves that elevated bedrails are often dangerous.[78]

Wheelchairs. Similarly, another patient was waiting in line for a laboratory test and fainted. The fall led to the amputation of a finger. The patient, suffering from chest pain, had been given drugs. The court found the hospital employee, a practical nurse, negligent in not providing a wheelchair. It was decided that a physician's order to use a wheelchair was not a prerequisite to a finding of ngeligence on the part of the practical nurse.[c190]

Belts. In some cases, restraints more effective than bedrails are needed. For example: a confused and hostile patient freed himself from a restraining belt, and then attacked another patient. The violent patient had frequently escaped from the belt. The injured patient recovered damages from the hospital because the injuries were a foreseeable consequence of the weak restraint.[c58]

Supervision. A hospital was sued for failing to provide protective supervision of a teenage female schizophrenic whose condition was allegedly made worse by her sexual activities in the hospital. The hospital claimed that limited supervision in an open ward with men and women present was beneficial to the patient and part of the needed treatment. The jury found in favor of the hospital. The appellate court upheld the decision, saying that the amount of supervision needed was a medical judgment.[c130]

MISUSING DRUGS

A 1982 case demonstrates effective defenses for allegedly negligent use of drugs. A patient developed hepatitis after twice in 1970 receiving halothane anesthetic in a clinic. It was known in 1970 that a small percentage of patients repeatedly given halothane will later contract hepatitis.

Nevertheless, there was no sure proof that halothane caused hepatitis in any given case, because no laboratory test could distinguish halothane-induced hepatitis from all other types. Nor, at that time, was there a test to identify patients susceptible to halothane-induced hepatitis. And the value of an eosinophil count, to detect white blood cells that react to allergic conditions, was questionable.

Testimony showed that even if a high eosinophil count had been done, the choice of anesthetic for the second operation would not have been changed. The federal appellate court for New Hampshire found in favor of the clinic.[c46]

The above case demonstrates four defenses to an accusation of negligent drug or anesthetic administration:

1. Though all drugs can have terrible side effects, there's usually no way to predict which patients will develop adverse reactions. So you can usually argue that the probable benefit of the drug greatly outweighed the small risk of adverse reaction.

2. On a slightly different tack, you can also argue that there's no proof that the adverse reaction resulted from the drug. Without taking any medication at all, people develop hepatitis, rashes, hearing loss, cardiac arrest, shortness of breath, and many other conditions attributed to drugs. Thus, the condition attributed to the drug may have been a result of the disease being treated, exposure to someone else with the disease, or over-the-counter drugs the patient took in the month before the adverse reaction.

3. In situations where there is a test that might have shown likelihood of the adverse reaction, question the validity of the test.

4. If there is a test—or if the patient had symptoms—that would have predicted the reaction, you could argue that the benefit of the medication still seemed to outweigh the possible adverse reaction. So not taking a test, or not taking warning signs into account, can be defended by asserting that, had such warnings been noted, the same treatment would have been given.

PROTECTING OTHERS

You may have a patient who is a danger to others, consciously intending to harm someone, or unknowingly unfit to drive because of seizures, diabetes, mental illness, or intoxication. If that patient injures someone, you can be held liable for damages. The rationale is that you might have prevented the damages had you acted on your knowledge of the patient's dangerousness.

Several defenses are effective when charged with failure to inform a third party of a patient's dangerousness. The basic stance is that such information is confidential. By law, confidences related by patients can't be given to other parties. (The changing rules on confidentiality and the duty to inform others were traced in Step 5.)

Contending that a patient's threat of violence was not believed is a valid defense that can hold, even when it's recorded on the patient's chart. Intoxicated or impulsive individuals make many threats that are not carried out. You need only visit an emergency room on Saturday night to hear patients who have lost fights vow they will "kill" those who beat them.

Perhaps the strongest defense is that state or federal law may prohibit you from reporting a patient's problem:

A paranoid schizophrenic and alcoholic patient collided with another car while driving on the wrong side of the road with his headlights off. A Veterans Administration psychiatrist was charged in the suit filed under the Federal Tort Claims Act by the occupants of the other car. The suit claimed that the patient should have been hospitalized and that the Department of Motor Vehicles should have been notified of his condition.

Federal law and regulations then in effect would have prohibited release of information to the Department of Motor Vehicles. So the court ruled that the psychiatrist had no ability or right to control the patient's conduct, and no duty to warn others of his dangerousness. That the psychiatrist felt the patient did not need hospitalization was good enough.[c83]

Thus, failure to notify third parties of the dangerousness of a patient can be defended on four points:

1. The information was confidential.
2. It was not believed to be true at the time.
3. The law prevented reporting it.
4. The patient had not previously injured anyone.

Protecting third parties from your patients. While some patients can be psychiatrically dangerous, others can be dangerous because of impaired driving. You may be sued for damages to your patient and anyone your patient drives into. Physicians have been sued in suits involving patients who were drunk, diabetic, and epileptic. Suits also arise because patients are on medications that make them drowsy and because they have blurred vision or eye patches.

If sued in such a situation your defense should include producing evidence that your patient was told that driving was dangerous. Your duty is to warn the patient, but you cannot be expected to control the patient.[c69,c73,211]

If you cannot find a written note documenting warnings given the patient, look for instruction sheets that may have been routinely given your patient in your clinic or emergency department. Many of these warn of driving with medications. Look to see if the patient was given the same medicine on the previous visits or in other clinics in which warnings were given. Check with the pharmacy to obtain evidence that the bottle containing the medication had a warning on it (this is almost universally done). See if your prescription was written in such a way as to preclude driving under the influence, as "Take two at bedtime for sleep."

CONTROLLING A DRUG-CRAZED PATIENT

Practitioners are sometimes faced with patients who, under the influence of hallucinogenic drugs, are out of touch with reality and injure others.

Drug charge. It's quite possible that shortly after seeing a doctor, a patient under the influence of a hallucinogen might have an auto accident, deliberately harm someone else, or commit suicide. If you were that doctor, you would likely be sued for not recognizing the danger, and for not taking steps to control the patient.

Six defenses. Faced with such a charge, you'll have six possible factors to base your defense on:

1. You didn't know that the patient had taken the drug.
2. Although it seemed possible that he was under the influence of a drug, evidence in his history or old charts indicated he was chronically or repeatedly intoxicated; therefore, detaining him

against his will during each or any period of intoxication seemed an unnecessary deprivation of his rights.

3. You thought his condition was due to alcohol alone, whether or not he claimed to have taken other drugs as well.

4. He gave no indication or warning of violent behavior.

5. He was with someone who seemed capable of watching him and who was familiar with the typical drug reaction.

6. Even though he seemed excitable or tended to be violent, you judged that detaining him against his will would likely cause more harm than good.

To bolster your defense based on Factor 1—you didn't know he had taken drugs—keep these things in mind: The history given by him and his friends was inaccurate or incomplete. Drug abusers are often afraid they'll be reported to the police and arrested for illegal drug use or possession.

Even if he and his friends tell the truth, as they know it, you may still be getting false information. After all, no one who buys drugs on the street really knows what he is getting. Street drug peddlers and suppliers are not known for following truth-in-labeling regulations. Someone who buys a drug on the street may receive LSD, PCP, marijuana, caffeine, Haldol—or just about any other drug—rather than the one advertised by the seller. Quite often, mixtures of drugs are sold containing such fillers as sugar or talcum powder.

PCP volatility. A drug that's cheaply produced and therefore often sold in place of other drugs is PCP, or phencyclidine, known on the street as angel dust. Eaten, snorted, smoked, or injected, PCP causes anesthesia and dissociation.[21] The user will not feel pain, and may be confused, go into a coma, have a seizure, or act normally. The effects differ from one person to another. Even in the same person the effects can vary minute by minute, hour by hour.

A patient under the influence of PCP who is restrained may struggle violently enough to cause the breakdown of his muscles (rhabdomyolysis). Chemical substances from the damaged muscles can then go to the kidneys and cause acute renal failure and death.[199] Consequently, take this warning from PCP expert Barry Rumack: "Other than those with life-threatening symptoms, the less done for these patients, the better."[232]Verifying that a hallucinogenic substance has been ingested can be difficult, time-consuming, expensive, or impossible. One of the difficulties in measuring chemical substances in blood or urine is that the patient may not want to give the sample because he does not want his drug abuse detected.

172

Even when samples are obtained, tests available at any given hospital are not likely to include all of the hundreds of possible substances that are abused. And even when the tests are available, they're often costly, slow, and insensitive.

For PCP, the most sensitive test is gas chromatography, which takes several hours. Less sensitive tests are not likely to detect mild intoxication. And even large ingestions of PCP will go undetected if the patient's urine is alkaline, since excretion of PCP in the urine depends on the pH of the urine.[21]

An emergency patient who was treated by one of the authors demonstrated many of the above points. The patient was brought in by friends because of a cut arm. The cut was down to the bone and had caused nerve and arterial damage. Yet he was alert, intelligent, walked normally, and spoke with better diction than most broadcast announcers.

When asked what cut him, he just said, "A knife."

When asked who cut him, he calmly explained, "I was trying to kill myself. I've been wanting to do it for six months, but I just got around to it tonight. I want to go home so I can finish it. Can I go home now?"

He was committed to a psychiatric facility, fortunately with no physical struggle. He denied any use of drugs, but a toxicology test showed he had taken PCP.

You can't commit someone just because he seems to be under the influence of a drug. That's especially true if he seems to be habitually taking drugs and functioning as well as he wants to function. Another recent emergency patient is a case in point:

A young woman came to the hospital with a small laceration. She and her friends said that she had been drinking alcohol and taking "white crosses"—amphetamines—all day. But she always took such medication, and there was nothing unusual about this intoxication or the alcohol on her breath. No drug-abuse counseling was desired. She was loud and slow to understand directions, yet basically oriented and cooperative.

In this case, we decided to ignore the fact that the patient was on possibly dangerous drugs, and to stress in the record that she had friends who were going to stay with her and had promised to return if anything unusual occurred.

PERINATAL NEUROLOGICAL DAMAGE

When a neurologically damaged infant is born, a malpractice suit often results, and the payments can be high. This led to a 1988 malpractice premium for obstetricians of over $50,000 per year in many locations. Florida obstetrician-gynecologists were facing premiums as high as $117,000 per year.[27]

Hypoxia near the time of birth, allegedly caused by the treating physicians, is often blamed for neurological damage. Scientific evidence, however, refutes the theories used to "prove" negligence in many such malpractice cases. For example, many infants with low Apgar scores at birth recover completely with no neurological damage.[228]

Low Apgar scores do not prove hypoxia. It is not accurate to equate birth asphyxia with low Apgar scores, a subject reviewed by Dr. George Giacoia.[97] In neonates born with low Apgar scores, cord blood gases can prove that hypoxia was not present. An already damaged neonate may be depressed at birth because of the strain of *normal* childbirth. Cerebral damage may have occurred weeks or months before delivery. Such cerebral damage may be the result of second trimester bleeding, acute or chronic maternal illness, or maternal drug or alcohol abuse. The neonate may also have tumors, degenerative disorders of unknown cause, or neuromuscular disorders. In addition, very low birth weight infants have immaturity of the central nervous system, which gives decreased muscle tone, reflex irritability, and respiratory effort. These 3 (of the 5) Apgar signs will have low scores because the infant is premature, not because it is hypoxic.

Maternal alcohol and drug abuse have well-documented effects on fetal development. It has been possible to make mothers answer questions concerning their use of drugs during pregnancy when a malpractice action for perinatal neurological injuries has been filed.[127]

As many as 375,000 infants every year could be impaired in some way by in utero drug exposure, according to a study by the National Association for Perinatal Addiction Research and Education in Chicago.[206] The National Institute of Drug Abuse estimates that 8 million of the 56 million American women between 15 and 44 use at least one of the four drugs: nicotine, alcohol, marijuana, or cocaine. Each of these drugs has been linked to birth defects. (See table 11–2 for a summary of information concerning perinatal neurological injury.)

Cerebral palsy. Delays in delivery and fetal hypoxia have been blamed for the development of cerebral palsy (CP), leading to expensive settlements. A defense to such charges would include explaining

174

TABLE 11–2. INFORMATION USEFUL FOR THE DEFENSE IN PERINATAL NEUROLOGICAL INJURY CASES[97]

Evidence of factors causing neonatal respiratory depression

Immaturity

Disorders of respiratory tract, thoracic cage, diaphragm, central nervous system, and congenital disorders (muscular or neuromuscular)

Previous damages events:
  Intrauterine infections
  Maternal alcohol or drug use
  Trauma during pregnancy
  Abnormalities of placenta or cord
  Maternal or fetal blood loss

Documentation useful to the defense

Fetal or cord blood pH to demonstrate absence of perinatal acidosis

Clinic and emergency department charts of mother demonstrating:
  Adequacy of prenatal care
  Drug or alcohol use
  Bleeding, trauma

Ultrasound examinations showing prenatal damage
  Condition of placenta
  Abruption
  Fetal abnormalities, such as cerebral infarction or intracranial hemorrhage

Post-partum CT or MRI studies of child's head showing nature of central nervous system abnormalities.

Condition of umbilical cord:
  Hematoma
  Knots
  Tears in the velamentous insertion

Condition of the placenta:
  A pale surface indicates transplacental hemorrhage
  Other abnormalities

Genetic studies of the infant

---

scientific literature that shows that the development of cerebral palsy is not related to substandard care during pregnancy or labor.[49] (See table 11–3.)

A study reported in the *Lancet* showed that substandard care during labor as defined in the article was not related to the incidence of cerebral palsy. Failure to promptly react to evidence of intrapartum asphyxia did not occur in any of the 34 deliveries of babies with cerebral palsy in the study.[192]

Defenses to specific charges

175

TABLE 11–3. FACTS ABOUT CEREBRAL PALSY

1. The prevalence of CP has not changed much over the years, despite increased intervention.
2. Most newborn asphyxia is not followed by cerebral palsy.
3. Imperfections in electronic fetal monitoring make the diagnosis of fetal asphyxia imprecise.
4. Fetal asphyxia may *follow* fetal brain damage.

The study found that substandard care during pregnancy was associated with an increased risk of fetal death and newborn convulsions. However, there was no increased risk of cerebral palsy. The study also showed that *the quality of prenatal care is more important than intrapartum care. This fact provides the basis for raising in court the possibility that a mother who sought no prenatal care may have caused her child's problems.*[192]

DEFENDING RETROLENTAL FIBROPLASIA CASES

Many unjustified malpractice claims have resulted from the incorrect assumption that retrolental fibroplasia (RLF, or retinopathy of prematurity, ROP) is an iatrogenic disease caused by the "excessive" use of oxygen in treatment premature infants. In fact, RLF has occurred in full-term and low birth weight infants who never received oxygen therapy. Studies have shown that RLF cannot be prevented by routine transcutaneous oxygen monitoring. This topic is reviewed in a manner which can be helpful malpractice defendants in pediatrics.[161]

The cause of RLF is unknown, but it is related statistically to a variety of factors. These factors include blood transfusions, intraventricular hemorrhage, apnea, infection, patent ductus arteriosus, genetic factors, and any disturbance in oxygen supply, either hyperoxemic or hypoxemic.

Look for genetic defects. An infant was born following prolonged labor associated with inadequate monitoring by residents and a medical student. Eventually a C-section was done. The baby's Apgar scores were 5 at one minute and 6 at five minutes. There were no seizures or other evidence of acute encephalopathy. However, progressive neurological deficits showed within weeks, and the patient ended up with spastic quadriplegia, poor vision and hearing, and marked mental retardation.

The jury voted 12 to 0 for the plaintiff on the issue of the standard of care. No damages were paid, however, because causation was not proven. The jury was convinced that the standard of care did not cause the neurologic deficits by two types of evidence. First, the defense contended there were no signs of perinatal brain damage, the Apgar scores being inconsistent with severe hypoxia. Second, an expert witness-geneticist testified that the patient had low-set ears, a high palate, abnormal palmar creases, rocker feet, epicanthal folds, and wide-set eyes. These were markers of congenital abnormality. Also, the variety and severity of the neurologic deficits suggested a congenital etiology.[222]

DEFENDING INTER-HOSPITAL PATIENT TRANSFERS

The defense to the accusation that transfer of a patient led to harm of the patient or was in violation of COBRA regulations lies in finding documentation of the items listed in the table 11-4. Also, factors proving the necessity of the patient transfer must be brought out. These factors are explained in the following discussion.

Reasons for patient transfers. When admission is needed, patients are often transferred to another hospital.[82]

The availability of special care at another institution is the reason for some transfers. Admitting physicians may request that a patient be transferred because of hospital staff affiliations, the desire to give one hospital business, or the convenience of making all rounds in one hospital.

Physicians and patients both may desire transfer to a public hospital when inability to pay is a factor. Patients without insurance or other resources feel that most doors in our nation's health system are closed to them and tend to go to public hospitals. However, in an acute situation, geographical and financial considerations are often temporarily ignored.

Financial considerations are significant. Urban public hospitals experience an annual average of $32,100 in bad debt on charity care per bed.[90]

Patient transfers are increasing and usually involve the poor. This trend will probably reverse in the early 1990s because of legislation in individual states, Federal COBRA legislation, and malpractice suits alleging damages from transfers. Patient transfers in Washington, D.C. increased from 169 in 1981 to 930 in 1985. A study at Highland General Hospital in Oakland, California found that of 458 patients transferred to the emergency department from other hospitals, 63% had no insurance, 21% had Medicaid, 13% had Medicare, and only 3% had private insurance. A study from Cook County Hospital in Chicago of 467 patients transferred to the emergency department from other hospitals found that 89% of patients were black or Hispanic, 81% were unemployed, and 87% were transferred because they lacked adequate health insurance.[15]

Sometimes a transfer cannot reasonably be expected to harm a patient. Patients with appendicitis, a broken arm or leg requiring surgery, and hundreds of other conditions can be safely transferred. It can even be argued that transferring an acutely injured patient will improve his chances of survival. In an article entitled, "Transfer of Unstable Patients: Dumping or Duty?" Olga Jonasson and John A. Barrett of Cook County Hospital in Chicago argue that many trauma patients are best sent to regional trauma center, which can expertly and quickly provide the needed care.[149]

Still, treatment may be needed before transfer. For example, fluids may be given, fractures splinted, and wounds cleaned. On the other hand, extensive X-rays and treatment may delay definitive, lifesaving surgery. Each case must be weighed individually to determine the safety of transfer. Look for documentation of the items in table 11–4 to show that your transfer was necessary, in the best interests of the patient, properly done, and (at the time) apparently safe.

TABLE 11–4. FACTS TO FIND WHEN DEFENDING A PATIENT TRANSFER

1. The reasons for the transfer
2. The wishes and attitude of the patient and family
3. Why the transfer was in the patient's best interest
4. Adequate medical facts, including *initial and final:* vital signs and physical examination at transferring hospital
5. Physician's signature on all charts
6. Details of the arrangements made with the receiving facility including the name of physician accepting the patient and medical records should be sent with the patient (test results, X-rays)
7. How the patient was transported (adequacy of personnel and equipment)

Handling the COBRA. In addition to worrying about patient care and being sued for malpractice, physicians now have to worry about violating federal regulations which affect patient transfer. On August 1, 1986, the COBRA law went into effect. This is the Consolidated Omnibus Budget Reconciliation Act, or Public Law 99-272. Four pages of this act (in Section 9121) affect emergency care, including patient transfers.[86]

COBRA requires all hospitals to examine and stabilize all patients who present to the emergency department. This includes patients who are unable to pay for the services. The stabilization must be done before transfer, and the medical benefits of transfer must outweigh the risks. The receiving hospital must agree to the transfer, and have adequate space and personnel. Medical records and a means of actually moving the patients must be assured by the transferring hospital. Physicians can be fined $25,000 for each violation, and hospitals can be suspended or terminated from the Medicare program for just one violation. Transferring at patient in active labor has brought a $25,000 fine to at least one physician.[92] Table 11–4 lists information you will want to piece together in defense of your COBRA or malpractice case that involves a patient transfer. Documentation is very important.[272]

Defenses involving other defendants

Even if the plaintiff who is suing you has named no one else as a defendant, a number of other individuals and organizations may pay at least part of the damages. Depending on the specifics of the case, your co-defendants and co-payers may include the workers' compensation board, the patient's employer, your employer or contractor, the person—or persons—who originally injured the patient before you rendered treatment, the hospital in which you saw the patient, the manufacturer or distributor of instruments that hurt the patient, drug manufacturers who did not adequately warn of complications, and a variety of insurance companies. All those parties can—and perhaps should—be your co-defendants.

As shown in Step 3, you can bring other defendants into the case by an impleader—a "third party complaint"—during pretrial pleadings. The next step will examine the various means you can use to make other parties co-defendants and share liability with you. And remember that it's never too soon to begin working with other professional colleagues on a cooperative, unified defense.

Application of the principles that follow will vary from state to state. So if one or more of the defenses are relevant to your case, your attorney will need to research the current laws and case precedents in your state.

WORKERS' COMPENSATION

In some states, a plaintiff who was injured and collected for disability under workers' compensation insurance can't collect again from

180   *PRESENTING YOURSELF AND YOUR CASE*

the practitioner who rendered negligent treatment. In such cases, though the negligent treatment may have increased the injury, the courts have held that the patient has been duly compensated by the workers' compensation payments.

In other states, however, workers' compensation payments to a plaintiff must be kept secret from the jury. Nor is the jury allowed to know that the plaintiff has received compensation for injuries from insurance policies or other payments. This arrangement, known as the collateral-source rule, can lead to the plaintiff receiving a settlement for damages from each of a number of sources.

Even when the jury is allowed to know about workers' compensation already paid, it may feel that the compensation was inadequate, and impose an additional award. In a 1981 case, a $1.5-million award was added to the workers' compensation paid: A Texas orthopedic surgeon damaged the popliteal artery while repairing a knee's torn meniscus; the plaintiff suffered severely impaired function of the leg and is likely to lose it.[c2]

Although information about collateral-source payments may not be admissible in court, such compensation from other sources may lead to an out-of-court settlement. You and your co-defendants should be more determined to resist a large settlement if you discover that the plaintiff has already been adequately and fairly compensated for medical costs, time away from work, and other losses due to the injury.

One psychologist brought a personal injury action against his fellow-worker, another psychologist, who shot him during a gun safety workshop at a state mental health agency. The state statute provided, and an Arizona appellate court agreed, that workers' compensation was the exclusive remedy for injuries caused by co-employees. Since compensation payments had been accepted, additional payments could not be obtained.[c32].

Similarly, a worker settled a claim with his employer following an injury. The employer filed a third-party action against the physician who had allegedly worsened the worker's injury. The complaint was dismissed because the employee's claim for contribution from the physician was barred by the previous settlement of the patient's claim.[164]

Absence of duty defense.   In general an employee will not be able to successfully sue a physician for medical malpractice when only an examination for a compensation carrier is performed. Courts have generally agreed that there is no physician-patient relationship created when an examination of an employee is conducted at the request of a worker's compensation carrier. The employee does not contract with the physician for services, and the employee does not seek medical advice or treatment.[146]

Therefore when a non-treating physician determines that an employee may return to work after an injury and the injury is exacerbated, the physician should not be liable.

If the physician is treating the patient, there is a physician-patient relationship and the physician may be found to have an additional duty to *adequately* communicate work restrictions to the employer as well as to the employee.[142] For example, the Alabama Supreme Court recently decided that it was not adequate to simply specify to the employer "light duty" with "no heavy lifting." A more clear definition of work restrictions would include a description of allowable bending, stooping, standing, and the amount of weight that could be lifted.[121]

ORIGINAL TORTFEASOR

The original tortfeasor is the one who first injured the plaintiff. It may be, for example, the driver of the car that struck the plaintiff. If the person suing you has recovered damages from the original tortfeasor, you may, in some instances, claim that compensation for all damages has already been made. This may be upheld, even if you or any other defendant has, in fact, negligently aggravated the injury.[114]

Two dental cases support the principle of satisfaction by the original tortfeasor. Both claims involved patients who had been negligently injured by one dentist, and had then gone to another dentist. The second dentist further injured the patient in each case. It was held in both cases that the settlement between the patient and the original dentist provided sufficient compensation and satisfaction; the second dentist wasn't liable.[c189]

A reverse judgment is also possible. In *Embrey v. The Borough of West Mifflin*, the plaintiff was in an automobile collision caused by a defective traffic signal. He suffered seven broken ribs, fractures of three lumbar vertebrae, and a splenic laceration. He died five days later from pulmonary edema and infection.

The jury found the nursing staff negligent for failing to ask for physician assistance when the patient went into respiratory failure. Expert witnesses had convinced the jury that the patient had not suffered any lethal injuries in the accident, so his death was the fault of the doctor and staff in the intensive-care unit.[213] The Pennsylvania appeals court in 1978 affirmed the verdict, and found the physician and hospital solely liable for the death of the plaintiff.[c60]

RELEASE OF TORTFEASORS

Releasing the original tortfeasor from liability has often released other persons who caused later injury. The release is a legal contract written when a settlement for damages is made. It's included in the settlement to prevent further claims, should the plaintiff later find more damage than originally discovered.

When a plaintiff is injured in an automobile accident, a claim is often settled with the other driver, or with the various insurance companies. The settlement contains a release stating that the damages have been compensated. It may also state that no further judgments will be sought against specific people, or that further injuries arising from the accident will not cause other legal action against anyone. On the basis of such releases, many medical practitioners have escaped liability for allegedly causing further damages to the already injured person.[c146]

The wording in such settlements and releases differs greatly, and the laws dealing with their interpretation vary from state to state. Such cases have been settled on various theories of justice. In a claim made against the Charleston Area Medical Center in West Virginia, for example, the court ruled that the case should be decided on whether the plaintiff intended to release other defendants when the original tortfeasor was released.[c191]

FELLOW SERVANT

If you're sued by one of your employees, you may escape unscathed through special defenses effectively used by employers.

The employer-employee relationship in some cases can evoke the fellow-servant rule: Because an employer has limited control over his employees' actions, he is not responsible for injuries caused to one employee by another.

You can also apply the assumption-of-risk rule: Employees should have realized they were assuming the risk of injury when they took the job. Employees in a psychiatric inpatient ward, for example, should realize they'll be exposed to violent patients. Likewise, most employees working in a hospital understand they'll be exposed to communicable diseases.

Just as in a patient's suit against you as the responsible practitioner, so you—in response to a suit by your employees—can extend the charge of contributory or comparative negligence to your fellow servants, as defined in Chapter 10.

If your employees are covered under workers' compensation, an award can be made regardless of whether you, as the employer, were negligent in the damaging action of your employee. Reason: Unlike malpractice cases, workers' compensation cases are not decided on the basis of fault. Accordingly, an injured employee should be able to receive adequate workers' compensation, even if your negligence caused the injury.

Such immunity from prosecution may also hold true if you or another professional colleague in your practice or hospital is negligent in treating another company employee. That employee may not be able to sue you for damages, but will be able to claim payment under workers' compensation.

Nevertheless, don't ever consider yourself safe. A 1979 Indiana decision ran counter to the fellow-servant rule, even though the state workers' compensation act was made the exclusive remedy for harm to an employee caused by negligence of another employee. An employee successfully sued the doctors who operated a factory clinic. Running contrary to the fellow-servant rule, the court ruled that the doctors in the clinic were independent contractors, not employees, and therefore were responsible for their own actions.[c162]

THE HOSPITAL

Specific policies and inadequacies may be used to make the hospital a co-defendant in your malpractice case. If found liable, in part, for the patient's damages, the hospital will then have to pay a portion of the award due the plaintiff. Over the years hospitals have had increasing exposure to liability. Nonprofit, nonproprietary hospitals were at one time generally immune to liability because they were considered charitable or public institutions. By the 1950s the defenses of governmental and charitable immunity had been substantially eroded, and hospitals were seen to be health care providers rather than custodial institutions. In the 1960s and 1970s the doctrine of corporate liability was applied. In the 1980s hospital liability was further expanded through application of the Uniform Commercial Code to allow recovery for injuries caused by defective tools of the medical profession. Courts have ruled that hospitals hold themselves out to the public as having special knowledge regarding the provision of medical services and inherent in this presentment is a warranty that hospitals will furnish patients with goods and services that are fit for their intended purposes.[c174,246]

The North Carolina Court of Appeals has listed the following duties of a hospital:[130]

1. To provide and <u>maintain equipment</u> reasonably suited for its intended use.
2. Not to obey instructions of a physician that are obviously negligent or dangerous (the physician *and* the hospital would likely be held liable for resulting problems).
3. To promulgate adequate <u>safety rules</u> relating to the handling, storage, and administration of medicines.
4. To make reasonable efforts to <u>monitor and oversee</u> treatment that is prescribed and administered by physicians practicing in the hospital.
5. To permit only <u>competent physicians</u> to practice at the hospital.

Failure to fulfill these duties has been referred to as corporate negligence, and it provides a basis upon which patients may sue hospitals. On the other hand, denial of medical staff privileges frequently results in physicians suing hospitals. Such suits are based upon state and federal antitrust laws, due process claims, and other theories. Thus, hospitals must balance the rights of health-care providers with the need to limit liability exposure.[130]

An example of a hospital being held responsible for equipment is the 1980 case of *Mosley v. Castillo and Mercy Hospital*. In this case the tip of a brittle catheter snapped off and migrated into a patient's iliac artery. An extensive arteriotomy was needed to retrieve it. The physician involved was able to make the hospital a co-defendant when it was found that the catheter was over 10 years old and had probably been sterilized over 30 times. Catheter instructions had warned against repeated sterilization. The hospital was found to have 50 catheters over 5 years old, half of which contained evidence of body fluids. Still, the court awarded $200,000 in compensatory damages and $750,000 in punitive damages against the physician *and* hospital.[13]

In another case $350,000 was awarded to the parents of a psychiatric patient who committed suicide by jumping from the 15th floor window of a hospital. Claiming that the window and other measures that should have been taken to restrain the patient were ineffective in preventing the suicide, the fault was put 50% on the hospital, 25% on the general contractor, and 25% on the window manufacturer.[89]

Hospital liability has been expanded even further by additional decisions made by courts in various states. Such decisions are somewhat binding as case precedents in the states in which they were made, and less significant in other states. For example, in 1965 the Illinois Supreme Court stated that if a physician fails to fulfill a duty owed to a patient, it becomes the nurse's duty to advise the hospital authorities so that appropriate action can be taken. Referring to this opinion, the Appellate Court of Illinois in 1985 concluded that hospitals must warn patients of the adverse effects of drugs that are administered by the hospital. This responsibility to warn included the need to tell of the danger of taking alcohol with drugs. This responsibility, the court said, could make hospitals liable to third parties injured when a patient mixed alcohol with medications.[95]

Here are some of the ways in which hospitals can be held liable for damages:

Facilities. If your hospital's facilities aren't adequate, you can't be expected to perform optimally. The laboratory, for example, may not make tests or blood for transfusions available at certain hours or with reasonable speed, may be slow to alert you to important abnormalities, or may not even do certain tests.

The radiology department may not have certain critical tests available, not provide readings at lunch hours and nights, not give accurate readings, not report serious abnormalities quickly, or not be located near the emergency department so studies for critically ill patients are delayed.

Nurses. Physicians depend upon nurses for evaluating and monitoring patients, relaying messages, giving medications, and many other functions. When a nurse performs in a negligent fashion, the physician often gets sued. In such cases the nurse and hospital (as employer of the nurse) should share responsibility for the problems created.[1,226] In one case the rescue squad told the emergency department nurse that a patient's blood pressure had been $^{60}/_{40}$. The patient's blood pressure improved, and the physician was never told of the transient hypotension. The patient was sent home and soon died.[88]

In another case the nurse failed to relay the mother's history that a child had suffered a tick bite. The diagnosis of Rocky Mountain Spotted Fever was missed.

In still another case the emergency department nurse did not tell the physician that a suicidal patient had taken tricyclics as an overdose. The physician thought that penicillin was the only medication taken. The true nature of the ingestion was described on "nursing notes," which were separate from the main emergency department record. Such notes are often written at the end of a nurses's shift. They do the patient no good while being treated. And, the physician has no chance to see such notes. Such notes can provide the basis for getting the treating physician in trouble later.

Hospital liability for physician negligence has been expanded by a number of decisions in several states.[259] In _Darling v. Charleston Community Hospital_,[c52] hospital liability was found for the actions of independent physicians practicing in the hospital. The basis for this responsibility was found in the standards of the Joint Commisssion on Accreditation of Hospitals, the hospital licensing act, and hospital's own bylaws.

Policies. An unfortunate hospital policy that makes it difficult for patients without health insurance to be admitted or get follow-up care can lead to a lawsuit when a critically-ill patient is turned away.[22] Written hospital policies and medical staff bylaws should be examined in every malpractice case. Such documents can provide protection for you—and they can sometimes also place liability upon the hospital.

Let's say you're blamed for a postoperative pulmonary embolus. Showing that you followed the hospital and medical-staff protocols to prevent that problem is a valuable defensive action.[171] Suppose the hospital's protocols state that all patients undergoing the procedure in question should be given 5,000 units of heparin subcutaneously after surgery to prevent a pulmonary embolus. The plaintiff's lawyer may find literature describing other precautions you should have taken. Regardless of what others recommend, if you followed the protocol judged best by your hospital's medical staff and standards at that time, you will have a strong defense.

A hospital can be negligent and liable for damages if it violated its own regulations or standards. In one case, a patient undergoing dental surgery suffered brain damage due to lack of oxygen. The hospital was held liable because it hadn't enforced its own rule requiring the presence of a physician during dental surgery.[c138]

Protections. Hospitals may be held liable for the negligence of their employees, even when the negligence resulted from employees not following hospital policies. In a suit against Bossier City Hospital

Commission in Louisiana, for example, an X-ray technician failed to strap a patient to a semi-upright table. The patient was unable to stand—a fact known by others, but not by the technician. Although hospital policy dictated that restraining devices or straps be used in such situations, both the hospital and the technician were found responsible for the patient's resultant injury.[c5] Similarly, as we noted in Chapter 11, hospitals have been found liable for not using bedrails and wheelchairs, even when protective devices were not ordered by the attending physician.

Hospitals are also responsible for seeing to it that patients give informed consent before any procedures are performed.[280]

Records.   Inadequate record keeping can lead to inadequate patient care and, consequently, hospital liability. In one case, a nurse failed to observe and record the symptoms of eclampsia. When the patient died, the hospital was held liable, the court ruling that the doctor might have prevented the death had he known of the patient's dangerous condition.[c80]

Nurses, technicians, interns, residents, and all other hospital employees have a responsibility to record and report to appropriate physicians information on the condition of patients.

Hospitals are also expected to provide their staffs with patients' previous medical records. Those records help physicians, nurses, respiratory therapists, and other health-care providers render appropriate treatment. When problems arise because a doctor can't obtain needed information, the hospital can be held liable. In a claim against Detroit General Hospital, for example, two cornea recipients lost sight in eyes that received transplants, because the corneas had been taken from a patient with diseases that should have barred him from being a donor. Hospital records of the donor were missing. Those records would have alerted the ophthalmology resident, who removed the eyes, to the inappropriateness of the donor. The resident was found not negligent. Liability of the hospital was upheld on appeal.[c151]

In an obstetrics case involving brain damage to an infant, the hospital claimed at deposition that the fetal monitoring strips no longer existed. It was 5 years since the case occurred, and the depositions of the physicians and nurses were largely based on what they remembered. A week before the trial, the hospital produced the fetal monitor strips. The testimony from the depositions was read back to the jury along with an analysis of the fetal monitor strips. The deposition testimony did not agree with the monitor strips, making it appear that the physicians had lied. This led to a $2 million verdict for the plaintiff.[134]

Reviews. Hospitals can be held liable for not operating a review system that identifies incompetent physicians. The assumption is that, once identified, such physicians may have the scope of their practice limited, or at least be required to obtain consultation before initiating treatment in certain situations.

The issue of hospital responsibility for identifying impaired physicians was raised in both the *Darling v. Charleston Community Memorial Hospital*[c53] and *Gonzales v. Nork*[c72] suits. In the latter case, the judge held the hospital liable for not having in operation a review process that would identify a neurosurgeon who performed laminectomies inadequately and unnecessarily, even though the hospital satisfied accreditation standards and had staff surveillance equal to the best of similar community hospitals.

One hospital was successfully sued after hiring and granting surgical privileges to a surgeon who had just completed his residency. The hospital had checked a list of the number and types of surgeries in which the surgeon had participated and had asked the prior hospital's administrator for an endorsement of the surgeon. The hospital was faulted for not determining exactly what role the surgeon had had in each operation and for not contacting the "mentors" of the surgeon for information. And, the hospital was faulted for failing to initially supervise the surgeon to evaluate the quality of his work. At trial it was argued that such investigation was impractical and unworkable. Still, the jury awarded the plaintiff more than five times the amount initially awarded by an arbitration panel in a case involving complications following a hysterectomy.[c91,54]

Additional cases [259] have recognized hospital liability to patients for failing to investigate physicians' qualifications or competence[c122] and failing to act on knowledge of prior lawsuits based on the same surgery negligently performed.[c149]

Some courts have not found hospitals responsible for the acts of treating physicians.[c34] Such decisions will vary according to laws and previous case precedents in the state and elsewhere, the facts of the case in question, the other factors.

Restrictions. Hospitals can incur liability because of restrictions they impose on their emergency physicians. Such restrictions can prevent a physician from examining a patient in the emergency room. The custom in many hospitals is to call the patient's physician before the patient is seen by the attending emergency physician. The resulting delay may be significant because the patient's physician is in surgery, traveling between hospitals, or otherwise unavailable. That delay can be eliminated if the triage nurse judges the patient to be in need of immediate attention.

Some emergency departments still allow patients to be treated and sent home—or admitted—without being seen by any physician at all. In such cases, a nurse tells the patient's regular physician on the telephone about the patient's problem, and then the physician prescribes some treatment. Yet attorneys generally agree that only a physician can make a diagnosis in an emergency.[156]

It's simply not sufficient for a nurse to evaluate an emergency patient. Nor is it sufficient for the doctor to evaluate by telephone a patient who has come to the emergency department.[113]

Restrictive staff call lists. Hospital call lists may force emergency department physicians to call inappropriate, incompetent, or fearful physicians. Physicians working in a hospital emergency department are usually required by hospital bylaws and the terms of their employment to follow the hospital on-call list. Unless an emergency physician has worked in a certain hospital for a long time, he will not know which consultants have which skills, and even then it will be difficult to avoid an incompetent consultant.

A hospital directive to follow a call list might be viewed as an interference in the practice of medicine. This directive keeps emergency physicians from complying with the usual and customary standards used in selecting a doctor to whom referrals are made. In general a physician making a referral has a legal obligation to be informed about the qualifications of the physician to whom the referral is made and to be reasonably assured that the physician is qualified.

> There are cases now starting to crop up where the emergency physician follows an on-call list and the physician on the list is an incompetent physician for that particular problem. There are hospitals that mandate all follow-up referrals be made to family and general practitioners, even if the problem is an orthopedic or other subspecialty problem. The emergency physician could be liable for referring to an inappropriate or an incompetent physician.[32]

When a patient is harmed by the improper actions of the attending physician, the emergency physician may also be sued. Attending physicians may make mistakes because of their limited abilities or because of pressures from the hospital and other organizations.

Needed care is sometimes not given because of economic pressures. Physicians fear for their hospital privileges:

> ...Physicians are forced to calculate charges using fee schedules negotiated with various preferred provider organizations and health maintenance organizations, as well as those provided by private insurance companies, Medicare and Medicaid....And if that isn't enough, physicians now face the prospect of losing their hospital privileges if they order too many tests or keep a patient hospitalized longer than the average for a particular condition.[220]

Other hospital demands on emergency physicians.   At times, emergency physicians are asked to fulfill the responsibilities of other physicians. This occurs most commonly when emergency physicians are required to write admitting orders for patients being admitted to other physicians. Emergency physicians become party to incomplete patient evaluations when they agree to read chest X-rays and electrocardiograms on inpatients who may be having pulmonary emboli or preinfarction angina: these tests usually show nothing in such patients.

An impleader or third-party complaint should be filed in cases in which the hospital has influenced any physician to call certain consultants or otherwise compromise patient care.

Hospital policies that keep patients from physicians.   Some hospitals still have policies that keep emergency department physicians from seeing emergency department patients. If patients are not ill, that is fine, but if someone is seriously ill, problems can result. In the following case the absence of emergency department physician liability was affirmed, but the staff physician ended up with a bad case and a high judgment in court.

A patient with a head injury was transferred to a neurosurgeon at 3:43 AM. The patient was somnolent and could not follow commands. Ten minutes after arrival the right pupil became dilated, while the left arm and leg became weak. The nurse did not ask the emergency department physician to evaluate the patient because of a hospital policy that a private physician's patient would be managed by the private physician. She thought the neurosurgeon would arrive soon, and she did not telephone him until 4:20 AM. The patient had an epidural hematoma and ended up with a spastic quadriparesis and mental impairment. The hospital settled before the trial, leaving the neurosurgeon as the only defendant at trial. The verdict was for $5 million.[224]

THE GOVERNMENT

If inadequate staff or facilities in a government-supported institution contributed to the bad outcome in your case, name the city, county, or responsible parties as co-defendants. For example, a 6-year-old boy who was being treated for a cut lip died when given incorrect drugs at an Army hospital. A Defense Department investigation concluded that the Army base involved lacked sufficient staff and money to treat the number of patients who used the facility. The case was settled for $1.44 million. In addition, Congress responded by allocating $7.7 million to add 210 staff members to the base.

Governmental policies often limit health care. If a suit arises in a case in which governmental actions led to inadequate care, the responsible parties should be named as co-defendants. Then, when damages are awarded, the physician may not have to pay the total amount. In New York City, for example, there is such a shortage of hospital beds that on many days there is not an empty bed in all of Queens or Brooklyn. Hospital beds had been taken out of service to meet federal occupancy requirements and state projections of the number of needed beds. When the need for beds increased in 1987, the beds (and related services) were not available. Thus, it is common for patients to wait for a bed on a stretcher in the emergency room for 4 days. In one hospital, on the average there are 20 medical-surgical patients and 10 psychiatric patients awaiting admission in the emergency department, literally within inches of each other. In many areas, the mechanism for efficient, organized quality care has broken down because the hospitals are full.[207]

If you are sued for taking care of an indigent, alcoholic, or mentally ill patient, make the government (if it is responsible) a co-defendant in your case. The federal government has drastically cut funds needed to treat the mentally ill in recent years. "Street people" are a constant reminder of the problem. Yet, when problems arise as a result of the poor condition of these people, physicians are likely to be sued. Problems in the mental health commmunity were worsened in 1963 with the Community Mental Health Facilities Act, which was intended to return 500,000 mentally ill to their communities. Now, only about 5% of the estimated 2 million Americans who are seriously mentally ill receive any community support or rehabilitation services. The Mental Health Systems Act of 1980 authorized an increase in federal funding for the mentally ill over 5 years, but it was repealed in 1981. Since then a 30% cut in federal funding has occurred. Response of most states to the burden of providing treatment, or even shelter, for the mentally ill has been much less than adequate.[14]

FEDERAL PROTECTION FOR PEER REVIEW

Peer review activities now enjoy some protection from federal law. The Health Care Quality Improvement Act of 1986 establishes criteria and due process steps for peer review. It also sets out a system of mandatory reporting of privilege reductions, license actions, and malpractice payouts.[180]

Under the Health Care Quality Improvement Act, which took effect November 14, 1986, doctors who participate in legitimate review or credentialing activities cannot be held liable for damages under federal law unless they knowingly spread false information about the physician being monitored. Starting in October 1989, the immunity extends to actions brought under state law, though states can accept the new protection before then. The law shields peer reviewers from the cost of defending themselves against unwarranted suits. A doctor who files frivolous charges against reviewers must pay all resulting legal fees and other defense expenses.[282]

Participants in peer review and quality control must not be in a position to financially profit from any peer review action against a colleague.[221] In one case members of the medical staff of the only hospital in Astoria Oregon sought to terminate the staff privileges of a general and vascular surgeon because of allegedly incompetent care. The physician resigned from the medical staff during the peer review proceedings. He later sued the physician peer reviewers, claiming their motives were not based on concerns about his quality of care, but rather were anticompetitive. A jury awarded $650,000 in damages, and in 1984 the federal district court trebled this to nearly $2.2 million, as required by antitrust law. This award was upheld by the U.S. Supreme Court in 1988.[75] One of the peer review physicians stated, "Even the Health Care Quality Improvement Act doesn't prevent being involved in a legal action.... If you're involved in peer review, you may be dragged through the mud. So why bother?"[194]

Confidentiality of peer review and quality assurance findings. When cases are discussed in hospital meetings there are often discussions of alternatives, and physicians often exaggerate mistakes that may have been made. It is often expected that records of such constructive discusssions be held confidential and not discoverable in any lawsuit that may arise. Decisions as to the discoverability of peer review and quality assurance committee records vary from state to state. Some protection can be obtained by discussing cases without using a patient's name, but open discussion is likely to be discouraged by the threat of lawsuits.[252]

Further immunity for peer review activities. In California hospitals are required to evaluate the competence of physicians who apply for medical staff privileges. A surgeon must have his performance at the operating table observed and evaluated by a proctor. The proctor is not expected to supervise or intervene in the surgical procedure.[250] When a proctor was sued for failing to intervene in a case being observed, the court found there was no relationship between the proctor and patient, or between the proctor and surgeon. Therefore there was no duty of care. Since the question of duty of care is a question of law, the court was able to determine the existence of a legal duty of care in this case, and summary judgment for the proctor was granted. The Court of Appeal upheld the decision.[c43]

Interestingly, if a proctor saw a situation needing his input, he would likely be immune from liability if he kept quiet, but liable for negligent acts if he acted. "In other words, when no duty to act exists, volunteering to act often raises a duty to act non-negligently."[250]

In Illinois, Chapter 111 $\frac{1}{2}$, Section 151.2, of the Illinois Revised Statutes gives members of a peer review committee immunity from civil damages, by way of actions of defamation or otherwise. This immunity is without reservation. It is unconditional, and it is not even necesssary that "good faith" be established to gain the benefit of the immunity.

HMOS AND OTHER THIRD PARTY PAYERS

HMO problems involve business considerations replacing medical thinking. "In an HMO, ethical problems derive from a simple fact: The less care physicians give their patients, the better the physicians' financial gain."[23]

Because of insurance considerations, a patient was sent from an emergency department with a myocardial infarction.[c135] The patient had gone to a hospital which did not participate in his Hospital Insurance Plan (HIP). The emergency department nurse spoke to a HIP physician who said the patient should see him that morning.

The nurse discharged the man, even though he had chest pain and shortness of breath. He died before seeing the HIP physician.

The mother of a five-month-old boy with a cough and fever wanted to take him to the emergency department of Children's Hospital of Wisconsin, Milwaukee. The child had already been seen in the emergency department twice within the previous five days. The mother claims that her HMO physician would not authorize payment and instead scheduled an office appointment for the next day. The child died before his appointment, and a $6 million lawsuit was filed.[42]

What to do if sued. If pressure from an HMO or insurance company caused you to compromise care, file an impleader or third-party complaint. At the trial let it be known that you fought for the patient's interests. Tell how HMO or other cost-containment mechanisms interfered with the quality of your care. Juries are receptive to such arguments.[181]

In addition to counseling physicians against expensive referrals and workups, many HMOs are structured in such a way as to delay specialist referral and diagnosis. A primary care physician or nurse-practitioner may serve as a "gatekeeper."[37] Instead of making an appointment with an easily-identified specialist, HMO patients often must make an appointment to see the primary care physician. Then, if that physician agrees, another appointment with a specialist can be scheduled. The delays are obvious.

HMO as co-defendant. HMO's create financial incentives that interfere with the physician-patient relationship. Therefore it has been claimed that physicians are agents of HMOs. This exposes the HMOs to indirect liability as the physician's de facto employer under the theory of apparent agency.[181]

Utilization review versus physicians. In *Wickline v. State of California* it was claimed that a premature hospital discharge, demanded by Medi-Cal utilization reviewers, resulted in the loss of a patient's leg. The physicians in the case had requested an 8-day extension of the hospital stay, but only 4 days were approved. The physicians did not object, and the patient lost her leg. The patient sued the state rather than the physicians. In 1982 she won a $500,000 judgment. Four years later an appellate court overturned that verdict, saying *"the physician who complies without protest with the limitations imposed by a third-party payer, when his medical judgment dictates otherwise, cannot avoid his ultimate responsibility for his patient's care."*[131a]

As the above cases show, death, disability, and malpractice suits will result if you let nonmedical persons make decisions for you. In such cases it will aid your defense if you can document phone conversations and letters sent to the third-party payer that dispute its decision.

FAILURE OF EQUIPMENT

Faulty equipment is not usually its operator's fault. The malfunction of a mechanical device or piece of machinery can lead to bad results or accidents. An arm of an X-ray machine may break and fall onto a patient; it may put out too much radiation and cause burns. A metal rod may break several months or years after being surgically implanted in a leg.[135]

In such cases, the operator's or doctor's actions are not the cause of the patient's injury. The equipment manufacturer may be responsible. Or the hospital may be liable if it failed to periodically test the equipment or hadn't followed routine or recommended preventative maintenance procedures. Even the injured party may be found liable for contributory or comparative negligence, if the patient didn't use a medical device properly and was injured as a result.[c140]

In most situations, doctors who aren't present during procedures they've ordered won't be held liable for any damages. Such procedures include X-rays and administration of medication.[126] If present, however, the doctor is responsible for seeing that hospital equipment, supplies, and medication are used properly.

One patient, for example, was awarded $25,000 for burns caused by electrocautery. The surgeon, anesthesiologist, and hospital were all held liable for damages. There was no evidence or explanation of why the burns occurred. But the court held that existence of the burns was *prima facie* evidence of negligence, and that put the burden of proof on the defendants.[c200] *Prima facie* evidence, if not rebutted or contradicted, is sufficient to sustain a judgment in favor of the issue it supports.

The practitioner or hospital can be held liable for not noticing equipment defects that would be detected on routine inspection. But they probably would not be held accountable for a hidden or "latent" defect. When the X-ray table collapsed, for example, the cause was a broken pin inside a sealed gear box. The defect was judged latent, so the practitioner was held not liable for the patient's injury.[c94]

In an equipment suit brought against the South Highlands Infirmary, a patient was scarred by a defective dermatome—a device for shaving off a thin layer of skin for transplant to another area. For this injury, the hospital, not the surgeon, was found liable.[c177]

A number of OBG physicians performed tubal ligations using a defective plastic clip. Even though it was not named in the suits, the clip manufacturer settled them. None of the physicians had to contribute to the settlements.[239]

In one case a surgical drape caught fire when a cautery was used during a dilation and curetage. A cotton gauze was being used to remove blood. The cotton began to smolder when it got close to the cautery, and the surgeon threw the gauze on the floor for the circulating nurse to extinguish. The cotton landed near the drape, which caught on fire and burned rapidly. At trial the surgeon held that throwing a smoldering sponge on the floor for a nurse to extinguish was an accepted practice. The manufacturer of the drape alone was found liable.[c150]

In another case, a supplier was held fully culpable. A patient died 26 hours after receiving a contaminated intravenous solution. The contamination was allegedly caused by a hairline crack in the bottle containing the intravenous fluid. The company that supplied the solution had to pay the patient's family $1.9 million; the hospital was not held liable.[c148]

FAULT OF DRUG COMPANY

A physician can hold a drug manufacturer liable for failure to inform about the hazards of a drug. In *Oksenholt* v. *Lederle Labs*, the plaintiff physician prescribed Myambutol to treat tuberculosis. The manufacturer's literature declared that the drug would not cause permanent loss of vision. Yet the patient of Dr. Oksenholt did suffer permanent impairment of vision, and got $100,000 from the doctor. Then Oksenholt's action against the drug company charged negligence and fraud in not telling of the dangers of the drug. The court noted that in the special relationship that exists between a doctor and a drug manufacturer, the doctor must rely on the company to provide accurate information about its drugs.[c134]

A physician who incurs liability because of a manufacturer's failure to inform about a drug's side effects may sue the company on an indemnity (repayment) or contribution theory.[204] The Oksenholt decision is unusual, in that it allowed the doctor to sue for the amount awarded the patient, plus his own damages, including loss of earnings and reputation.

To sum up: When you're sued, you may be able to share liability with an insurance carrier, drug company, equipment manufacturer, hospital, or other defendant. And you can get compensation from them. As you'll see in steps 14 and 15, whatever the damages, there are many ways to pay and defray the costs of a malpractice case.

IT IS DECIDED

The charges and defenses of all parties are finished. The jury has rendered its verdict. The court has made its final judgment. The appeals are finished. The case is closed; it can't be opened again.

Its cost and effects, however, are not over. Steps 14, 15, and 16 will show you how to pay your costs—whoever won the case—and then step solidly and positively into the future with your psyche, family, and practice intact.

Malicious Prosecution and Other Types of Countersuits

Countersuits are seldom indicated and rarely won. However, you should consider filing a countersuit if it is justified.

Malicious prosecution suits are the best known type of "countersuit." In fact, there are a number of different reasons, or "legal theories," that can be used as a basis to sue your patient and his attorney. These include malicious prosecution, suing without the patient's permission, defamation (libel or slander), abuse of process, prima facie tort, invasion of privacy, infliction of emotional distress, and conflict of interest.[218,262]

Though you must recognize the need for the suit and initiate it, an attorney will probably be needed to help you file and carry out the lawsuit. Malpractice insurance companies *should* be glad to support the filing of such suits because they have been demonstrated to reduce the number of malpractice claims filed.

For example, in the 18 months following the Berlin case, the number of malpractice suits filed against doctors in the greater Chicago area was down 42%, even though Dr. Berlin "lost" his countersuit. In the suits that did occur after the Berlin case, fewer doctor co-defendants were named. In 1975 in Cook County, the total number of physicians named as defendants in malpractice suits was 1,499. In 1977, the number was 628, a reduction of 58%.[25] In a meaningful way, Dr. Berlin clearly "won" his countersuit.

WHY COUNTERSUE?

Medical practice as we know it may soon end unless the number of malpractice suits is decreased. Already 2 billion dollars a year is paid in awards to patients and their attorneys. Many physicians have gone out of practice or moved to states with lower insurance rates. Other physicians have eliminated "high risk" procedures from their practices. For example, many board certified obstetricians will not deliver babies. The number of malpractice suits and amounts of awards are increasing rapidly.

Lawyers have learned that they can file a malpractice suit and collect a few thousand dollars in settlement. This is true because it is easier for the physician and less expensive for his insurance company to settle than to take the case to court. Physicians are afraid of not settling out of court. Too often juries will take the attitude that sick or injured patients need money to live on, and there is nothing wrong with taking it from the rich doctor or insurance company, even if the physician gave competent care.

Most types of countersuits are more easily won if the malpractice case is decided in your favor, but that is not always necessary. Case precedents and laws have been changing recently. These changes in the law give attorneys a responsibility to the people they sue. Attorneys are now obligated in many jurisdictions to investigate lawsuits before they are filed to see if there are grounds for a lawsuit. This change in the law will reduce the number of frivolous malpractice suits if physicians countersue in appropriate cases.

THE HISTORY OF COUNTERSUITS

Countersuits arose out of the frustration and desparation that came during the malpractice crisis of the mid-1970s.[120] The number of countersuits that have been filed is relatively small.

In the past, insurance companies have not paid for the court costs and lawyers' fees associated with countersuits. Possibly because the cases have been so unsuccessful, lawyers will not usually take a case on a contingent fee basis. Also, many attorneys believe that anyone should be able to sue for any reason they please, the court deciding the validity of the claim. The fact that defendants in unwarranted suits are hurt is considered an unavoidable cost of our system of justice. Even when a countersuit is successful, the time and effort involved is more costly than the award.[158] Million dollar awards and settlements do not occur with physicians on the receiving end.

200

DEPOSITION TRANSCRIPTS CAN DOCUMENT WRONGDOING

The transcript of your deposition will document unfair questioning tactics of the opposing attorney. Any malicious or emotionally distressing treatment you receive during your deposition will be documented.

If there is no foundation for the claims made against you, all the depositions taken for the case will document this. Your patient's deposition may document the fact that he did not want to sue you or that claims of damages have been exaggerated by his attorney.

YOUR RELATIONSHIP TO THE PATIENT'S ATTORNEY

You are not a client of the patient's attorney. You are a so-called "third party." As stated in the *New York University Law Review,* "Attorneys generally owe a duty of care solely to their clients, and courts therefore seldom hold them liable for negligence resulting in injury to third parties...third party plaintiffs have been denied compensation and attorney misconduct has not been deterred....Bar association grievance committees alone cannot sufficiently police attorney misconduct. They lack the funding, the power, and the inclination to stalk attorney incompetence....Clients may not have sufficient interest to bring suit—they may be untouched by the attorney's conduct, they may be bankrupt, or they may even have benefitted from the attorney's negligence.[70]" This situation is changing. Federal laws, some state laws, and some state courts have begun to recognize the duty of attorneys to investigate the reasonableness of lawsuits before they are filed.

COUNTERSUITS: USE ONLY WHEN INDICATED

You should initiate a countersuit only when it is clear that your malpractice suit was unfounded. If you can understand why the malpractice suit may have seemed justified, do not bring a countersuit just because one of the theories for countersuing listed in this chapter seems to fit.

Countersuing is a difficult project that should be undertaken only after much consideration. Countersuing costs time and money. You can be countersued for countersuing. There are few case precedents (previous successful countersuits).

Most lawyers and judges believe that everyone should be able to sue anyone for anything, the court deciding if the suit should be sucessful. Still, few attorneys will sue another attorney. Those who do may have few friends and may be labeled as mercenaries.[110]

MALICIOUS PROSECUTION COUNTERSUITS

Though it has received much publicity, this classical type of counter-suit is quite difficult to win. Malicious intent (malice) must be proved in a malicious prosecution countersuit. It is necessary to have won the malpractice case before the suit can be initiated. Therefore, if unfair legal practices help the patient win a malpractice suit against you, this type of countersuit is not possible.

This Catch-22 situation does not exist when suing under other legal theories. For example, you can claim you were defamed whether or not you won the malpractice suit.

The deposition transcript can document malice. During your deposition it is likely you will have to put up with insulting, upsetting, unfair, and even illegal treatment from the lawyer suing you. Every malpractice suit will insult and upset the physician involved. Some amount of unfairness must be endured without complaint so that justice can be done in unclear cases. Still, if the abuse is excessive, the deposition transcript will document this (see table 13–1).

TABLE 13.1. NECESSARY ELEMENTS OF A MALICIOUS PROSECUTION SUIT

1. A judicial proceeding was initiated or continued by the patient against the physician.
2. The physician prevailed in this proceeding.
3. There was no probable cause to institute the proceeding. The malpractice suit was entirely without foundation in fact.
4. The proceeding was instituted because of malice or intent to obtain revenge.
5. The physician sustained injury.

Note that if you lose your case, you cannot claim malicious prosecution. If your case is settled for some amount of money, it will probably not be possible to claim malicious prosecution. If the suit is dismissed or abandoned, a malicious prosecution suit will be possible. However, dismissal on technicalities such as the statute of limitations may not suffice. State laws differ on whether a malicious prosecution suit can be filed before the original suit against the physician has been settled.

Probable cause is established if the opposition can find an expert witness to support its claims. Lack of probable cause is not proven by the absence of such a witness.

The definition of malice varies from state to state. Malice may be defined as reckless disregard for the truth, motivation by ill will, or forcing a settlement without a reasonable belief that the suit has merit. Malice is easiest to prove when there is evidence of intent to injure or annoy the physician. It is possible to argue that malice existed because of proven anger provoked by aggressive attempts to collect bills or impersonal care.

States disagree on what constitutes damages. Some states require variously defined "special damages," though tort reform in some states has changed this. Traditionally spsecial damages included such things as actual money losses, time lost from work, medical expenses, and loss of consortium. In the *Berlin v. Nathan*[C18a] case it was ruled that certain losses are common to all physicians being sued. These usual damages could not be claimed as damages in a malicious prosecution suit, the Illinois court ruled. Such losses include defamation of character and reputation, mental distress, time away from practice, increased malpractice insurance rates, and attorneys' fees. This reasoning seems to imply that because all physicians being sued suffer these loses, they have nothing to complain about! As stated by Rothblatt (1983),[218] courts have a "general disdain for malicious prosecution suits."

The Court of Appeals of Tennessee upheld a jury award of $11,500 to a physician whose countersuit against his patient and her attorney was based on malicious prosecution and abuse of process.[268] In this case,[C139] the patient was told she might have gonorrhea and that laboratory tests would be needed to confirm this. A week later she returned to the physician and found she had not had gonorrhea. A year later she filed a suit claiming that the physician was negligent in diagnosing gonorrhea because he took tests that took unnecessarily long to yield results. It was claimed that the physician was receiving kickbacks from the laboratory. It was determined that the patient did not receive culture results promptly because she had not called the office as instructed. The claim that the physician was receiving kickbacks was suggested by the patient's attorney and had no basis in fact.

Perhaps the most well-known countersuit is that of Dr. Berlin. Though the laws have been changing since Dr. Berlin's countersuit, the case shows the attitude that courts have concerning countersuits in general. In Dr. Berlin's case it was ruled that "willful and wanton conduct does not amount to malice." Therefore physicians should not be able to recover "for willful and wanton filing of a frivolous lawsuit."[25]

Such rulings, which draw a fine line between malice and willful and wanton behavior, need to be challenged by means of jury trials and appelate court proceedings. Some juries might find that malice does exist in such cases. Some appellate courts might find that willful and wanton actions in the pursuit of undeserved monies was malicious.

HOW THE LAW IS CHANGING

In a recent case the Kansas Supreme Court determined that an attorney must conduct a reasonable investigation to find the true facts of a case before filing a civil action on behalf of his client.[C131] According to this decision, when determining if an attorney had malice when filing a lawsuit, a jury may consider that the attorney had a duty to investigate.[104] Such court decisions, along with the change in Rule 11 of the Federal Rules of Civil Procedure described below, give attorneys the responsiblity of investigating cases before they are filed.

ADDITIONAL TYPES OF COUNTERSUITS

There are other types of countersuits that can be supported by your deposition and the depositions of other witnesses. The specific types of countersuits to be considered here include charges of attorney negligence, suing without the patient's permission, defamation, abuse of process, prima facie tort, invasion of privacy, outrage, infliction of emotional distress, and conflict of interest. Keep the requirements of these countersuits in mind when giving your deposition and planning the depositions of others with your attorney.

Attorney negligence: the law changes in 1983. Countersuits based on the claim of attorney negligence have failed in the past because such claims could only be made by clients of the negligent attorney;

the patient's attorney did not owe a duty of competence to third parties such as the physician.

A change in the rules governing the filing of lawsuits came in 1983. The FEDERAL RULES OF CIVIL PROCEDURE are the recognized standard of practice in federal courts. These rules are, usually after some delay, adopted in most state courts. Rule 11 was revised, effective August 1, 1983. Rule 11 deals with the signing of documents which initiates a lawsuit. Rules 11 states, in part, "The signature of an attorney or party constitutes a certificate by him that he has read the pleading, motion, or other paper; that to the best of his knowledge, information, and belief formed after reasonable inquiry it is well grounded in fact and is warranted by existing law."[77]

The requirement of a "reasonable inquiry" is new. This requirement of reasonableness will provide the foundation for countersuits that were not possible a few years ago.

In 1983 a Louisiana physician was awarded $80,000 when a malpractice suit against him was continued after the plaintiff's attorney knew that the physician was not one of the physicians caring for the patient. The case was overturned because the statute of limitations had run.[7,196]

Suing without the patient's permission. In many malpractice suits every physician involved in the case is sued. If you can show that the patient did not want you sued, you may be able to recover for damages. This situation may occur when the family physician of many years refers a patient to a specialist who has a poor result. The patient may have had a reasonable suit against the specialist but never intended to bring suit against his regular family physician. Document such information during the deposition of your former patient early in the course of the lawsuit.

Donald R. Huene, M.D. was sued for malpractice without his patient's approval. Dr. Huene had inserted an intramedullary rod into the patient's broken femur. When the rod later broke the patient wished to sue the surgical devices firm that made the rod. The patient's lawyer also sued Dr. Huene.

The suit against Dr. Huene was dismissed for failure to prosecute. This type of dismissal qualifies as a favorable termination of litigation for purposes of malicious prosecution.[111]

Dr. Huene could not find an attorney willing to help him sue. He successfully handled the case himself. The court ruled that "The mere filing by an attorney of an action against a particular defendant which is unauthorized by his client presents a prima facie case of malicious prosecution—in that an action filed without authority is filed without probable cause." The court also noted that it was easy to infer malice "when, as here, the attorneys have a large financial stake in the cause, and their compensation is contingent on the outcome."[135]

During your patient's deposition, have your attorney find out for the record whether suing you was the patient's idea.

Defamation. Defamation will occur if the opposition makes statements about your case to the press or to other physicians. Libel is defamation involving the written word. Slander is defamation involving spoken accusations. The usual defenses to a defamation suit are consent, truth, lack of publication, and privilege.

The pleadings of your case include the summons, subpoenas, and other papers filed in the course of the suit. The pleadings are considered privileged communications. They are confidential and cannot be made the basis of a defamation suit as long as they stay in prescribed legal channels. You will only have a chance of winning a defamation suit if you can show that the statements were improperly given to the press or other parties. Unfortunately, attorneys have the right to write defamatory matter when filing pleadings, and newspapers have the right to publish the pleadings in many cases.

Save newspaper articles relating to your case. Find out how the information for the articles was obtained. Lawyers are often quoted in the press about the malpractice cases they are pursuing. Physicians have been slow to prosecute lawyers for such public discussions of privileged information.

Examples of public statements that have been held to be actionable (grounds for a lawsuit) include statements which charge that a physician is guilty of gross negligence or impute to the physician a general lack of ability or integrity.[218] Statements that charge the physician with negligence in one case without implying a general lack of ability are not considered defamatory. For example, to say that a physician failed to make a diagnosis would not be defamatory, but to say the physician overtreated his patients would be. In the first case one is saying that a mistake was made; in the second case the integrity of the physician is being defamed.

Consent is a valid defense to the charge of defamation. If you permit newspaper stories to be printed about you, there is no telling where it will end.

Another defense to a charge of libel is to claim that the damaging statement was true. In about half the states, truth is a defense only if the communication was published with good motives and for justifiable ends.[91] Another defense to a charge of libel is "privilege." The law permits the publication of certain types of

206

public records and documents. In many states it is possible for newspapers to report the contents of complaints and other papers filed with courts at various stages in a lawsuit. The newspapers have the defense called "privilege" to protect them from libel. Therefore the unproven, often ridiculous claims made in complaints and other papers filed during a lawsuit can be published.

Like many areas of law, the entire field of libel is undergoing a complete re-examination. An editorial and several articles in the *Chicago Tribune* on October 29, 1988 reviewed proposed Illinois legislation. These articles provided a plan of action which can be taken by anyone, at least in part, regardless of existing legislation. First, the plaintiff must ask for a retraction. If the defendant agrees, the plaintiff can't sue. If the defendant refuses, either side can demand that the case be tried on the truth of the report. The person who loses must pay legal costs and attorney fees.

Defamation without a malpractice suit. A neurosurgeon moved from Wisconsin to Arizona. An attorney who had known him wrote to physicians in Arizona saying the neurosurgeon had been hospitalized because of drug overdoses and possible suicide attempts, and he had been the primary medical witness in malpractice actions in the state of Wisconsin. A jury found the letter was defamatory and not true. The neurosurgeon was awarded $250,000.06.[38]

Abuse of process. Abuse of process is improper use or perversion of a process. Action for abuse of process is different from malicious prosecution in that the process (the lawsuit) was not necessarily maliciously initiated. The main point is that the lawsuit was carried out for purposes not intended by the law.

The law does contain a remedy for the thousands of nuisance suits that embarrass physicians and cost insurance companies: "If a malpractice suit is instituted by an attorney who knows or should know that there is no reasonable basis for the claim, and his or her motive for bringing the action is to force a nuisance settlement, an abuse of process action may lie."[218]

Abuse of process is not proven simply because the case was not thoroughly investigated before a lawsuit was filed.

An abuse of process suit might succeed when a suit is brought for the purpose of making a physician drop his claim for fees[28] or to obtain the physician's free testimony.[255]

Dr. Jerome Levine performed a myelogram and later back surgery on a patient. She had no significant complications or problems after her treatment. Insurance would not pay the bill. When the physician tried to collect his bill, the patient threatened she would sue for malpractice if the physician continued to ask for payment. When the patient and her attorney were sued for abuse of process, they settled out of court. The patient's lawyer said, "What are you trying to do? I'm faced with having to defend a case I won't get paid for—and the client could even turn on me because I filed the action for her that led to this countersuit."

A 1980 case[C29] brought $35,000 in compensatory damages and $50,000 in punitive damages in a countersuit based on abuse of process. An 86-year-old woman suffered multiple injuries in an automobile accident and was later sent to a nursing home. A malpractice suit was filed when she developed bedsores. The suit was filed without consulting another physician, examining the hospital records, or submitting the claim to the local screening panel. The physician won the jury trial. He countersued, and his award of $85,000 was upheld by the Supreme Court of Nevada. He was allowed compensation for damage to his reputation, extreme embarrassment, humiliation, mental suffering, and inconvenience.[268]

Read the court's comments about your case, especially if it is appealed. Judges may comment on attorney's improper conduct and rule on procedures and charges made. Such comments might support your countersuit for abuse of process.

Prima facia tort. This action is sometimes referred to as a case of first impression, or an act without precedent to govern it. *Prima facie* tort is usually used when no other basis to sue is available. No other legal theory may fit the case, or the statue of limitations for other types of suits may have run.[260]

A *prima facie* tort has been defined as the intentional infliction of harm, resulting in damage, without excuse or justification, by acts which would otherwise be lawful.[25] Though the means of inflicting harm would, in most circumstances, have been legal, damages were inflicted without excuse.

In one lawsuit a physician was sued for malpractice even though he had no association with the patient during the illness that led to the patient's death. The purpose of suing the physician was to obtain information from the physician. The trial court ruled against the physician who claimed that a *prima facie* tort existed. The Appellate Court reversed this decision, saying that *prima facie* tort did exist. A higher appellate court later ruled against the physician.[C59]

Invasion of privacy. Private facts revealed in judicial proceedings are not privileged. Such facts are revealed to the general public. Invasion of privacy can also be claimed in most states if the opposition taps your telephone or sends investigators to observe your office or home.

Respect your own privacy, and make sure the patient's attorney does also.

Outrage and infliction of emotional distress. Two developments in law have led to a number of lawsuits based on the tort of "outrage." The first is the increasing belief that people are liable for emotional injuries they inflict on others. The second is the recognition that professional persons (if not others) have a responsibility to identify any foreseeable consequences of their actions (see table 13–2).[123]

TABLE 13-2. REQUIREMENTS FOR AN OUTRAGE SUIT

1. The outrageous conduct was intentional or reckless.
2. The conduct offended generally accepted standards of decency and morality.
3. The conduct caused emotional distress.
4. The emotional distress was severe.

Outrage suits have been used against physicians more than by physicians.[123] Examples of some "outrageous" activities that have brought or been part of successful suits are: telling a sports journalist that a retired football player had a terminal illness when this was not true; failing to dispatch an ambulance; and attempting to intimidate expert witnesses.

Conflict of interest. A conflict of interest is said to exist when someone is biased for or against an issue when neutrality was supposed. For example, a physician sued his insurance company because a malpractice case was settled without his permission. The law firm that represented the physician in his suit was the same which represented the insurance company. A conflict of interest thus existed.[161]

COUNTERSUITS AND YOU

Most readers will not ever file a countersuit. However, if attorneys know that a large number of physicians are aware of the many types of countersuits, attorneys may investigate more carefully before filling suits and act more reasonably during lawsuits.

PAYING FOR IT
(THIS WAY OUT)

Settling out of court

Although we've taken you through all the steps of presenting your case in court, keep in mind that 95 percent of all personal injury suits filed are settled out of court, rather than decided in a trial.[124] Along with automobile accident and workers' compensation claims, malpractice suits are the personal injury cases most frequently resolved out of the courtroom. These tips may help you decide if, when, how, and with whom to take the step of settlement.

WHEN CAN YOU SETTLE?

A lawsuit may be settled at any time. How you perform at your deposition (Step 7)—and how well you and your attorney handle the other preparations described in the other steps—will determine your bargaining strength if and when the issue of settlement comes up.

WHO CAN SETTLE?

Your input as defendant in making a settlement depends on the wording of your insurance policy and other special arrangements you may have made with your carrier.

Your policy is a contract. It may give the insurance company the right to negotiate and complete a settlement without your permission. If you're sued and don't want a settlement made without your

213

permission, ask the company to tell you what is happening at every stage of the negotiations.

That's what Dr. Rogers did when he was sued. Despite his request to preview any settlement, the law firm retained by his insurer settled before trial for $1,250 without his permission. The Illinois appellate court held that Dr. Rogers had suffered damages because of the settlement. This defendant-turned-plaintiff specifically suffered:

1. Loss of opportunity to pursue a malicious prosecution suit.
2. Loss of patients.
3. Increase in malpractice insurance premiums.
4. Legal fees and costs.

The court also held that Dr. Rogers had the right to sue the attorneys who'd been retained by his insurer to defend him.[c161,55]

In a similar case, another physician went beyond suing the law firm which had settled his case without his permission. The physician also collected a settlement of $250,000 from his insurance company.[c9]

WHEN THE CARRIER REFUSES TO SETTLE

It often happens that a physician-defendant wants to accept a settlement offer that insurance would cover, but the insurance carrier refuses. When the verdict later exceeds the amount of coverage the issue raised is: "Was the insurance carrier guilty of a bad faith refusal to settle?" To fulfill its responsibility to the physician-defendant, it is generally felt that the carrier should have believed that it had a good possibility of winning the suit when the settlement was refused.[231]

The California Supreme Court ruled that the size of the final judgment furnishes some idea of how reasonable it was to refuse a settlement, so carriers should be held liable for the excess judgment when the verdict is much greater than the policy limit. When there is relatively little difference between the coverage and the jury verdict, the carrier might avoid liability.

In New York and Ohio cases, carriers have been held responsible for payment of verdicts in excess of coverage when they failed to inform the policy holder about the settlement offer.[231]

What to do when your carrier refuses to settle. Malpractice expert Jack E. Horsley offers this advice: "To lay the foundation for an action against the insurance company who refuses to settle when a settlement could be completed within the policy limits, the insured physician should send a letter by certified mail to the insurance company. In it he should state, in substance, that he demands that the settlement be completed at the level available within the policy limits and that if the company fails, he intends to insert this as a waiver of the policy limits. He should add that he intends to hold the company to pay any verdict, including whatever might be returned in excess of the policy limits."

WHY SETTLE?

If yours is clearly a case of negligence, it may be better to settle out of court.

The plaintiff may be willing to settle for an amount covered by your insurance. The plaintiff's attorney, if it's early in the course of events, will be happy to settle for a moderate fee, and avoid the time-consuming, expensive process of preparing a case for trial. You, too, will be spared the time, expense, and bother of going through the long process of being sued.

It will be over quickly with less publicity than if you go to trial. In fact, you can stipulate in your agreement that the amount of the settlement be kept secret.

If you can't reach a settlement in an unfavorable situation, you may find yourself in front of a jury with a hopeless, defenseless case. If punitive damages are not sought, it may be wise to admit liability openly and ask that the judge or jury make a settlement on the basis of actual damages. The processes of presenting evidence, questioning witnesses, rebutting charges, and making convincing arguments will be eliminated.

Here are four more personal advantages in asking for an early settlement on the basis of the damages:

1. Events that might stimulate anger against you are kept out of evidence (the jury won't hear about it).
2. Witnesses who would elicit sympathy for the injured plaintiff won't be called to testify.
3. Admitting fault reflects your willingness to be accountable and accept responsibility for your error.
4. If you disagree with the extent of damages, the jury will be more likely to give due consideration to your requests if you openly admit to being liable.[16]

Some insurance carriers have found that costly malpractice suits can be avoided if physicians alert them of untoward outcomes. Lawsuits are avoided when the insurance company contacts the injured patient or relatives to offer a reasonable settlement. When delays, attorney fees, and the uncertainties associated with a lawsuit are explained to patient and family, rapid settlements usually result.[58]

INVOLVE OTHER PARTIES IN SETTLEMENTS

Frequently one or more defendants settle with the plaintiff before trial. Then the jury awards a relatively large award that must be paid by the defendants who had not yet settled. In such cases it is possible that the defendants who did not settle will try to collect what they had to pay from the defendants who did settle. Malpractice expert Jack E. Horsley has the following suggestions for avoiding such problems.[216]

1. Try to bring everybody involved in the suit into the settlement. If you do not get the other defendants to go along with you, there is a remote chance you would still be open to indemnity or contribution suits from any one of them. This might depend on previous express agreements.
2. To act independently, you must be certain that none of your co-defendants can claim that something you did wrong put him or her at risk.
3. The release should cover all contingencies. When defendants unite in the settlement, include cross-waivers of indemnity rights. If there's even one holdout, try for a clause stating that the party you're settling with holds you harmless from further liability to anyone involved in the case.
4. Check your malpractice coverage. Most policies insure against any and all claims arising from your practice. But some insurers contend they have no obligation to defend or pay for indemnity claims. In such situations a general comprehensive liability policy with a seven-figure umbrella, to protect against all types of claims (including indemnity), can be useful.

DOES PAYING MEAN ADMITTING GUILT?

Paying a settlement is not an admission of negligence or guilt. When a settlement is made, a contract is written. This contract should state

216

that the settlement is not an admission of guilt. It should also contain the stipulation that no further claims will be made against you, your estate, or any other parties.

The amount of the settlement should be kept confidential. So should the fact that the case was settled. Involved parties should be prohibited from talking to news reporters.

While these confidential arrangements will help, you will be damaged by even groundless nuisance suits. "If the malpractice crisis has taught doctors anything, it's that there are no nuisance suits."[53] Certainly, if a nuisance suit goes to trial, jury sympathy can lead to large settlements. Even with cases settled out of court, however, there are problems. Insurance and staff applications ask about the number and types of dispositions of previous malpractice cases.

A national data bank was put into operation in 1989 to permanently document information concerning such "black marks" against physicians. A $15.9 million contract was awarded to an information systems firm to collect and report adverse actions on licensing, hospital privileges, payments related to any malpractice claim or settlement, disciplinary actions taken by professional societies, and peer review actions that affect clinical privileges for over 30 days. The data bank was authorized by the Health Care Quality Improvement Act of 1986 and the Medicare and Medicaid Patient and Program Protection Act of 1987. The information is not to be made available to the general public. Hospitals will be required to check with the bank before hiring or granting privileges to physicians. Hospitals will be required to consult the bank every two years for updates on MDs. The information in the data bank will only be available to plaintiff's attorneys if a hospital is sued and has failed to obtain the data bank information on a practitioner in the manner required by law.[98]

WILL INSURANCE BE RAISED?

Probably so, even if you settle without a trial. As with any type of insurance, once a claim is made against you, your rates are likely to be raised. This rate change is understandable. Even when no fault is found in your treatment, the cost of responding to a claim is significant. Repeated claims against a practitioner can be very costly to the insurer, even if all the cases are successfully defended. It can easily cost an insurance company $20,000 to prepare and defend a simple, successful case in court.

WHAT PRICE ARBITRATION?

About 25,000 malpractice suits are filed each year against health-care professionals and/or hospitals in the United States.[73] Because of that large and growing number of suits, and the delays and costs in the court system, many states have legislation providing for arbitration of malpractice cases. Yet in most states the arbitration is not binding, unless both parties agree that it should be.

A review board made up of a lawyer, a physician, and another knowledgeable person would be ideal. But any board consisting of a few members who are informed, educated, and previously exposed to malpractice cases will likely make better and faster decisions than a jury.

In some cases, however, a jury may be more competent to judge a malpractice case against a health-care professional than a panel of physicians and lawyers. The jury can be instructed in the relevant legal principles. Expert witnesses can explain the medical factors involved.

In contrast, a panel might consist of physicians who have no training in the medical specialty involved, and lawyers with little experience in negligence or personal injury cases. Medicine and law have become so complex and specialized that it's not unusual for a highly competent orthopedic surgeon to have no idea of what to do for an overdose of medication—or a gynecologist not to know how to handle a serious head injury.

A board of specialists in the area of medicine involved would have the best chance of really understanding a case. But a panel of peers might be considered to be biased.

One argument in favor of review boards and arbitration is the recognized sympathy of jurors for a disabled patient. They feel the patient needs some payment for the injury, and assume that the rich doctor or employer of other involved practitioners has insurance and other resources that will easily pay a large settlement. So the question of whether the defendant was actually responsible for the plaintiff's injury may become a secondary consideration.[267]

A panel of experts will usually not be swayed by such considerations. They know that in our society various agencies try to help the disabled. They're also not as likely as a jury to be swayed by impeachment or personality of the practitioner.

Various types of screening panels have been tried in several states in recent years.[59] Many medical groups and malpractice defense lawyers were initially in favor of screening panels, expecting that they would reduce the number of claims. Some plaintiffs' attorneys also were all in favor of the panels, thinking that they would encourage early settlement in obviously meritorious cases.

Arbitration by review boards or panels has not, however, worked well enough to gain general support. Their Constitutional validity also remains in question.[c182, 155]

Arbitration programs have not always been administered well.[168] In some states, the process associated with the panels has caused delays. And plaintiffs' attorneys are not always deterred from going to trial in cases that panels have judged nonmeritorious.

The situation in New York illustrates several problems in malpractice arbitration: In 1983, the head of the New York State Trial Lawyers Association filed suit to abolish the screening panels that hear all medical liability claims. Under state law, a panel composed of a judge, a lawyer, and a physician must hear a malpractice claim before it can go to court. But it has been difficult getting physicians to sit on those panels, especially specialists such as neurosurgeons, endocrinologists, and gastroenterologists. So some plaintiffs must wait four years to get a panel convened.

Part of the problem in obtaining panelists is that the plaintiffs' attorneys have insisted, in many cases, that physicians serving on the panels have no prior association with the defense lawyers. If and when a panel finally judges the plaintiff to have a strong case, the plaintiff often then demands an extremely high settlement.[11]

If screening panels function in your jurisdiction, your attorney should get the answers to these vital questions:

1. Is arbitration optional?
2. Are panel determinations binding?
3. Is evidence discovered at the panel admissible in court?
4. How much delay and expense might the panel cause for your case?
5. How well has the panel functioned?
6. Have the decisions been reasonable?

Binding arbitration may provide a more objective view of the medical and emotional issues than one could expect from a jury. For example, in a San Francisco case, an 8-year-old girl was brought to several pediatricians in her usual clinic complaining of headache and vomiting. No tests of any kind were taken, and her old chart was not consulted; it would have shown she was losing weight. On her third visit a pediatrician diagnosed dehydration due to viral gastroenteritis. She was admitted and given an IV containing dextrose. When it was discovered that her blood sugar was 1,530 mg% she was given half normal saline. She developed cerebral edema and was left with mental retardation, hemiparesis, and behavioral problems. In this case the arbitrators settled the case for $500,000, while it is believed that a San Francisco jury would have awarded at least $2 million.[227]

Even if your case is submitted to a review board, don't lose track of the questions, dangers, and advantages of out-of-court settlement mapped out in this chapter.

The next step takes you through the monetary maze that a court case creates.

Paying off the cost

The verdict is in. Even if you win, you still must pay. The cost of malpractice litigation is high—and rising rapidly. The number of awards of $1 million or more have tripled in three years. The total awarded to suing patients topped $2 billion in 1983. And physicians now pay $1 billion a year for malpractice coverage.[270, 271]

This chapter takes you through the costs of your win or loss and the ways to pay them. Let's begin with what to do if you win, then turn to the consequences you could encounter in countersuing, going bare, going beyond your coverage, voiding your insurance, sequestering your assets, going bankrupt, and reorganizing.

Even if you've won, you're still likely to have lost thousands of dollars in filing fees, court costs, and perhaps additional attorneys' fees. And that's not counting the cost in time that you, the attorneys, and your staffs have spent preparing your case.

STRUCTURED PAYMENTS SAVE MONEY

Structured payment schedules are an alternative to lump sum payments of malpractice awards. Structured payments spread an award over a claimant's predicted lifetime.[18] At least 17 states now call for periodic payments in malpractice cases, and 11 others allow them. Structured payments are probably used even more in pretrial settlements than following court decisions.

Structured settlements often combine one or more annuities with a lump sum payment. The annuities provide for long-term care and lost earning capacity. The lump sum payment provides for immediate expenses such as attorneys' fees and modifications to the patient's home. Annuities and life insurance policies can provide for care of children if a parent remains disabled or if the parent dies.

The annuities cut the cost of a settlement by as much as 25% since compounding of interest or dividends on invested money provides for future payments.

Many plaintiffs are better off with structured payments. Such scheduled payments can provide a guaranteed income, lower tax payments, and a fund to pay for medical and other personal care expenses. These payments can be designed to vary with national inflation and health care costs.

Plaintiffs' attorneys may oppose structured settlements because they can lower attorney fees. In such cases, modification of the settlement can often bring agreement.

A recent Florida case provides an example of a family's needs not being met.[205] A woman entered the hospital for childbirth. She had a cardiac arrest during a caesarean section and was left permanently comatose. After 30 months of litigation, $3.45 million was awarded. Of this $1.8 million was put in trust to pay for her medical expenses, and $1.65 million (45% of the total) went to the attorneys. Her disabled husband and six children were left with nothing.

THE COLLATERAL SOURCE RULE

One would hope that money the plaintiff receives from insurance and other sources would decrease the award received from physicians and other defendants. The collateral source rule is contrary, stating that such payments are not to be deducted from the damages assessed.

Liability tort reform has improved this situation. In some states the collateral source rule has been eliminated and either the judge or jury can consider a plaintiff's other sources of compensation in determining damages. In other states there is a mandatory offset of the amount of other compensation against the award of damages.[122]

JOINT AND SEVERAL LIABILITY

Joint and several liability is the so-called "deep pockets" rule that permits full recovery of an award from a minor-fault defendant.[225]

Laws have been proposed to permit several, and eliminate joint, liability in malpractice cases. Under such laws, each defendant would be liable only for the amount of damages due to his percentage of fault. Such laws would seem desirable but can cause problems for physician-defendants in at least two ways. First, minor-fault (and poorly insured) defendants will not be excused from cases early-on for fear that some percentage of the liability will be judged to be theirs. Second, defendants would be encouraged to blame each other for the damages, giving plaintiffs more "proof" of liability.[225]

SHOULD YOU COUNTERSUE?

You were found not negligent, not liable. Yet you still feel you were charged and prosecuted maliciously—and at a loss to your reputation. So you're tempted to countersue. Before you do, make sure you understand that it would be long, expensive, and hard to win—and that your countersuit could be countersued. If you do countersue, you'll have to show that the original suit against you was brought improperly or without probable cause, and that you consequently suffered specific damages.[25, 100] Chapter 13 in this book discusses countersuits.

SHOULD YOU GO BARE?

Either as a result of or in fear of losing a malpractice claim, some doctors have "gone bare"—they've dropped their insurance coverage. Their (wishful?) thinking runs along these lines: "If I don't have insurance, there's less chance I'll be sued, because my patients will know there won't be any quick settlement. And if I am sued, and lose, they probably won't go to the trouble of taking all my assets."

When a physician is unable to pay the malpractice award, co-defendants, such as the hospital, often wind up paying the bill. For example, in one case the physician had $100,000 of insurance, but the award was for over $4 million. The hospital, which was also found liable, had to pay the balance.[34] In such situations, the doctrine of joint and several liability will be relevant. Under joint and several liability, which is the law in many areas, a plaintiff can choose to satisfy a judgment from any or all defendants, regardless of their relative contributions to the damages.

Whether going bare would work for you can't be determined. Regardless, you have three good reasons to carry insurance:

1. The cost of defending a case can be significant even if you win. When you lose, you may have to pay the settlement out of your personal assets. Insurance will cover much of those costs.

2. Accidents do happen, and patients do get injured. So it's only humane that funds be available to compensate the victim of your mistake. A plaintiff with a legitimate claim is more likely to be compensated adequately if you have insurance.

3. Many states and hospitals require physicians to have malpractice insurance.[34]

Therefore, going bare makes little sense financially, and shows little sense of compassion.

GOING OVER YOUR COVERAGE

What can the winning plaintiff get from you if the award is more than your insurance will pay? Perhaps your personal property and future earnings. So you must take an active part in protecting your resources. The first step is to review your malpractice insurance policy and its disclaimers.

Some policies don't cover cases involving fraud, libel, slander, criminal actions, and certain forms of vicarious liability. You can also find yourself uncovered if you don't report your case promptly to the insurance company, help obtain evidence and prepare your defense, and meet with your attorney. Some policies also relieve the insurer of responsibility for paying awards if you've failed to notify the company of loss of license to practice, communicated with the plaintiff's attorney without the company's approval, or given false information in obtaining the coverage.[c4]

Many policies require that you immediately send the company all papers served concerning a malpractice case. Responses to such papers must be made within certain time limits, or a default judgment can be made against you. And the company may not pay in such cases. What's more, even when no papers have been served, many policies require you to notify the company of any information that indicates a claim may be made in the future.

Be wary of policies that provide "pure-loss" coverage. Pure-loss coverage will pay only the actual damage award. "Ultimate net loss" coverage will provide for the award as well as attorneys' fees and costs.[53] This is critical since a large proportion of malpractice claims, win or lose, are defended at a cost of $10,000 or more.

224

In a personal injury case, the award is made to compensate the injured party. An attempt is made to "make the person whole" by means of a cash allocation. If the jury feels that the malpractice was deliberate, criminal, indifferent, or grossly negligent, it may award additional damages. Such additional amounts are called exemplary, punitive, or vindictive damages. And some malpractice policies don't cover them.

The Illinois State Medical Society (ISMS) defines a criminal act as the "willful violation of a statute, ordinance, or regulation imposing criminal penalties." Damages awarded for such criminal acts are not covered by the ISMS malpractice insurance.

Willful malpractice. A jury may award punitive damages when the defendant's behavior was "willful and wanton," rather than just negligent.[44] Punitive damages can also be awarded if the defendant acted with malice.

In the case of *Stogsdill* v. *Manor Convalescent Home*, plaintiff Stogsdill lost her leg after a small wound became gangrenous during more than three months of negligent treatment. The jury awarded punitive damages, but the decision was reversed because there was no proof of willful or wanton behavior.[c184]

Punitive damages are not as closely tied to the degree of injury as are awards for negligence. They're based more on the nature of the defendant's wrongdoing than on the result of it. Indifference to the safety of a patient can justify a punitive damage award.[c175]

Gross misconduct. The insurance carrier may refuse to pay in cases of alleged gross misconduct. In *Zipkin* v. *Freeman*, a psychotherapist, Dr. Freeman, induced his patient, Mrs. Zipkin, to leave her husband, turn her savings over to him, and become his mistress. Freeman's insurance carrier refused to pay the damages because the therapist's conduct was not in the line of professional duty.[c204]

Guarantee. If a practitioner guarantees the result of a treatment or operation, liability can be claimed on the theory of breach of contract. Thus, liability can occur even when there's no negligence or malpractice; the guaranteed result simply was not obtained. Your insurance policy may not pay the judgment in such a case.[c114]

Slander. Acts of libel and slander involve written or verbal defamation of another party. Such acts will not likely be covered by a malpractice insurance policy. For example, St. Paul Insurance Company, the issuer of a comprehensive nursing home liability policy, was not required to defend or pay damages when the Talladega

Nursing Home and its owners interfered with the running of a rival nursing home by alleged slander.[c181]

Another slander suit was brought against a physician who had been deputized by the Florida Board of Medical Examiners to investigate another physician. The first doctor allegedly made slanderous remarks at an informal press conference, charging the other with performing unnecessary and incompetent surgery. The court ruled that making such statements was not covered by the investigating doctor's professional service policy.[c28]

Vicarious liability. Some policies don't cover vicarious liability—the wrongdoings of your employees, residents, students, partners, co-shareholders, and other parties. Insurance companies don't want to be responsible for the actions of unknown persons. Policies are available to cover specified other persons, but don't assume that your policy covers them.

Some policies don't cover liability incurred because of your position in a hospital, clinic, or other business. Others don't cover work done in a government institution. Some become invalid if you lose your license to practice medicine, or to prescribe drugs.[44]

No claims made. Malpractice insurance is based on either occurrence or claims-made. An occurrence policy covers acts that occur while the policy is in effect. A claims-made policy covers malpractice that takes place while the policy is in effect—*if* the claim is made while the policy is still in effect.

Thus, if you're sued for malpractice after changing insurance companies or retiring, a claims-made policy won't be of any use. Many suits are brought a year or more after allegedly negligent care was given, so continued coverage is important.

Most claims-made policies guarantee that you'll be able to buy some sort of continuing coverage if the policy is ever terminated. Such continuing coverage is called claim-reporting endorsement or tail coverage.

Tail and nose coverage. Tail coverage for a claims-made policy gives protection comparable to an occurrence policy. It can be costly, but consider that you paid a lower initial cost for the original claims-made policy. Buying tail coverage allows you to increase your coverage limit. And that might be advantageous if awards are running higher than when you bought the original policy.[139]

An unusual policy is offered by the Physicians Insurance Company of Ohio. Called Career Assets Protection, it covers you from the policy issue date back to the beginning of your practice. It can add to insurance previously obtained, and cover periods when you went bare. This "nose coverage" policy provides protection of up to $5 million and is available to doctors in Ohio only (call 1-800-435-0863).[273]

Claims-made malpractice insurance may have a hidden tail. A few courts in New Jersey, Mississippi, and California have found that claims-made coverage is contrary to public policy.[223] In other words, such policies take money from physicians but provide inadequate benefits to physicians or injured patients. It is too early to see if courts in the various states will begin to order insurance companies to treat claims-made policies as if they had been occurrence policies, but it has happened in at least one case already. Check the case precedents in your state if you lack a tail.

DON'T FORGET YOUR UMBRELLA

Umbrella insurance policies can extend the protection of regular property and automobile insurance. They are also useful in protecting from liability related to slander, defamation of character, and false imprisonment. While personal umbrella insurance does not reduce the need for malpractice or other practice-related insurance, it can help in areas not always covered by malpractice policies.[261]

PROTECTING YOUR ASSETS

If a malpractice judgment goes against you, especially if it goes beyond your coverage, you may want to consider the following ways to protect your personal assets.

Discuss your plans with an accountant and an attorney. Each must be familiar with the laws of your state. Timing and intent for sheltering assets are important. You cannot shelter assets for the purpose of keeping them from creditors, even future creditors. Assets must be transferred for purposes such as divorce, estate planning, or to make sure that your children will be provided for in case of your death.[17]

Sequestering earnings. If the plaintiff's award is more than you now have, you may be tempted to sequester (in effect, hide) some of your coming earnings. But that's illegal—and futile. Even if you're insured, unreasonable settlements can wipe out your resources.

In a case of brain damage to a newborn, the initial award was $2 million, plus monthly payments totaling $21 million more if the child lived to age 66. The baby was seen at birth by an obstetrician and seemed to be fine, but later had difficulties and suffered severe brain damage. Two of the physicians named in the case had insurance that made payments. The hospital also made a payment. Two other physicians involved had no insurance and claimed they had no assets. The plaintiff's attorney was not barred from investigating the physicians' assets.[176]

In another costly case, a posterior plaster splint was applied following foot surgery. When the patient complained of burning in her foot three days later, the cast was removed. A blister had formed, leaving a four-inch scar. A $200,000 settlement was obtained and upheld on appeal.[c54]

The latter case shows that large awards can be made to patients who suffer minor, common complications of medical care.

Transferring funds.   You can put your assets in someone else's name. But doing that with your earnings is really not enough. To avoid losing assets through a suit, you must make them the actual property of someone else, and you must give up control of them—a form of "legal sequestration."

You can, for example, set up a trust for your children's education. But the terms of the trust prevent you from getting any of the money, even if you need it.

All such funds have to be set up before the act of alleged malpractice. If you do it after, the court would see that you created the trust to avoid paying your damages, and declare it fraudulent.

Deeding your house.   In some states you can will or "deed" your house to someone else before you die, yet continue to live in it until your death. This arrangement is called a "life estate." If you arrange it before the malpractice action, your house can't be taken from you. You could, however, be evicted, and your house could be rented until you die. It would then go to the holder of the deed.

The homestead exemption.   Some states have a homestead exemption law that prevents residences from being claimed by creditors. In Florida, Minnesota, Kansas, and Texas, homesteads of any value are protected. Other states have limits on how much value is protected, while some states have no homestead exemption at all.[253]

Exempt assets.   Certain types of properties (in addition to homesteads) are exempt from creditors in each state. For example, in Florida, life and disability insurance policies and annuities are

PAYING FOR IT (THIS WAY OUT)

exempt assets. It is possible to put millions of dollars into such policies.[253]

Divorcing your spouse. An anesthesiologist unwilling to pay $25,000 a year for malpractice insurance made an extreme move to protect personal assets. He divorced his wife, but continued living with her in the same way and place.

In the divorce settlement,the doctor kept his retirement and pension and profit-sharing plans; his wife took the house, all life insurance policies, and other property. Money for their children's education was put in bank accounts. And his wife's alimony paid for home maintenance.

All that wouldn't work under the laws of many states. A plaintiff's attorney could claim that the ex-wife was a common-law wife. Under common law, belongings are not separate. And a court could easily see the arrangement as a ploy to avoid responsibility— and declare it invalid or fraudulent.

Pension funds. Some authorities feel that pension funds may not need sheltering from malpractice actions, as they are fairly well protected by the Federal law on pensions (ERISA). However, pension funds are not always protected from bankruptcy or divorce actions.

GOING BANKRUPT

When things don't go well for a business, it can go bankrupt. Individuals can do the same. Bankruptcy is a civil, not a criminal action. The legal basis for bankruptcy is the Bill of Rights of the United States Constitution (Article 1, Section 8), which did away with debtors' prisons.

A new federal bankruptcy act, Public Law 95-598, went into effect on October 1, 1979. In the prior fiscal year, 196,976 people had filed for bankruptcy; the following year, 452,732 filed.[254]

The procedure for going bankrupt is not complicated. First, an accounting of all debts and assets must be made. The next step is the settlement, stating what you can keep and what you must pay to creditors. It's important to wait until all judgments against you are made, so they can be included in the settlement. Once you have settled, you can't file for bankruptcy again for six years.[182]

The assets you can keep when going bankrupt are listed in the federal law. States also have their own lists of exemptions: 18 states allow the filing party to choose between the federal and state lists of exemptions; 32 states require the bankrupt party to use the state list.

(States that allow a choice are: Alaska, California, Connecticut, Hawaii, Massachusetts, Michigan, Minnesota, Mississippi, Missouri, New Jersey, New Mexico, New York, Pennsylvania, Rhode Island, Texas, Vermont, Washington, and Wisconsin, plus the District of Columbia.)

In some instances, the wife can use one list while the husband uses the other. Because property in marriage is usually considered to be jointly owned, both husband and wife file. If both husband and wife use the same (state or federal) list, the property they can retain is double the amount an individual could keep.

Bankruptcy proceedings are a matter of public record. They may be publicized in the newspapers.

The purpose of the bankruptcy law is to allow you to make a fresh start. Therefore, not all personal property is taken. The federal list of exemptions include:

- $7,500 debtor's interest in real-estate value.
- $1,200 debtor's interest in a motor vehicle.
- Household items, clothes, and appliances, not to exceed $200 in value for any given item.
- $750 in tools of the trade.
- Unmatured life insurance, including accrued interest, dividends, or loan value up to $4,000.
- Prescribed health aids.
- Miscellaneous disability, social security, pension, and other benefits.

A married couple using the federal list of exemptions could retain more than $20,000 in assets, not including the $200 per item for household appliances, clothes, and other belongings. So you could, for example, stock your home with food before filing for bankruptcy.

Warning: Transferring property to friends or relatives within a year of declaring bankruptcy would be considered a criminal act. It would also jeopardize your bankruptcy. Paying off certain debts within 90 days of filing bankruptcy would likewise be considered improper and invalid. Furthermore, if you do file for bankruptcy, others responsible for your debts will still be responsible for them. They would include co-signers on loans.

Debts not discharged (excused) by bankruptcy include taxes, wages owed to employees, debts incurred by criminal means, debts not listed on the bankruptcy schedule (agreement), debts associated with alimony and related expenses.

REORGANIZING

Bankruptcy may not be your best move for several reasons: the bad publicity, the principle of the matter, and the need to give up valued assets. Fortunately, there's another way out: reorganization. It says that bankruptcy is undesirable, and a settlement is to be made. In the settlement, you can bargain about which, if any, personal assets will be taken. Binding promises can be made for future payments to satisfy debts. The debts can be reduced by agreement, but not below the amounts the creditors would have received under a bankruptcy settlement.

The laws and principles that apply to payments of creditors vary from state to state, and change from time to time. And efforts are being made to change the federal law because of the large increase in the number of bankruptcies. So when you consider filing for bankruptcy, or taking any other action based on material from this book or any other source, consult an attorney who knows the current malpractice and financial management laws in your state.

THE LEGAL END

If you've followed all the steps we've traced, you should be able to function positively and effectively throughout the litigation process. You should be able to figure out what information and which witnesses must be found, brought out, and used to prepare your best defense. And you should be ready to present it to your best advantage. In sum, you should now be equipped with the strategies and tactics needed to meet the real charges and complete the battles in your malpractice contest—now and in the future.

GOING HOME

Your defense isn't made entirely on the legal front. The most critical battle is the one you have to fight against yourself—on the home front. What the battle is about, and how you can win it, are the subjects of the next and final step.

Getting on with your life and family

Malpractice can be spelled stress. Just the thought of being sued probably sends waves of anxiety through you. So if and when the thought becomes reality, be prepared for an onslaught of emotions that may hit you and your family. It can include fear, pain, anger, guilt, helplessness, and despair. And you may also begin to wonder how your family life can possible survive the pressure.

The assault on your psyche can upset your stomach as well as mind. Insomnia, headache, stomachache, and compulsive eating are some of the physical signs of emotional upheaval.[71]

"He awoke in the middle of the night with stomach pain so sharp he was afraid he had cancer," recalled one defendant's wife. "It was a spastic colon. Then I started getting dizzy spells, and I've been on hypertension medication and diuretics ever since."

Can you do anything to ease the stress and avoid some of its negative effects? Yes! Even when you feel at your worst and believe you're being stripped of all your physical, emotional, and economic assets, you can still control your health, dignity, and family life. Your personal life in the malpractice lane can be more than midnight snacks, tranquilizers, and all-night pacing. You still have your health and your family—and you'll want to have them when this is all over. As the old song goes, "No, no! They can't take that away from me."

This last chapter offers suggestions to help you and your family turn the negative pressures of a lawsuit in positive directions.

BELIEFS DETERMINE EMOTIONAL REACTIONS

One particularly helpful source for dealing with stress is *A New Guide to Rational Living* by Doctors Albert Ellis and Robert Harper. Every health-care professional could benefit from this book, anytime. But we prescribe taking it in large daily doses upon receipt of a summons and throughout a trial.[38] The suggestions that follow apply some of the book's concepts to what you may face in the malpractice experience.

A critical Ellis and Harper point: Our beliefs about events in our lives determine our emotional reactions to them. So if you're feeling emotionally upset about your lawsuit, you probably believe that your security and self-worth are also on trial—that if you lose this case, you're worthless as a practitioner and as a human being.

Such false beliefs—not the malpractice charge itself—cause anxiety and depression.

Compare these responses to a lawsuit:

One doctor's spouse, fearful that the malpractice suit against her husband would bankrupt the family, went on a frantic spending spree. Another bit the bullet, saying, "I still have a house to run and children to educate. This suit is big, but it will pass. It's not a disease we'll have for the rest of our lives. So we will do whatever we must to get through each day, and be one day closer to the end of it."

The first spouse panicked in response to her belief that the suit meant financial ruin. But the rational thinking of the second spouse enabled her to adapt to the situation and minimize the stress.

Here's another example of how your thinking can affect your feelings and actions:

Let's say that you have a fight with a close friend. The problem isn't just the fight; it's what you believe about it: "Friends don't fight. Our friendship is ended forever. And I'll even lose other friends as a result." Such unsubstantiated beliefs about the effects of the fight create a reaction of depression.

Replacing those thoughts with more reasonable and positive ones can put your situation in a new light and reveal that the conflict need not be a catastrophe.

Try this position: "It's too bad that we fought, but this is not a disaster. It's inevitable that friends sometimes disagree, but we'll both cool down—and we'll still be friends."

In that way, you can regret the fight, but not set yourself up for sleepless nights, stress, and depression. And you'll be able to reflect rationally on what happened. Perhaps you really didn't do anything wrong; your friend was just in a bad mood. Maybe it was your fault so you owe an apology. Thinking rationally will help you feel better and that will allow you to act better—not unproductively fixing blame, but constructively changing your behavior and relationships.

CONCEDING DEFEAT

How can a fight with a friend compare with a lawsuit? It can't; a malpractice charge is a hundred times worse. Yet both events are essentially the same in the way irrational thoughts can cause emotional distress in both situations. Try this scenario to see how your thoughts about an event can hurt you:

You come home after a particularly full and harried day with your patients, pick up the newspaper, and spot the headline: "Doctor sued for $1 million." And you are the doctor. Then you learn that your spouse and children have already been asked about your "malpractice." Unless you're made of stone, the emotional consequences for you are pain, panic, and depression.

Remember, it's not the lawsuit itself that's causing those severe reactions; it's what you're telling yourself about its effects, as you imagine them. You've short-circuited into self-destruction.

Don't surrender to negative thinking. Instead, look out of the warning signs of self-defeat so you can turn them around:

Signs of self-defeat. Here are five sure signs of someone conceding defeat in a malpractice case. Are these thoughts in your mind?

1. "I'm going to lose this suit and my license, too. I'm ruined in this community, and won't ever be able to practice medicine again."
2. "This suit is frivolous and unfair, but people will come to doubt my competence as a doctor. I'll be worthless when my patients and peers abandon me."
3. "I know this suit is valid. I really did make a mistake. I'm guilty and worthless as a healer, and as a human being."
4. "It's absolutely horrible and unfair for this to be happening just when my practice is getting going. I'm still a fortune in debt and just beginning to have a little free time with my family. This is the end of my career and my marriage."
5. "I've lost control of my life. It's now in the hands of a lawyer and a jury. This damn suit will probably leave me depressed for the rest of my life."

234

Don't victimize yourself. Put those negative and irrational propositions in your mind on the stand for cross-examination. Once you begin to dispute such destructive thoughts, you'll feel better. Free from anxiety and depression, you'll be able to see constructive changes you can make, in both your practice and in your private life.

REVERSING SELF-DEFEATING THINKING

Let's examine those five admissions of defeat to see how they can be disputed and replaced with constructive responses.

1. Counter catastrophizing. The first admission of defeat is: "I'm ruined." It sounds like total surrender—a bitter end.

"There we were in our dream house," said the spouse of one doctor who was sued. "Then all of a sudden the roof caved in."

That is catastrophizing. Sure, there's a remote chance you'll need to move your practice, and an even more remote possibility you'll lose your license. Certainly, it's wise to make plans to deal with potential crises. But worrying won't change either the past or the future So do everything you can to keep your fears from coming true, but don't obsessively ruminate on them. Follow the advice of Ellis and Harper: "Live fully and creatively, and accept the inevitable dangers and risks."[73]

You have absolutely no reason to leap mentally from being summoned to being run out of town. Many malpractice charges are frivolous and are settled without going to trial. So concentrating on all the potentially harmful consequences of going to court is as useful as contemplating everything that could go wrong when you get on an airplane.

If you find yourself uselessly worrying, yell *stop* to yourself. If the internal scream doesn't work, zap yourself on the wrist with a rubber band. Do that every time you catch yourself indulging in more than two minutes of nonconstructive thinking. It's more beneficial to go on preparing your defense, treating your patients, being with your family, and rereading medical texts.

Use this counter to catastrophic thinking: "Even if I have to leave town or lose my license, I'll still survive. But I'm really jumping to highly unlikely conclusions. Instead of wasting time on them, I'm going to play with my children, take my wife to dinner, and read something positive before I go to bed tonight."

2. Preserve your worth. Saying, "I'm worthless," is really saying that your self-worth depends on the approval of others. Even if you're sure you took the proper medical action, you may feel devalued by the negative, misinformed opinions of community members. True, we all want approval from others; but we don't need it. It's unrealistic to think that everyone will always be pleased with you.

You'll feel better if you tell yourself: "I'm sure I gave the proper treatment in this case. Even so, some colleagues and patients will think ill of my work because of the negative things they read in the paper and hear around town. But I can't control their thinking. If they choose to check the facts, they'll be set straight. I know that I still have worth, whether they approve of me or not. In fact, this is a good time to see who my friends really are."

Even if you feel abandoned, you are not alone. Many others have been—and are now going—through what you face. And if you know your treatment was right, things will probably turn out all right.

"The newspaper that headlined my husband's alleged negligence didn't bother to print the not-guilty verdict," noted one victorious wife. "But he got only one crank call, against scores of supportive letters and calls from his patients. Then his colleagues elected him chief of pediatrics at the hospital."

3. To err is human; to forge on is fine. Disputing your negative thoughts when you know you made a mistake is particularly difficult. The pain of remorse is almost inevitable if you made a serious error. Still, there's no use condemning yourself, doubting your worth, or wallowing in guilt. So don't say: "I'm damned." You are human. Humans err.

One bad judgment doesn't make you a bad person or bad doctor. One bad turn can be turned around. Assess your abilities and your performance. Then start to correct your deficiencies.

It may hurt to make the needed changes. If you made a mistake because you were too rushed, perhaps you should reduce the number of patients you see, though that could also reduce your income. Even so, making constructive changes that may prevent future mishaps is preferable to endangering your patients and your practice. If the error resulted from not knowing the latest techniques, maybe you could use a skills-training course or a retraining program.

But the first thing to do is to resist discrediting yourself. Try this redeeming thought: "I did make an error in treating this patient. I am responsible for it; but I refuse to damn myself for it. I intrinsically have worth. I'm not going to wallow in guilt. I'll update my skills. It may mean a loss of income, but I'm going to start making changes in my lifestyle and practice this minute."

Improvement can come from better use of the time you have.

Take a tip from what the wife of one doctor told us: "When we take a trip, he plays medical cassettes for five hours at a stretch."

4. Don't curse what's unfair. "It's unfair!" you may cry. Unfortunately, that may be true. The fact is you are being sued. But just dwelling on how awful it is could make you a nervous wreck.

At best, a malpractice suit is unpleasant. But even at its worst, it isn't unbearable. You're being unrealistic if you expect everything to always go smoothly and well. Certainly, after many hard years in training, you can hope that your life will begin to get easier. But you're in for lots of anxiety and depression if you demand that life must treat you better, and think you can't stand it when it doesn't. Stop insisting that life shouldn't be like this. Accept the fact that life isn't always fair.

So what should you do? Hold on to what's good, and improve what isn't. Start, for example, by coming up with the best defense you possibly can, and at the same time increase communication with your spouse.

The worst thing you can do is to feel so sorry for yourself that you just try to escape the whole thing. Medicating yourself with whiskey each day may reduce the pain of the trial; it can also erase your chances of winning the case, and put a barrier between you and those who love and want to help you.

Don't think your marriage and family can't survive the pressure. Yes, it's possible the stress could result in divorce. But with rational planning and positive action, you stand a good chance of coming out of the crisis with an even stronger family life. Try this approach:

"It's really rough having to deal with this malpractice mess on top of keeping up my practice, paying out lots of money, and getting close to my family. But I got through a lot of tough years of training, and I'll get through this. Dwelling on this injustice would do as much good as it did to worry about how unfair it was that I had to stay up and study every night in med school.

"I won't worry about my wife leaving me over this. She's stuck with me through many hard years, and I believe she'll tough this out, too. I'll share my feelings with her, and ask for hers. Actually, this will motivate us to work harder on our marriage. I'll do my best to make it work."

That won't guarantee that you'll win your case or save your marriage. But it can decrease the tension and anger—and increase your chances of staying together. "When you get to something colossal like a lawsuit," mused one beleaguered wife, "you remember all the mini-disasters and decide you'll live through this, too. You grow. Adversity does that. You sort of prove your mettle."

5. Retain control. It's tempting to throw up your hands in surrender and say, "I've lost control of my life!" That can happen only if you let it. That discouraging attitude can lead to withdrawal and depression, and with it, abdication of control over your emotions and assets.

Don't assume that the misery is only externally caused. Some individuals give up in a crisis. Others overcome the most severe stress by choosing to change their attitudes.

You had the self-discipline to get through the gruelling years of medical training. Will you now readily give up control of your own destiny just because you face a tough battle on unfamiliar ground?

A malpractice charge can cause much real hardship. But someone who has controlled and mastered other areas of his or her life should be able to apply the same strengths to a lawsuit. Whatever has happened, or will happen, you should be able to assess the situation, put it in a rational frame, get set to take positive action, and say: "Yes, I'm being sued. But I won't give up because of it. I'll learn to take the frustration and not feel helpless. I'll work to defend my case and try to improve the present unjust system of compensating malpractice claims. That way I'll increase my self-discipline, power, and efficacy. By controlling my thinking, I'll control my emotions and actions, too. So instead of putting my future in the hands of accusers and detractors, I'll be the one calling the shots of my emotional and behavioral well-being."

HOW YOUR FAMILY CAN HELP

Your malpractice case is a case of secrecy. You instinctively may think your family can help if you tell them all about it. Don't. With all the loyal, well-meaning intentions in the world, your family can inadvertently hurt you.

Don't tell all. Don't tell your family all the details of the case. As noted in Step 2, it's wrong to bare all to your family in discussing a patient's case. It's equally wrong to discuss malpractice developments. It's also a breach of confidentiality.

All members of your family may have done a good job keeping secrets in the past. Nevertheless, this time may be different. They can't legally help your defense; but they can hurt it by trying to help it. When talking to friends about your suit, they'll try to defend you and the family name—and may reveal things they shouldn't. That information will likely be passed on—and be misquoted.

Don't give them the chance to damage your case or image by trying to spread a "good" word about you. If they're also spreading a bad or confidential word about your former patient, it could prove to be a "bad" word about your personal and professional ethics and your practice.

Let your spouse and children know that confidentiality on both professional and legal grounds forbids you from sharing the details in this case. But that doesn't mean that you should stop sharing your feelings with them.

Don't shut out your spouse. Always be careful not to shut out the partner who once vowed to stick with you for better or for worse, and has done so for years. Your spouse may begin to withdraw because you seem to want or need isolation and silence.

"He wouldn't talk about it," recalled one wife. "So I never knew what was going on. That fed my anxiety, which I communicated to our daughters, and they became insecure."

Go out of your way to bring out your spouse's feelings. Ask for and listen to what your partner is thinking. Your spouse, for example, may even help you think more rationally and positively about the meaning and the implications of your lawsuit—and then help you dispute any unrealistic and damaging attitudes.

Here's how one wife shouted her spouse out of his self-pitying spell: "Why do you take this thing so personally? Settle it, so we can get back to living!"

Just as your spouse can help you out of your pit, it's up to you to help your partner think rationally. Watch carefully for any signs that your self-absorbed ruminating is making your spouse feel you're not interested in his or her needs and fears. So if you see your spouse pulling away, pull up a chair, sit down, and talk. Vent the anger, hurt, and rejection. But don't cast either blame or an unmanageable burden on your wounded partner.

Remember that when you suffer a painful blow, your family members recognize, feel, and react to the pain, because you're all part of one body. If you pull back from them, they may in turn pull away from you. Then, instead of giving each other the support you all need, everyone can end up suffering in isolation, blaming each other for not meeting your common needs.

Don't forget your children. You may think that all your hard work on the case, both at the office and in your study, is a sure sign to your children of how much you care for them and their future. But they may see it as a sign that you no longer care or have time for them.

Your spouse will probably be able to talk about the personal hurt and pain much more easily than your children will. Instead of saying they feel badly, they're more likely to just act badly. Children who aren't adept at verbalizing their sorrow and anger often act them out to get attention and close the emotional distance between you and them. Their own brand of "malpractice"—misbehaving—won't help ease the tension in your home. Take time for them. Tell them how much you love them. Affirm something good they're doing. And do something with them.

Don't withdraw physically or emotionally. Whatever you do, don't withdraw from your family. You need them now, and they need you. Even if you can't hold them in your confidence with case details, you can hold them in your arms. Physical contact and affection form a vital counterattack to the feeling that everything is falling apart. It tells them that, come what may, the family is not coming apart. Hug your spouse and children. Show them you care and that you're still there.

Tell them how you feel. Don't shut out your family with silence. You can't give them the details of the case, but you can and should give them your feelings, and ask for theirs. Sharing feelings can bond you closer.

Tell them your frustrations. Let them know how aggravating it was for you to spend two hours talking with your attorney after you worked a full day. But tell them, too—if true—that you came up with some good evidence or tactics that will help your case. And tell them when you need to rest, be alone, or think things through after a long, hard verbal battle in court. But at the same time tell them that you also need and want to do something with them after you're rested. And then do it.

Time your lawsuit talks. If you and your family want to talk about what happened with your lawyer or in court, put a time limit on the discussion. Set a maximum daily dose for the subject. And stick to your time limit. Then they'll get the basic information—a sense of what's happening and its effect on you—and you'll get the chance to air what you feel about your case, attorney, accusers, and colleagues.

Such limited discussions will help keep things in perspective. Encouraging yourself, spouse, and children to talk about other issues and to do other things will remind all of you that there's a lot more going on in your lives than just the lawsuit.

Take time to do something together. Positively the best counter to catastrophizing is recasting. Do something new—or something old that you all love but haven't done lately—that will bring the family together. If the pressure has closed in around the house, take a day or a weekend away with your spouse. Go out to a game or concert or event your children are participating in. You'll be getting away from your lawyer and closer to them—and what's important to them.

Come home. Don't let your preoccupation with the case reduce you to no more than an occasional occupant of your home. You might be there physically, yet be absent mentally and emotionally. Not only must you share some of yourself and your ordeal with your family; you must also let them share with you what's happening to them.

Your spouse and children may not be as directly affected as you by the day-to-day details of the case. Nevertheless, your reaction to those details can have drastic negative implications for their daily well-being. It's up to you to make life at home a positive counter to the daily problems generated in court.

Your family will surely react in some way to what's hurting you. So let them help you make your home the place where mutual love and support are exchanged every day.

A FRIENDLY ENDING

Your spouse can be your best friend at a time like this. And your children, too, can be your trusty friends. But don't expect them to shoulder an unbearable share of the burden. While you certainly will have to take the lawsuit home with you, you don't have to—and shouldn't—leave it there.

"He wouldn't go out," said one wife. "He'd say, 'I have to study this deposition.' I'd shout back, 'Why are you punishing yourself? You're punishing us, too!'"

After the summons comes, you may tend to avoid friends and stay home. You may think you have no time for fun. In fact, it's the time you need fun and friends more than ever. Friends, particularly other medical couples, can be excellent sources of support. They can help get your head and your body away from the suit and into some needed recreation. Social contacts and activities will show you that life and the world go on.

WHAT'S LEFT?

If you expect—or get—the worst in a malpractice judgment, your family may be forced to ask: "If most of our possessions and money were taken away, what would we have left?"

That question can put you in a deep depression. Or it can motivate you to renewal. Your best answer would be a decision to spend the time it takes, and the money you have, to develop those things that can't be taken away from you—health, love, learning, faith, and worthwhile pursuits.

You need no one to tell you that a malpractice suit—potential or actual—is a crisis in your life. But perhaps you can take some comfort from the Chinese word for crisis: It also means opportunity. So take your malpractice crisis as a real opportunity to strengthen your practice, your knowledge, yourself, and your family.

Glossary

Further information can be obtained from legal dictionaries, such as *Black's Law Dictionary*, from which some of these definitions were derived in part.[30]

Abandonment. Failure to fulfill a contract. Malpractice charge made when a practitioner stops giving care during the course of a patient's illness.

Abuse. Excessive or improper use or treatment of something or someone. (See child abuse.)

Abuse of process. Improper use of legal procedure.

Ad damnum. "To the damage." The clause in a complaint that states the plaintiff's claim for money damages.

Admissible evidence. Evidence that can be introduced in court. In federal courts, admissibility of evidence is governed by the Federal Rules of Evidence. Information that would not be admissible in court can be investigated in a deposition.

Adverse witness. A witness prejudiced for or against the party questioning the witness. (See hostile witness.)

Agent. Someone authorized to act for someone else.

Allegation. Assertion of claim in pleadings that states what the plaintiff expects to prove.

Answer. Reply written by the defense attorney to the plaintiff's complaint, defining the grounds for the defense, admitting or denying allegations, and listing arguments for preventing recovery of damages. (See pleadings.)

Arbitration. The settlement of a dispute by an impartial third party.

Argumentative questions. A question that suggests an answer favorable to the person asking the question. The argumentative question may consist of a statement instead of a question: "You killed the patient, didn't you?"

Assault. Willful attempt or threat to injure another person. Assault may occur without any physical contact or bodily harm. (See battery.)

Assumption of risk. "Non fit injuria." Subject cannot claim damages for an injury caused by a danger which he or she knew about, yet voluntarily chose to be exposed to and take the risk that the danger entailed.

Attorney's lien. Document describing the right of an attorney to obtain payment for services. A copy of an attorney's lien may be given to a defendant as a means of announcing a lawsuit.

Authoritative. Person or written work commonly held to be correct. To state that someone or something is authoritative is to implicitly agree with every detail the person has ever written or every detail in a specified written work. To concur instead only on the accuracy of particular statements of the author or work is to avoid making authorizations beyond your awareness or intent.

Badger. To harass or torment.

Bankrupt. Unable to pay one's debts. The federal Bankruptcy Act of 1978 allows for reorganizing a debtor's financial condition rather than taking the debtor's assets.

Battery. Criminal battery is the unlawful beating or use of force on another person without consent. Technical battery occurs when a health-care practitioner administers treatment that goes beyond what has been consented to by the patient. Assault and battery are punishable under civil and criminal proceedings, (See assault.)

Best evidence. Rule that original documents, X-rays, and other best evidence be entered in court. Copies should only be used if the originals are not available.

Bias. The predisposition to decide an issue in a certain way.

Bill of particulars. Statement defining the details of a claim. (See pleadings.)

Body language. See *nonverbals*.

Borrowed servant. A person temporarily working under the direction of a master who is responsible for the actions of that "borrowed servant" in certain circumstances of close supervision. If a nurse who is an employee of a hospital performs an act under the direct supervision of a physician, the doctor, rather than the hospital, might be held responsible for that nurse who acted as a borrowed servant.

Breach of contract. Failure to act as required by a contract. A contract may be implied and initiated when a doctor undertakes the responsibility to treat a patient.

Breach of duty. Failure to provide the usual standard of care to a patient.

Brief. Written statement, prepared by an attorney for a court, that summarizes a case and tells how specific laws are relevant to the case.

But for. Test whether the plaintiff would have suffered harm "but for"—or in the absence of—the actions of the defendant.

Captain of the ship. Holds the surgeon in an operation responsible for the negligence of nurses and others working under the direct supervision of that surgeon. Recently, some courts have decided not to uphold this doctrine, and thereby made nurses—and the hospitals that employ them—liable for their negligent acts. (See borrowed servant.)

Case precedent. See precedent.

Causation. Implication that the damage suffered by the plaintiff was a direct result of the action—or inaction—of the defendant.

Child abuse. Mistreating, molesting, or causing serious physical or emotional injury to a minor. (See abuse.)

Circumstantial evidence. Testimony not based on personal observations of the witness.

Civil. Relating to private rights. A civil wrong, or tort, is a wrong against another individual. A criminal wrong is an act against the state. Murder, assault, and battery can be prosecuted as criminal as well as civil wrongs. Some malpractice insurance policies do not cover criminal acts. A physician might be charged with a criminal act simply because the statute of limitations has run for the relevant civil proceedings.

Civil lawsuit. Legal action designed to protect personal rights, or to correct and compensate for damages done to individuals (See crime and tort.)

Claimant. Plaintiff. One who sues.

Claims-made policy. Insurance covering lawsuits filed and alleged acts of negligence that occur during the life of the policy. Because many suits are filed years after the alleged acts of negligence occurred, claims-made policies by themselves may provide insufficient malpractice coverage.

Closing arguments. Summaries given to the jury by each attorney at the end of a trial.

Co-defendants. Parties being sued in the same lawsuit.

Collateral source. Defendant's payment will not be reduced because the plaintiff has been paid by another source. For example, if a plaintiff who has won a claim of $100,000 in damages has already received $80,000 in insurance benefits, the defendant physician would still be required to pay the plaintiff $100,000 (See Step 12 for exceptions to the rule.)

Common law. Statutory law refers to laws passed by the legislature. But, the legislature cannot think of everything that might ever happen, so courts have to decide right and wrong every time a law does not exactly fit. The collection of court decisions establish case law, also called common law. Case decisions in one state are not necessarily followed in other states. Case decisions in lower courts have less weight than decisions of higher courts. Decisions in courts lower than an appellate court carry very little weight. State courts do not always follow federal decisions or laws. Appellate courts, even in the same state, often disagree when deciding an issue.

Comparative negligence. When injuries are judged to be due in part to several different parties, including the plaintiff, the negligence—and liability—of each party can be determined on a percentage (comparative) basis. (See contributory negligence.)

Complaint. Often the first legal paper filed to announce a malpractice claim and give a brief account of the facts of the case. (See pleadings.)

Confidential. Information given by a patient to a health-care practitioner is normally to be kept secret. However, a practitioner may be held liable for not sharing certain "confidential" information, as in the case of a dangerous or threatening patient who injures someone else. When a malpractice suit is active, considerations of confidentiality are relaxed while in court, but not at other times.

Conflict of interest. Situation in which a person in a position of duty and trust is given opportunity to betray that devotion and trust. For example, an attorney cannot represent two sides of a disagreement simultaneously.

Consent. See informed consent.

Contingency fee. Payment a plaintiff agrees to give an attorney will be a specified percentage of (contingent on) the damages paid to the plaintiff.

Contract. Agreement about what will or will not be done. Most contracts in business are made in writing. In medicine, a practitioner has an implied contract with a patient once treatment is undertaken—and will be held to that contract to give competent, continuing care, even if the patient fails to follow treatment or pay bills.

Contractor. One who performs work under a contract. (See independent contractor.)

Contributory negligence. The patient (or another person) contributes to the injury. Comparative negligence is a type of contributory negligence, not recognized in all states, in which negligence is measured in terms of percentage. Thus, a patient with a million dollars worth of damages who was 30% responsible for the damages, might claim his or her physician owed him $700,000. See also negligence.

Counterclaim. Claim made by the defendant against the plaintiff. For example, a physician being sued for malpractice might make a counterclaim for the bills for treatment that had not been paid by the plaintiff.

Countersuit. Lawsuit brought by the defendant against the plaintiff or plaintiff's attorney. A suit charging the plaintiff with malice would be difficult to prove. Easier to win would be a claim of a poor standard of practice or harassment of the practitioner by the plaintiff's attorney, which would be a malpractice suit against the attorney.

Crime. An act judged to be against a state or the country. (See civil lawsuit and tort.)

Cross-examination. The questioning of a witness by the opposing attorney. The material covered in cross-examination is limited to that introduced previously during direct examination.

Damage. Personal or property loss. Or, injury caused by accident, negligence or the intentional act of another person. In a malpractice case an attempt is made to "make the person whole," to undo the damages, by means of a cash settlement. If a jury feels that the malpractice was done in a deliberate, criminal, indifferent, or grossly negligent manner, additional damages may be awarded. These additional damages may be called exemplary, punitive, or vindictive damages. Some malpractice policies will not cover such additional damages.
The physician being sued might suffer damages because of the lawsuit. He or she might countersue, asking for recovery for his damages. See special damages and special injury.

Damages. The amount of money a plaintiff is awarded for injuries suffered.

Deadlocked jury. A jury that cannot reach a decision. (See hung jury.)

Deep pocket. A physician or other person with a bank account or insurance policy healthy enough to make it worth an attorney's time to sue.

Defamation. Injury to a person's reputation by acts of libel (writing) or slander (speech).

Defendant. The person being sued and asked to pay damages to the plaintiff.

Demurrer. Declaration by the defendant stating that even if the accusations made were true, there would be no basis for a suit against the defendant. For example, the claims do not state that the defendant's negligence was a proximate cause of the patient's injury.

Deponent. A deponent is one who testifies in a deposition. The person being questioned.

Depose. To depose is to give information in the form of a deposition.

Deposition. A meeting in which various parties, including the defendant, are asked a series of questions. The deposition will be recorded and used to define the facts of the case, the limits of memory and knowledge of the defendant, and the extent and meaning of entries in the medical record. The record of the deposition can be used as evidence in court.

Deposition transcript. The written record of the deposition. The deposition transcript is a word for word account of what is said during a deposition. Nonverbal actions may also be recorded. The deposition transcript is a legal document that can be quoted in court. Attorneys frequently study, index, and cross-reference deposition transcripts. The deposition transcript is proof of any admissions a defendant might make during hours of long questioning.

Diligence. Due diligence is the degree of care which could be expected from a prudent practitioner under similar circumstances. This is the standard to which a practitioner is normally held when facing a malpractice charge.

Direct examination. The questioning in court of a witness by the attorney who called that witness. This is normally the first questioning in court experienced by a defendant.

Directed verdict. The trial judge may enter a decision, a directed verdict, when a party has failed to present a case with sufficient evidence for jury evaluation.

Disability. Loss or lack of the ability to work, to enjoy legal rights, or to receive governmental payments.

Disclosure. Divulgence or explaining of information and evidence.

Discoverable. Information is discoverable if it is suitable for examination during a deposition. Any information that might be expected to lead to facts relevant to the case in question is discoverable. Much information that would not be admissible in court will be discoverable.

Discovery. The finding of information, e.g., by private investigation, depositions, interrogatories, and examination of evidence.

Discovery rule. The statute of limitations starts to run when the patient knows about, or when a diligent patient would have been able to recognize, the negligent act of the practitioner.

Duty. Obligation or commitment. A health-care practitioner has a duty to continue competent treatment of a patient once treatment has started.

Employee. A person hired by an employer to perform duties.

Employer. The employer (e.g., family physician or hospital administrator) has the responsibility to control the details of how the duties of employees are performed. (See respondeat superior and independent contractor).

Entrap. To bring unexpectedly into danger or to entangle. To entrap in a conversation is to confuse or cause the other person to make contradictory statements.

Evasive answer. An evasive answer is an answer that does not admit to or deny a fact in response to a question in a direct manner. Rule 37 of the Federal Rules of Civil Procedure treats an evasive answer as a failure to answer. It provides a mechanism for obtaining a court order that demands the question be answered.

Evidence. Matters of fact or proof on which belief or decision is based.

Examination before trial (or EBT). A deposition.

Exculpatory. Excusing from guilt or fault. Exculpatory clauses in treatment consent forms that hold health care personnel free of liability for negligence are generally held to be invalid.

Exemplary damages. Awards beyond what would compensate the plaintiff for injuries suffered, likely to be added when fraud or other deliberate or criminal actions have occurred. Such awards, often not covered by malpractice insurance, are meant to deter future misconduct.

Exhibit. An exhibit is a document or an object that can prove something. Exhibits used in medical malpractice cases include medical records, X-rays, drawings, and anatomical models.

Expert witness. Someone recognized by the court as qualified by reason of training or experience to give expert testimony on the case and subject being tried.

Federal rules of civil procedure. A body of rules that govern all civil actions in United States District Courts. Most states model their rules of civil procedure on the Federal Rules.

Fellow servant. Fellow employee.

Fellow servant rules. Provision invoked by employers to decrease their liability when an employee injures another by claiming that the injuring employee was responsible for the damage to the other employee. Workers' compensation insurance has eliminated the need for this argument in many cases.

Fraud. An intentional lie that has the purpose of causing another to part with a valuable or to give up a legal right. Fraudulent acts would probably be considered criminal acts and would not be covered by most malpractice insurance policies. Fraud can extend the statute of limitations. For example, telling a patient that a postoperative complication is normal and will spontaneously clear up, would probably allow the patient to sue later than if the complication had been immediately acknowledged.

Frivolous. Not sufficiently supported by evidence. Lawsuits can be proven to be frivolous by depositions taken of various parties, such as the patient. The information obtained during such depositions can make a countersuit possible.

Going bare. Practicing medicine without having professional liability (malpractice) insurance.

Good faith. An abstract quality with no technical meaning or statutory definition. An honest belief and intention. Good faith settlements may not be final: when the opposition claims it has "new" evidence about your case, they may ask you to pay more depending on the terms of your "good faith settlement."

Good Samaritan law. Statute that protects from malpractice claims the health-care practitioner who renders free and voluntary emergency care outside of medical facilities.

Gross negligence. The intentional failure to perform a duty in reckless disregard of the consequences to others. See also *negligence*.

Guilt. Violation of a criminal law. A defendant may not be "guilty" of malpractice, a civil wrong; yet one may be guilty of criminal charges filed along with a malpractice claim.

Harassment. Words, gestures, or actions that annoy, alarm, or verbally abuse another person.

Hearsay. Secondhand testimony provided by rumors or unconfirmed reports. (See inadmissible evidence.)

Hostile witness. A witness prejudiced against the questioning party. (See adverse witness.)

Hung jury. A jury that cannot reach a verdict (See deadlocked jury).

Hypothetical question. A question posed to a witness in relation to a situation that is supposedly similar to the case at hand, in order to allow the expert to express an opinion which will help the jury make an informed judgment about the present case.

Immaterial. "Matter" that is unimportant, unnecessary and meaningless to the case at hand.

Immunity. Freedom from penalty or obligation.

Impeach. Denounce, castigate, or discredit.

Impeachment. The process of proving a person to be untrustworthy or a liar. Impeachment of physicians can be accomplished by finding inconsistent statements made during questioning. When read before a jury, the physician is made to look dishonest.

Impleader. Document that names a third party as a defendant. (Same as third-party complaint.)

Implied contract. See contract.

Inadmissible evidence. Testimony or matter that cannot be legally brought before the court (See hearsay.)

Indemnity. Exemption or protection from liability, penalty, or loss.

Independent contractor. One who performs under a contract with no controls on how the work will be done; only the result of the work is specified by the contract. A hospital might be held less liable for the act of an independently contracted physician who operated in the hospital than for the practice of a physician employed by the hospital.

Independent expert witness. Not subject to control or influence from another party. To avoid the bias of experts who are hired by each side in a malpractice case, "independent" expert witnesses are sometimes used. If the expert is somehow tied to one party, or is "hired for unrelated work" by one party, his or her independence would be open to question.

In evidence. The facts of a case which have been established as true are considered in evidence.

Informed consent. A patient may accept or reject treatment based upon an evaluation of information about the treatment and its possible effects that would be given by a reasonably prudent practitioner. What information is an adequate prerequisite for treatment may depend upon the emotional state of the patient or the urgency of the situation.

Injury. Physical or psychological harm. Damages are the amount of compensation the plaintiff is awarded for suffering the injury.

Interrogatories. A written list of questions given to witnesses or defendants to obtain information that would be difficult to obtain from memory at a deposition.

Intimidation. To purposely deter another from action by putting that person in fear. Some attorneys feel that intimidation is an important part of taking a deposition.

Invasion of privacy. The unwarranted publicizing of one's private affairs with which the public has no legitimate concern. Or, the wrongful intrusion into one's private activities in such a manner as would cause an ordinary person mental suffering or humiliation. See defamation, libel, slander.

Judgment. The decision of the court.

Jurisdiction. The legal and geographical territory in which a court has power to interpret and apply the law (e.g., appeals cases in California).

Lawsuit. A case of action placed before a court for decision.

Leading questions. Framed to control, direct, or cause the witness to answer in a manner that would serve the needs and support the case of the questioning attorney.

Legal theory. The reasoning, based upon statutes and case precedents, that supports an action.

Liability. Obligation, responsibility, or duty to pay.

Liable. Legally responsible or under obligation.

Libel. Defamation of a party by printed means. (See also slander.)

Life estate. Agreement in which a living beneficiary receives use of, and income from, property. When the beneficiary dies, the property goes to the person who had given the life estate.

Likely. More then 50 percent chance of occurring. Same as probable. More than possible. A question about a rare event can be answered by saying that its occurrence is very unlikely, but anything can be said to be possible.

Locality rule. Obsolete "rule" that medical professionals should be held to the standard of care practiced in their own locality. Thus, if all physicians in a town were out of date in their practice, all would be excused. It is now recognized that practitioners in all parts of the country have access to education and consultants through transportation, telephone, tapes, and other media.

Loss of consortium. Loss of affection, companionship, sex, and other benefits when a spouse or other close person dies or is severely injured. Payment for such loss is often sought in malpractice claims.

Magistrate. A public civil officer. U.S. magistrates have some, but not all, of the powers of a judge. A magistrate may decide whether or not a deposition question must be answered. If many conflicts arise during a deposition, the deposition may be held in the presence of a magistrate so that immediate rulings on disagreements can be made.

Malice. Intentional wrongdoing against another person without justification, or wanton disregard for another's rights, welfare, or reputation.

Malicious prosecution. Difficult to prove counterclaim that a lawsuit has been brought without probable cause and with malicious intent.

Malicious prosecution lawsuit. A malicious prosecution lawsuit claims that a physician was sued with malice and for no good reason. A number of facts need to be proven to support the claim of malicious prosecution. The proof can sometimes be obtained by making sure that the depositions of the physician and of other parties document the necessary information. The facts that must be proven to support a claim of malicious prosecution are:

1. A judicial proceeding has been initiated or continued by the patient against the physician.
2. The physician prevailed in this proceeding.
3. There was no probable cause to institute the proceeding.
4. The proceeding was instituted because of malice.
5. The physician sustained injury.

See also, *damage, special damages, probable cause, malice.*

Malpractice. Negligence or misconduct on the part of a health-care practitioner, lawyer, or other professional that causes injury and leads to a civil suit. Failure to use the degree of skill and knowledge exhibited by other professionals in similar circumstances is usually involved in the claim.

Malpractice insurance. See professional liability insurance.

Material. Substantial and important.

Mental anguish. Pain, fear, and anxiety that follow a damaging or endangering physical or mental injury or loss.

Meritorious. Legally proper and deserving.

Mistrial. Invalid or erroneous trial.

Motion. Request made by an attorney. It may be accepted or denied by the court. Dozens of different motions may be made, whose purpose might not be apparent to the uninitiated at the time they are made.

Narrative answer. An answer in which the witness speaks without interruption. The usual question and answer format is put aside. When being sued for malpractice, you are not required to answer questions that require a narrative answer, such as "Tell me everything you know about the patient."

Neglect. Failure to perform one's duties.

Negligence. The failure to do something that a reasonable person would do, or the doing of a thing that a reasonable and prudent person would not do. As applied to medical malpractice, negligence is failing to act in the manner a reasonable, prudent, average practitioner of similar standing would act. See also *gross negligence*.

Non fit injuria. See assumption of risk.

Nonverbals. Gestures, facial expressions, and other actions that communicate meaning. A large part of communication is not what is said, but how it is said. Nonverbals can intimidate during depositions. It really does not matter what a person is saying if he or she has an angry look, is shaking a fist, or is leaning toward you.

Nusiance. An unwarranted or unlawful activity that leads to annoyance and damages to another. A term often applied to medical malpractice cases. See *frivolous*.

Nurse practice acts. State laws that define professional activities in which nurses may legally engage. Some states limit the right of nurses to diagnose problems and prescribe treatments.

Objection. Statement used to make the court aware that the objecting attorney believes a statement, procedure, or evidence entered by the opposing attorney is not proper and should not be allowed.

Occurrence policy. Insurance for acts of alleged negligence that occur during the life of the policy, thus providing coverage even when a claim is filed after the policy has been terminated. (See claims-made policy.)

Off the record. During a deposition a conversation may be held "off the record." If all attorneys present at the deposition agree that the conversation should be off the record, the reporter will probably not record the conversation. However, it is still permissible that after the conversation is held, the plaintiff's attorney recite the contents of the conversation onto the record and into the deposition transcript. One should therefore hold off the record conversations where they cannot be heard.

Opening statements. Verbal summaries given by opposing attorneys to the jury at the beginning of a trial.

Outrage. Affront, insult, and abuse. One type of countersuit is the outrage suit. The requirements for any outrage suit are:
1. The outrageous conduct was intentional or reckless.
2. The conduct offended generally accepted standards of decency and morality.

3. The conduct caused emotional distress.

4. The emotional distress was severe.

Pain and suffering. All intangible damages, including discomfort and mental distress.

Patient privilege. Right of a patient to have information given to a practitioner held secret. This right is usually waived in court when the patient sues the practitioner.

Perjury. Lying under oath.

Petition. Written request.

Plaintiff. Person who sues. (Also called the claimant.)

Plaintiff's attorney. The lawyer of the person who is suing.

Pleadings. Formal statements of claims and defenses, including the complaint, answer, and bill of particulars.

Possible. Anything that could happen under the circumstances. (Less than likely and probable.)

Precedent. Previous court decision on a similar case. Courts try to follow principles used to decide previous cases.

Prejudice. Bias or preconception.

Preponderance of evidence. Enough testimony to prove something to be more probable than not. "A fair preponderance of evidence" is the degree of proof needed in a civil (malpractice) case. In a criminal case, guilt must be proven "beyond a reasonable doubt."

Prima facie. "At first glance." Before further investigation.

Prima facie evidence. That which seems to be correct and will be accepted by the court as fact if not contradicted in rebuttal by other evidence.

Prima facie tort. Intentionally inflicting damages without excuse or justification by acts that would otherwise be lawful.

Privilege. A right or exception before the law. For example, the right to keep secret the information discussed with one's attorney or physician. See also *confidential*.

Probable. Same as likely. (See also possible.)

Professional liability insurance. Malpractice insurance. Policy covering legal counsel and costs of alleged lack of standard skills, misconduct, or negligence in performing professional responsibilities to the client.

Proof. Clear demonstration. That which causes people, or convinces a jury, to believe something.

Proximate. Closely related or causative.

Proximate cause. Malpractice implies that the damages suffered by the plaintiff were the direct result of the action, or inaction, of the defendant.

Punitive damages. Funds awarded to a plaintiff, beyond the amount needed to compensate for injuries suffered, "to make the person whole again" and to discourage the defendant from performing further negligent acts. Punitive damages are usually not covered by insurance policies.

Reasonable doubt. See preponderance of evidence.

Rebut. Contradict or oppose by countervailing proof or argument.

Rebuttal evidence. Testimony given to disprove arguments given by the opposing party.

Redirect examination. Re-examination of a witness by the attorney who called the person to testify. The questions are limited to material introduced by the opposing attorney during cross-examination.

Refresh memory. Acceptable way a witness may admit inability to remember a detail at question during testimony in court, and ask to look at a medical record or other evidence to "refresh my memory." However, it is not acceptable to say you need to look up a detail because you don't remember it; you would then be accused of having no memory of what happened.

Release. Giving up a right. When compensated for an injury, a plaintiff may sign a release barring further recovery for the injury, and releasing from liability any health-care practitioners who cared for the injury.

Relevant. Concerning and related to the issue at hand.

Remittitur. Order by a judge for a plaintiff to remit (give back) part of an unreasonably large award.

Reorganization. An alternative to bankruptcy by which a debtor adjusts and sets up a payment schedule to honor at least part of the debts owed.

Res ipsa loquitur. "The thing speaks for itself." Means of proving negligence which depends on the fact, obvious to any lay person, that the injury would not have occurred in the absence of negligence. No expert witness is required to present complex arguments or facts proving guilt.

Res judicata or Res adjudicata. "The matter judged." Decided by previous lawsuits whose precedents will be followed.

Respondeat superior. "Let the master answer." The employer (master) is responsible for the actions of employees (servants).

Satisfaction. Compensation or payment of the damages set in a court decision.

Servant. Employee or helper who is under the control of an employer or master.

Settlement. Pretrial agreement or court disposition concerning difference between parties in a lawsuit.

Slander. Defamation by the spoken word. (See also libel.)

Special damages. Damages not usually suffered. Special damages are defined differently in various states. Some courts have held that a physician cannot recover damages resulting from a frivolous lawsuit unless the damages are different than those usually suffered in a malpractice lawsuit. Thus, it would not be possible to recover damages from losses such as defamation of character, mental distress, increased insurance rates, and attorney's fees. The deposition can document various forms of insult and harassment that might not be considered usual. See damage.

Special injury. Deprivation of liberty or property. Some courts have not held as special injury humiliation, embarrassment, emotional anguish, subjection to public scorn, ridicule, injury to reputation, and increased liability insurance premiums.

Speculation. Theorizing about a matter you really do not know about. You are not required to speculate about anything, and you should not speculate. It is normal to feel a need to speculate when questioned repeatedly about a matter, but such questioning is an effort to cause a person to make inaccurate statements. Unless you wish to be proven a liar, do not speculate.

Standard of care. The level or degree of competence under which a professional is expected to perform duties to a client (patient).

Stare decisis. "Let the decision stand." Follow previous court decisions on similar matters.

Statute of limitations. A limit to the time in which a lawsuit must be filed. For example, in many states a malpractice suit must be filed within two years of when the alleged negligence took place. The statute of limitation is extended in many states by various rules. For example, the foreign body rule may extend the statute in cases involving a foreign body (piece of needle, pacemaker, or IUD). If the case involved a minor, the time might be extended until the child becomes an adult.

Statutory law. Law enacted by a legislature. (See common law.)

Stipulations. Stipulations are agreements made by opposing attorneys on matters they are able to decide. During depositions this can include the manner of making objections, verifying the accuracy of the deposition transcript, and the need for signing the deposition transcript. Some attorneys will ask their opponent if he agrees to "the usual stipulations." An agreement is sometimes obtained without it being clear what the usual stipulations are. In such a situation, the physician witness should be told what has been agreed to and refuse to proceed until he has been told.

Subpoena. An order to appear at a certain time and place. A subpoena *duces tecum* orders the production of papers and other evidence.

Subrogation. Substitution of one party for another (e.g., an insurance company may sue someone its client had the right to sue).

Substantial. Of significant value. (Same as material.)

Suit. A legal action or case in court in which a plaintiff seeks compensation for injury.

Summary judgment. Court decision based on the belief that there is no significant evidence or basis in law to support a claim for damages.

Summations. Talks to the jury near the end of a trial in which each attorney, and sometimes the judge, reviews the main points of the case.

Summons. Document which establishes that a court has jurisdiction over a defendant and orders the person to appear before the court.

Superior. One who can direct another (e.g., employer to employee).

Supersedeas bond. Money that must be paid by a defendant who is appealing a judgment. Even though an award for damages has been appealed, a fee (the supersedeas bond) must be paid by the defendant until the final judgment has been made.

Testimony. Information given under oath.

Theory. The legal foundation on which a case is based.

Third party. A third party is a person who did not take part in a transaction. For example, a physician is a third party when a patient and lawyer decide to sue the physician. The responsibility of the patient's lawyer to act reasonably toward the physician has increased in some jurisdiction in the last few years.

Third-party complaint. Document (impleader) filed by the defendant stating that some other party is liable at least in part for the damages attributed to the defendant.

Tort. A private or civil wrong or injury (besides breach of contact). Usually a tort is handled by an action for damages (attempt to get money to right the wrong). See also *civil*. The elements of every tort action (including a malpractice action) are:
1. Existence of legal duty from defendant to plaintiff.
2. A breach of that duty.
3. Damage as a proximate result of the breach of duty.

Tortfeasor. A party who commits a tort, a legal violation.

Transcript. A written record. See *deposition transcript*.

Verdict. The veredictum is the "true declaration" or decision made by a jury.

Verification. Affirmation of accuracy.

Vicarious liability. Responsibility for the acts of others (e.g., a hospital's accountability for the acts of its nurses).

Vindictive damages. Punitive awards made because of anger.

Voir dire. "To speak the truth." The process of questioning and choosing jurors.

Waiver. Voluntarily giving up a right, such as the right to verify the accuracy of your deposition transcript.

Wanton. Malicious, immoral, or reckless action that lacks consideration for others.

Willful. Conscious or deliberate.

Willful or wanton misconduct. A reckless disregard for the safety of others. Willful or wanton misconduct is the failure to exercise ordinary care to prevent injury to a person who should be known to be in danger because of the act being performed.

Wrongful death. Statute allowing that the death of a person may be grounds for a civil suit.

Wrongful life. Lawsuit that charges a health practitioner with being responsible for the life (undesired birth) of an individual (e.g., following an unsuccessful sterilization procedure or failure to give genetic counseling).

References

1. Aaronson DW and Lescoe RJ: Darling decision after 20 years. *Medical Malpractice Prevention.* July/August 1986, pages 31–32.
2. Aaronson DW: Standard of care...not standard of perfection. *Medical Malpractice Prevention.* September/October, 1987, page 13–13.
3. Alton WG: Malpractice—A Trial Lawyer's Advice for Physicians (How to Avoid, How to Win). Boston: Little, Brown & Co. 1977.
3A. American Heart Association: *Textbook of Advanced Cardiac Life Support.* Dallas: American Heart Association, 1987.
4. *American Medical News:* College, MDs named in surgery death suit. July 12, 1985, page 7.
5. *American Medical News:* Drug fails to prevent pregnancy; rape victim sues. February 8, 1985, page 45.
6. *American Medical News:* Illinois court rules against "wrongful birth" suits, 17, Mar 4, 1983.
7. *American Medical News:* Louisiana physicians win $80,000 in countersuit against lawyer, patient. March 2, 1984, page 1.
8. *American Medical News:* MDs immune from liability in reported child abuse. November 14, 1986, page 35.
9. *American Medical News:* MDs protest $4.4 million attorney's fee, 3, Dec 24, 1982.
10. *American Medical News:* New liability experts born. December 2, 1983, page 27.
11. *American Medical News:* New York lawyers group sues to end liability screening panels, 3, Mar 11, 1983
12. *American Medical News:* Patient wins conspiracy suit, $5.1 million in damages, 14, Feb 4, 1983.

13. *American Medical News:* Reusing catheter leads to $950,000 lawsuit. April 13, 1984.

14. Ansberry: Community facilities for the mentally ill are few and overburdened. *The Wall Street Journal,* September 25, 1987, page 1.

15. Ansell DA and Schiff L: T Patient Dumping. *JAMA,* 257(11): 1500–1519, 1987.

16. Appleman JA: Preparation and Trial. Vienna, VA: Coiner, 1967.

17. Ardman C: Doctors without malpractice coverage seek to shelter assets. *Physicians Financial News,* February 15, 1987, page 33.

18. Astrachan A: Why a plaintiff's lawyer hates a structured settlement. *Medical Economics,* April 18, 1988, pages 157–169.

19. Barr D: Why good doctors must start breaking bad laws. *Medical Economics,* September 5, 1988, pages 19–30.

20. Bauer WB: Physicians losing respect: don't blame all of medicine's problems on lawyers. *American Medical News,* 60, Jan 21, 1983.

21. Bayer MJ and Norton RL: Solving the clinical problems of phencyclidine intoxication. *ER Reports,* 4(2), Jan 24, 1983.

22. Belli M: How doctors get sucked into malpractice suits. *Medical Economics,* 76, Jan 24, 1983.

23. Berenson RA: Dealing with financial risks and ethical dilemmas. *Consultant,* September 1987, pages 100–105.

24. Bergman D: The clinical gambler. *Emergency Decisions,* September 1988, page 7–8.

25. Berlin L: Countersuit, In *Legal Medicine,* edited by JA Everett. Baltimore: Urban and Schwarzenberg, 1980.

26. Berman AL and Cohen-Sandler R: Suicide and the standard of care: optimal vs acceptable. *Suicide and Life-Threatening Behavior,* 12(2): 114–122, 1982.

27. Bianco A: Washington scene. *Legal Aspects of Medical Practice,* 14(9):8, 1986.

28. Birnbaum IM and Parker ES: *Alcohol and Human Memory.* New York: John Wiley & Sons, 1977.

29. Bishop J., Garr DR and Marsh FH: Video v. malpractice. *Physicians' Video Guide,* October, 1985, page 16–18).

30. Black HC: *Black's Law Dictionary.* St. Paul: West Publishing Company, 1979.

31. Blackwell BR: The drug defaulter. *Clinical Pharmacology and Therapeutics,* 13:841, 1972.

32. Blaylock P: The legal revolution in the emergency department. Part 2— The perils and pitfalls. *Legal Aspects of Medical Practice,* 14(12), 1986.

33. Boisaubin EV and Dress R: Informed consent in emergency care: Illusion and reform. *Annals of Emergency Medicine* 16:62–67, 1987.

34. Bond C: You and the bare physician. *Medical Times,* 111(1): 86–92, 1983.

35. Boyarsky S: Informed consent. *Legal Aspects of Medical Practice* 16(5):1, 1988 (speaking of Melvin Belli's works).

36. Boyd JR, Covington TR, and Stanaszek WF: Drug defaulting II— analysis of noncompliance patterns. *American Journal of Hospital Pharmacology*, 31:485, 1974.

37. Breo DL: 'Couldn't wait' to leave HMO. *American Medical News* July 29, 1988, page 3.

38. Brodsky SL: *Psychologists in the Criminal Justice System.* Champaign: University of Illinois Press, 1972.

39. Brooten, KE: Fortify your liability protection. *Private Practice*, March 1987, pages 20–25.

40. Brooten KE: What a malpractice attorney looks for in medical records. *Physician's Management*, 36, Nov 1982.

41. Brown JM, Helling DK, Burns EA, Burmeister LF, and Rakel RE: patient care telephone calls received in family practice offices. *The Journal of Family Practice*, 14(3):527, 1982.

42. Burda, D: HMO's may cause legal headaches for hospitals. *Hospitals*, February 5, 1986.

43. Burns JR: Emergency hospital services guidelines. *New York State Journal of Medicine*, 81:1691, 1981.

44. Butt ET: Exclusions for vicarious liability. *Illinois State Medical Insurance Services Exchange Commentary*, Mar 1980.

45. Butt ET: Recent developments in medical malpractice law. *Illinois State Medical Insurance Services Exchange Commentary*, Mar 1982.

46. Caplan H: We can't afford to prolong so many hopeless lives. *Medical Economics*, 62, Dec 29, 1982.

47. Cassell EJ: The relief of suffering. *Archives of Internal Medicine*, 143:522, Mar 1983.

48. Cassileth BR, Zupkis RV, Sutton-Smith K, and March U: Informed consent—why are its goals imperfectly realized? *New England Journal of Medicine*, 302:896, 1980

49. Cerebral palsy: Is substandard care at fault? *Patient Care*, September 15, 1988, pages 19–20.

50. Cerny JH: Courtroom known-how. In *Observations by a Court Reporter.* Cincinnati: WH Anderson Company, 1958.

51. Chang G and Astrachan BM: The emergency department surveillance of alcohol intoxication after motor vehicle accidents. *JAMA:* 260(17): 2533–2536, 1988.

52. Chapman S: Incompetent physicians—a legal mine field. *Physician's Management*, 206, Mar 1983.

53. Chapman S: 10 questions doctors ask most about malpractice. *Physician's Management*, September 1986, pages 124–131.

54. Cody NC: Liability for granting surgical privileges. *Legal Aspects of Medical Practice* 16 (1): 4, 1988.

55. Cooper A: Settlement of medical liability lawsuits without physician's consent. *Journal of the American Medical Association*, 248:1980, Oct 22, 1982.

56. Cooper TR: Medical treatment facility liability for patient suicide and other self-injury. *Journal of Legal Medicine*, 20, Jan 1975.

57. Couch JB and McCabe JJ: Retrolental fibroplasia: All is not lost—truth and justice prevail. *Legal Aspects of Medical Practice* 13(1):5–8, 1985.

58. Crane M: A tactic that's heading off malpractice suits. *Medical Economics*, October 17, 1988, pages 101–106.

59. Curran WJ and Hyg SM: Screening panels in malpractice cases, some disturbing process reports. *New England Journal of Medicine*, 302:945, Apr 24, 1980.

60. Cusumano CL: *Malpractice Law Dissected for Quick Grasping.* New York: Medicine Law Press, 1962.

61. Danner D: *Pattern Interrogatories: Medical Malpractice.* New York: The Lawyers Cooperative Publishing Company, Bancroft-Witney, 1973.

62. Davenport J: The trickiest malpractice trap of all. *Medical Economics*, February 15, 1988, pages 83–87.

63. Davis JM: Good-bye, Bendectin, old friend. *Postgraduate Medicine* 75(7):20–24, 1984.

64. *Diagnostic and Statistical Manual of Mental Disorders—3d Ed (DSM-III).* Washington, DC: American Psychiatric Association, 1980.

65. Dinman BD: The reality ad acceptance of risk. *Journal of the American Medical Association*, 244(11):1226, Sep 12, 1980.

66. DNR policy to be required at hospitals. *American Medical News*, June 19, 1987.

67. Dotson BL: *Notice to Health Care Providers.* Washington, DC: US Dept of Health and Human Services, Office for Civil Rights, May 18, 1982.

68. Drasin GF: These doctors broke the countersuit barrier. *Medical Economics*, 70, Oct 25, 1982.

69. Dunner DL: Affective disorders. In *Current Therapy,* edited by HF Conn. Philadelphia: WB Saunders, 1981.

70. Eisenberg, ES: Attorneys' negligence and third parties. *New York University Law Review* 57(126): 126–163, 1982.

71. Eisenberg H: Overlook victims in a malpractice suit—the doctor's family. *Medical Economics*, 252, Mar 6, 1978.

72. Eisenberg H: How private eyes expose phony malpractice claims. *Medical Economics*, 80, Jul 19, 1982.

73. Ellis A and Harper RA: *A New Guide to Rational Living.* North Hollywood, CA: Wilshire Book Co. Copyright © 1975 by Institute for Rational-Emotive Therapy, New York.

74. Everett JA: *Legal Medicine,* Baltimore: Urban and Schwarzenberg, 1980.

75. Fackelmann K: *Physicians Financial News* 6(12):1, 1988.

76. Fauman B, Terranova J, and Tupin JP: The violent patient. *Patient Care,* August 15, 1987, pages 142–156.

77. *FEDERAL RULES OF CIVIL PROCEDURE.* 1983 Edition. St Paul, Minn.: West Publishing Company

78. Feldman WS: You're sued (damned) if you do and You're sued (damned) if you don't. *Legal Aspects of Medical Practice* 16(9):3, 1988.

79. Ficarra BJ. *Surgical and Allied Malpractice.* Springfield, IL: Charles C. Thomas, 1968.

80. Fine ER: What to do when the doctor's wrong. *Nursing Life*, 22, Nov/Dec 1982.

81. Fish RM and Ehrhardt ME: *Malpractice Depositions, Avoiding the Traps.* Oradell, NJ: 1988.

82. Fish RM and Ehrhardt ME: *Preventing Emergency Malpractice.* Oradell, NJ: Medical Economics Books, 1988.

83. Flamm MB: What law schools teach about doctors. *Medical Economics*, 276, Feb 21, 1983.

84. Fla. lawyers delay ads on pain damage limits. *Physicians Financial News.* 6(19):21, 1988.

85. Flynn TC, Ward RW, and Miller PW: Emergency department thoracotomy. *Annals of Emergency Medicine*, 11:413, Aug 1982.

86. Frew SA, Roush WR, and LaGreca K: COBRA: implications for emergency medicine. *Annals of Emergency Medicine* 17:835–837, 1988.

87. Fuerst M: Lawsuit could mandate screening. *Medical World News*, March 28, 1988, page 19.

88. Fuller BL: One couple's approach to malpractice protection—get a divorce. *Medical Economics*, 130, Oct 16, 1978.

89. Furrow BR: *Malpractice in Psychotherapy.* Lexington, MA: Lexington Books, 1980.

90. Gage LS and Andrulis DP: Our nation's greatest public hospitals. *JAMA* 2576(14): 1942–1943, 1987.

91. Galvin, M: *Media Law, A Legal Handbook for the Working Journalist.* Berkeley, CA: Nolo Press, 1984.

92. Gapen, P: Physician fined for patient dumping draws support from Texas doctors. *Physicians Financial News* 6(19):2, 1988.

93. Garcia RR: What to be ready for if you testify in a child-abuse trial. *Medical Economics*, December 9, 1985, pages 133–143.

94. Garvey MJ: In the middle of the malpractice trial, the plaintiff died. *Medical Economics*, 77, Jan 10, 1983.

95. George JE and Quattrone MS: Hospital liability to nonpatients: A case report. *Journal of Emergency Nursing*, 13(1):52–53, 1987.

96. George JE: Physician responsibility and the law. *Annals of Emergency Medicine* 14(12):1239, 1985.

97. Giacoia, GP: Low Apgar scores and birth asphyxia. *Postgraduate Medicine* 84(2): 77–82, 1988.

98. Gianelli DM: Data bank to chronicle licensing, malpractice actions. *American Medical News*, January 13, 1989, page 13.

99. Gianelli DM: MDs, not parents, end up making 'Baby Doe' decisions—report. *American Medical News*, December 2, 1988, page 1.

100. Ginsburg WH: Could you break the countersuit barrier? *Medical Economics*, Oct 25, 1982.

101. Gold BA and Chapman S: Quiz: What an attorney might tell a patient. *Physician's Managements, 81, Dec 1982.*

102. Goldberg RL: Patients who leave the hospital against medical advice. *Physician & Patient*, 38, Jan 1983.

103. Goldfrank LR: *Toxicologic Emergencies*, 2d Ed. East Norwalk, CT: Appleton-Century-Crofts, 1982.

104. Goldman JK: Lawyer beware! New developments in attorney's liability. *The Journal of the Kansas Bar Association*, page 88–96, Summer, 1981.

105. Goodman CE: Pathophysiology of pain. *Archives of Internal Medicine*, 143:527, Mar 1983.

106. Gordon D and Summer M: The state of the states. *Options*, October 1987, pages 13–18.

107. Gordon, D: See you in court. *Options*, October 1987, pages 8–43.

108. Grateful Med Computer Program: MEDLARS Management Section. National Library of Medicine. Bethesda, MD 20894. 800 638-8480 or in Maryland 301 496-6193.

109. Gray JE: The radiation hazard—let's put it in perspective. *May Clinic Proceedings*, 54:809, Dec 1979.

110. Gray PB: A lawyer who sues other lawyers wins cases but few friends. *The Wall Street Journal*, Wednesday, November 5, 1986, page 1.

111. Gregory DR: Defamation redress and unauthorized suit. *Legal Aspects of Medical Practice* 10(3):2, 1982.

112. Guthrie A. Presly A, Geekie C, and MacKenzie C: The effect of alcohol on memory. In *The Psychopharmacology of Alcohol*, edited by M Sandler. New York: Raven Press, 1980.

113. Halleck SL: *Law in the Practice of Psychiatry, a Handbook for Clinicians*. New York: Plenum Medical Books, 1980.

114. Harney DM: *Medical Malpractice*. Indianapolis: Allen Smith, 1973.

115. Harris JH: High yield criteria and skull radiography. *Journal of the American College of Emergency Physicians* 8(10): 438–404, 1979.

116. Hayt E: *Medical Legal Aspects of Hospital Records*. Berwyn. IL: Physicians Record, 1977.

117. Hemenway C: Reaction mixed on using videotapes as malpractice defense. *Physicians Financial News* 6(2):1, 1988.

118. Henry GL: Legal rounds; Patients who leave against medical advice. *Emergency Medicine*. June 15, 1985.

119. Hersey N: Standards of performance in expanded practice. *American Journal of Nursing*, 72:88, Jan 1972.

120. Hirsh HL: Countersuits: Where angels fear to tread? *Legal Aspects of Medical Practice*, February 1979, p 29–31.

121. Hirsh HL: Dispatching unwanted patients. *Legal Aspects of Medical Practice* 14(1):7, 1986.

122. Hirsch HL: Malpractice crisis of the '80's. Part 3—Professional liability tort reform. *Legal Aspects of Medical Practice* 13(12):2–8, 1985.

123. Hirsh HL: Outrage gains in suits against MD's. *Legal Aspects of Medical Practice*, November 1979, pages 41–42.

124. Hirsh HL: Prescribing drugs to known abusers. *Legal Aspects of Medical Practice* 13(11):2, 1985

125. Hogan D: *The Regulation of Psychotherapists*, Vol 3. Cambridge, MA: Ballinger, 1979.

126. Holder AR: *Medical Malpractice Law*. New York: John Wiley & Sons, 1975.

127. Holder AR: *Medical Malpractice Law*, 2d Ed. New York: John Wiley & Sons, 1978.

128. Holder AR: The physician as fellow servant. *Journal of the American Medical Association*, 223:1203, Mar 5, 1973.

129. Holley CR: *Trial of a Civil Lawsuit*. Norcross, GA: Harrison, 1978.

130. Hollowell EE: Medical staff credentialing. *Legal Aspects of Medical Practice* 15(9):2, 1987.

131. Holoweiko M: How defense attorneys are shooting down hired guns. *Medical Economics*, 78, Nov 23, 1981.

131a.. Holoweiko M: Watch out for these new liability risks. *Medical Economics*, April 18, 1988, page 66–87.

132. Holroyd JC and Brodsky AM: Psychologists' attitudes and practices regarding erotic and nonerotic physical contact with patients. *American Psychologist*, 32:843, Oct 1977.

133. Horsley JE: You don't have to play the other lawyer's game. Page 168 in John M. Curtin: I came to defend my patient. Instead, I helped hang him. *Medical Economics*, December 5, 1988, pages 165–168.

134. Horowitz and Richman: The latest trends in malpractice. *Physician's Management*, January 1987, pages 92–96.

135. Huene DR: I handled my own countersuit—and won. *Medical Economics*, Dec 6, 1982.

136. Hunt RC and Wiley ED: Operation Baxstrom after one year. *American Journal of Psychiatry*, 114:974, 1968.

137. Illinois Department of Registration and Education, *Special Committee on Licensing Examinations: A Blueprint for Occupational Licensing Reform*. Springfield, May 1978.

138. Illinois State Medical Insurance Services: Anatomy of the malpractice claim. *Antidote* 1(1):1, 1983.

139. *(ISMS) Illinois State Medical Society Exchange Commentary*, 3(3), Sep 10, 1980.

140.. Ingram B, Keifetz N, and Watkins T: A stark look at DNR by the book. *Medical Tribune* 30(2):1, 1989.

141. Jankowski CB and Drum DE: Diagnostic correlates of discharges against medical advice. *Archives of General Psychiatry*, 34:153, 1977.

142. Jevicky, JE: Duty to adequately communicate work restrictions to patient and patient's employer. *Legal Aspects of Medical Practice* 16(1):2, 1988.

143. Jevicky JE: Joint liability for patient's death? *Legal Aspects of Medical Practice* 14(11):5, 1986.

144. Jevicky JE and Woodside FC: An error in judgment following standard method: Still liable? *Legal Aspects of Medical Practice* 15(1):5, 1987.

145. Jevicky, JE and Woodside, FC: Expert physician: immune from civil liability for statements in his evaluation report. *Legal Aspects of Medical Practice* (16)7:11, 1988.

146. Jevicky, JE and Woodside FC: Hired examining physician not liable to malpractice. *Legal Aspects of Medical Practice* 15(10):5, 1987.

147. Jevicky JE and Woodside FC: Preventing patient from suing twice for same claim. *Legal Aspects of Medical Practice* 16(2):5, 1988.

148. *JAMA*, 234:534, 1977.

149. *Jonassen O and Barrett JA: Transfer of unstable patients: Dumping or duty? JAMA, 257(11): 1519, 187.*

150. Jonassin O and Barrett JA: Transfer of unstable patients: Dumping or duty? *JAMA*, 257(11):1519, 1987.

151. Kardener SH, Fuller M, and Mensh IN: A survey of physicians' attitudes and practices regarding erotic and nonerotic contact with patients. *American Journal of Psychiatry*, 130:1077, Oct 1973.

152. Karson M: Regulating medical psychotherapists in Illinois—a question of balance. *John Marshall Journal of Practice and Procedure*, 11:601, Spring 1979.

153. Kelly R and Smith BN: Posttraumatic syndrome—another myth discredited. *Journal of the Royal Society of Medicine*, 74:275, 1981

154. Kogan M: the troubles do-it-yourselfers face going to court. *Americans for Legal Reform* 7(3)14–18, 1987.

155. Ladimer I: Medical malpractice arbitration. In *Legal Medicine Annual*, edited by CH Wecht. East Norwalk, CT: Appleton-Century-Crofts, 1978.

156. Ladimer I, Solomon JC, and Mulvihill M: Experience in medical malpractice arbitration. *Journal of Legal Medicine*, 2(4):433, 1981.

157. Letourneav Z: Legal Aspects of the hospital emergency room. *Cleveland Law Review*, 16:60, 1960.

158. Levine JI: I beat a malpractice blackmailer. *Medical Economics*, February 23, 1976, p. 65–71.

Levonian WP: I won my countersuit—but lost most of my practice. *Medical Economics*, March 16, 1987.

159. Lindenmayer JP and Kline NS: The depressed patient. In *Principles and Practice of Emergency Medicine*, edited by GR Schwartz

160. Littenberg B: Aminophylline treatment in severe, acute asthma. *JAMA*, 259(11):1678–1684, 1988.

161. Lucey JF and Danagman B: A reexamination of the role of oxygen in retrolintal fibroplasia. *Pediatrics* 73(1):82–96, 1984.

162. Lydon, DR: Children's rights when parents refuse treatment. *Legal Aspects of Medical Practice*, July 1986, page 4.

163. Lydon DR and Woodside FC: Expert testimony in malpractice lawsuits. *Legal Aspects of Medical Practice* 15(3):7, 1987.

164. Mancini MR and Gale AT: *Emergency Care and the Law*. Germantown, MD: Aspens Systems Corp. 1981.

165. Mandell MS: Ten commandments for defendant-doctors. *Postgraduate Medicine*, 70:303, Dec 1981.

166. Marco CH: Legal checkup. *Physician's Financial News* 6(21):40, 1988.

167. Marco CH: Risk of liability? *Legal Aspects of Medical Practice* 10(1):2, 1982.

168. Margolick DM: Mediation isn't a cure for patients' claims. *National Law Review*, Feb 4, 1980.

169. Martin MJ: Psychiatric aspects of patients with compensation problems. *Psychosomatics, 11:81, 1970.*

170. Marx JA and Rosen P: Current concepts in penetrating abdominal traumas. *Digest of Emergency Medical Care*, 2:2, Oct 1982.

171. McCabe JJ: Defending the orthopedic surgeon involved in the recurrent problems giving rise to malpractice actions in that specialty. In *Medical Malpractice*, by SH MacKauf and H Kolsby. New York: Law Journals Seminar Press, 1981.

172. McCabe JJ: Liability for abandonment. *Legal Aspects of Medical Practice* 13(8):2, 1985.

173. McCabe JJ: What to do if you are sued for malpractice. *Journal of Legal Medicine*, 21, May/Jun, 1974.

174 McGinn PR: Birth defect link to Bendectin not proved, judges say. *American Medical News*, September 16, 1988, page 16.

175. McGinn PR: Good Samaritan Law cover MDs in hospitals.

176. *Medical Liability Monitor*: "Deep-pockets" theory operates in $4-million case: two MDs, hospital pay up: "bare" doctors don't, 6(12):1, Dec 1981.

177. *Medical Liability Monitor*: Hospitals must treat, feed all defective infants or lose funds, 8(3):7, Mar 1983.

178. Meire HB, Farrant P, and Wilkins RA: Place of ultrasound and radiography in obstetrics. *British Medical Journal*, 1:882, 1978.

179. Meisel A: The "exceptions" to the informed consent doctrine: Striking a balance between competing values in medical decision making. *Wisconsin Law Review* 1979, 412–488.

180. Meyer H: HCQIA sets criteria, due process steps for peer review. *American Medical News*, May 27, 1988.

181. Meyer H: Lawyer: Suits blaming HMO controls for malpractice may have jury appeal. *American Medical News*, July 29, 1988, page 1.

182. Milberg AS and Shain H: *How to Do Your Own Bankruptcy.* New York: McGraw Hill, 1978.

183. Miller DS and Butler EF: Legal aspects of physician-patient communication. *Journal of Family Practice*, 15:1131, 1982.

184. Mohammed MD: Patients' understanding of written health information. *Nursing Research*, 13:100, 1964.

185. Mole RH: Radiation effects on pre-natal development and their radiological significance. *British Journal of Radiology*, 52:89, 1979.

186. Montemarana VA: Euthanasia and the law. *Newsweek*, 83:45, Jan 28, 1974.

187. Montgomery WH, Donegan J, and McIntyre KM: Cardiopulmonary resuscitation and emergency cardiac care. *JAMA* 255(21):2905, 1986.

188. Morrill AE: *Trial Diplomacy.* Chicago: Court Practice Institute, 1973.

189. Morris WO: *Dental Litigation.* Charlottesville, VA: The Miche Co, 1977.

190. *New England Journal of Medicine* 317:426, 1987.

191. New York State Court of Appeals opinions concerning: in the matter of John Storar, in the matter of Father Philip K Eichner. *New York Law Journal*, 185(63):1, 4–6, 1981.

'192. Niswander K, Henson G, and Elbourne D: Adverse outcome of pregnancy and the quality of obstetric care. *Lancet* 2:827–831, 1984.

193. Northcutt N: *Adult Performance Level Study*, Austin, TX: University of Texas, 1975.

194. O'Brien C: Full immunity for peer review suffers a blow...Supreme Court reverses Patrick. *American Medical News*, May 27, 1988, pages 1, 22.

195. O'Keeffe DF and Conway GL: Physician discipline professional conduct. *New York State Journal of Medicine*, March 1988, pages 146–148.

196. Palmisano DJ: Key malpractice prevention strategies. *Physician's Management*, May 1986, pages 128–137.

197. Parker ES and Noble EP: Alcohol consumption and cognitive functioning in social drinkers. *Journal of Studies of Alcohol*, 38(7): 1224, Jul 1977.

198. Parker MA: Risk of malpractice escalates in breast cancer screening. *Diagnostic Imaging*, July 1988, pages 82–85.

199. Patel R, Das M, Palazzolo M, Ansari A, and Balasubramaniam S: Myoglobinuric acute renal failure in phencyclidine overdose, report of observations in eight cases. *Annals of Emergency Medicine*, 9(11):549, Nov 1980.

200. Peck L and King JN: Increasing patient compliance with prescriptions. *Journal of the American Medical Association*, 248:2874, Dec 3, 1982.

210. Perr IN: Blood alcohol levels and "diminished capacity." *Journal of Legal Medicine*, 28, Apr 1975.

202. *Personal Injury Newsletter*: Locality rule inapplicable to nationally certified medical specialists, 21(14), Jan 9, 1978.

203. *Personal Injury Newsletter*: Michigan recognizes child's cause of action for loss of jparental consortium, 25(1), Jul 6, 1981.

204. *Personal Injury Newsletter*: Physician can sue drug manufacturer failing to inform about the hazards of prescription drugs, 25(4), Aug 17, 1981.

205. *Physician's Financial News*: $3.4 million malpractice award adds up to zero. April 30, 1988, page 21.

206. Pinkney DS: Drug-addicted newborns increasing; MDs, hospitals face care dilemma. *American Medical News*, February 3, 1989, page 2.

207. Pinkney DS: N.Y. hospitals spilling over. *American Medical News*, February 5, 1988, page 1.

208. Plum F and Posner JB: *Diagnosis of Stupor and Coma*. Philadelphia: FA Davis, 1972.

209. Prosser WL: *Handbook of the Law of Torts*. St Paul: West, 1964.

210. Putka G: After the cemetery, grieving pet owners head for the courts. *The Wall Street Journal*, Wednesday, August 24, 1988, page 1.

211. Rasinski-Gregory, D: Duty to warn is not duty to control. *Legal Aspects of Medical Practice* 13(9):8, 1985.

212. Redfield RA: *Cross Examination and the Witness.* Mundelein, IL: Callaghan & Co. 1963.

213. Robinson D, Abramson NS, Grenvik A, and Meisel A: Medicolegal standards for critical care medicine. *Critical Care Medicine,* 8:524, Sep 1980.

214. Robitscher J: The uses and abuses of psychiatry, lecture 1. *Journal of Psychiatry and Law,* 333, Fall 1977.

215. Rosenberg AR and Goldsmith LS: *Malpractice Made Easy.* New York: Books for Industry Inc, 1976.

216. Rosenberg L: Don't count on a malpractice settlement to protect you. *Medical Economics,* December 10, 1984, pages 62–70.

217. Roth LH, Meisel A, Lidz CW: Tests of competency to consent to treatment. *American Journal of Psychiatry,* 134(3):279, 1977.

218. Rothblatt HB: *Handling Health Practitioner Cases.* Chapter 28: Physicians' Countersuits and Defamation, page 407–423. The Lawyers Co-Operative Publishing Co. Rochester New York and Bancroft-Whitney Co. San Francisco, California, 1983.

219. Rothman DA and Rothman NL: *The Professional Nurse and the Law.* Boston: Little Brown & Co, 1977.

220. Rothman SA: Fighting the system for the sake of your patients. *Private Practice,* September 1987, pages 9–13.

221. Rubsamen DS: Carriers urged to aid peer review by closing antitrust coverage gap. *Physicians Financial News* 6(12):10, 1988.

222. Rubsamen DS: 'Cause" was vital issue in decisions awarding $8.4 million vs. no damages. *Physicians Financial News,* June 15, 1986, pages 18–19.

223. Rubsamen DS: Claims-made malpractice insurance—A look at some judicial skepticism. *Physician Financial News* 7(5):37, 1989.

224. Rubsamen DS: Delay in treating epidural bleed leads to $5 million liability verdict. *Physicians Financial News* 6(19):21, 1988.

225. Rubsamen DS: 'Deep pockets rule change in suits may backfire on doctors in California. *Physicians Financial News* 4(14):1, 1986.

226. Rubsamen DS: Failure to execute proper peer review costs hospital $600,000 judgment. *Physician's Financial News,* October 15, 1987, page 21.

227. Rubsamen DS: Objectivity of binding arbitration can be advantageous to the defense. page 28 *Physicians Financial News,* page 28.

228. Rubsamen DS: Study of perinatal injuries points to ways of reducing the tragic toll. *Physicians Financial News.* 6(5):25, 1988.

229. Rubsamen DS: Unjustified punitive damages claims restricted by new California Law. *Physicians Financial News,* January 15, 1988, page 33.

230. Rubsamen DS: Unusual California case results in $19.9 million award to plaintiff. *Physician's Financial News,* October 15, 1988, page 23.

231. Rubsamen DS: Who pays when doctor suffers loss after insurer refuses a settlement? *Physicians Financial News,* January 30, 1987, page 20.

232. Rumack B: Phencyclidine overdose, an overview. *Annals of Emergency Medicine,* 9(11):595, 1980.

233. Russell O: *Freedom to Die—Moral and Legal Aspects of Euthanasia.* New York: Human Sciences Press, 1975.

234. Rust M: S. Fla. Tort reform: too little, too late? *American Medical News,* May 20, 1988, page 1.

235. Sachs T: Proof of the corpus delicti by the use of extrajudicial confessions. *Michigan Law Review,* 48:1197, 1950.

236. Sanbar SS: Myocardial infarction: Loss of a chance of survival. *Legal Aspects of Medical Practice* 16(9):1, 1988.

237. Sawyer TD and Picken M: Defending the hospital emergency room. *For the Defense,* Sep/Oct 1980.

238. Schlauch RW, Reich P, and Kelly MJ: Leaving the hospital against medical advice. *New England Journal of Medicine,* 300(1):22, Jan 4, 1979.

239. Schutte James E: The malpractice crisis, up close and ugly. *Medical Economics,* February 15, 1988, pages 175–182.

240. Schutz BM: *Legal Liability in Psychotherapy.* San Francisco: Jossey Bass, 1982.

241. Schwartz HI: Legal and ethical pitfalls in family practice psychiatry. *American Family Physician* 35(5):103–108, 1987.

242. Seibert JJ, Bryant E, Lowe BA, and Fiser R: Low Efficiency radiography of children. *AJR* 134(6): 1219–1223, 1980.

243. Shandell RE: *The Preparation and Trial of Medical Malpractice Cases.* New York: Law Journal Seminars Press, 1981a.

244. Shandell RE: Acute abdomen problems of differential diagnosis. In *Medical Malpractice,* by SH Mackauf and H Kolsby. New York: Law Journal Seminars PRess, 1981b.

245. Shaw A, Randolph JG, and Manard B: Ethical issues in pediatric surgery, a nationwide survey of pediatricians and pediatric surgeons. *Pediatrics,* 60:588, 1977.

246. Shemonsky NK: Alabama Supreme Court expands hospital liability. *Legal Aspects of Medical Practice* 13(8):3, 1985.

247. Shemonsky NK: American Heart Association's ACLS guidelines are not controlling. *Legal Aspects of Medical Practice* 16(3):13, 1988.

248. Shemonsky NK and Flannery FT: ED employment arrangements. *Legal Aspects of Medical Practice* 15(2): 7, 1987.

249. Shemonsky NK: Fractured jaw not a foreseeable consequence of misdiagnosis of syphilis. *Legal Aspects of Medical Practice* 16(4):10, 1988.

250. Shemonsky NK and Flannery FT: Medical peer review activity is protected. *Legal Aspects of Medical Practice* 16(2):5, 1988.

251. Shemonsky NK: MDs admission of negligence replaces expert witness requirement. *Legal Aspects of Medical Practice,* 14(6): 2–3, 1986.

252. Shemonsky NK: Missouri Supreme court holds peer review committee records are discoverable. *Legal Aspects of Medical Practice,* 13(10):6, 1985.

253. Silverman TN: Best ways to protect your profesional and personal assets. *Physician's Management,* October, 1988, pages 77–97.

254. Silvers WL and Harkness RM: *I Filed Bankruptcy and I'm Glad I Did.* Muncie IN: Bryden Press, 1979.

255. Singer and Giampietro, The countersuit, y, *Litigation* 18, 1979.

256. Slavicek JJ and Berger E: *The Simplified Guide to Personal Bankruptcy.* New York: Crown, 1975.

257. Slocum K: Florida lawyer wins big malpractice suits, and loves doing it. *Wall Street Journal*, January 11, 1988, page 1.

258. Smith HW: Some medico-legal aspects of pain, suffering and mental anguish in American law and culture. In *Pain and Suffering*, edited by L Crue. Springfield, IL: CC Thomas, 1970.

259. Smith WB: Hospital Liability for physician negligence. *JAMA* 251(4):447–448, 1984.

260. Snevel, HF: Doctors get a new weapon. *Legal Aspects of Medical Practice*, September, 1978, pages 58–59.

261. Steinberg C: Sales of "umbrella" insurance rise as personal liability cases grow. *Physicians Financial News*, page 8, April 30, 1987.

262. Stern DN: Causes of attorney malpractice claims. In Pfennigstorf, W: Types and causes of lawyer' professional liability claims: the search for facts. American Bar Foundation Research Journal 253:255–302, 1908.

263. Strauss S: *The Pharmacist and the Law.* Baltimore: Williams & Wilkins, 1980.

264. Strodel RC: Attorney-physician professional relationships. In *Medical Evidence*. Springfield, IL: Institute for Continuing Legal Education, 1980.

265. Suber DG and Tabor WJ: Withholding a life-sustaining treatment for the terminally-ill, incompetent patient—who decides? Part 2. *Journal of the American Medical Association*, 248(19):2431, Nov 19, 1982.

266. Swartz HM and Reichling BA: Hazards of radiation exposure for pregnant women. *Journal of the American Medical Association*, 239(18) 1907, May 5, 1978.

267. Tagliaferro P: Malpractice—another perspective. *New York State Journal of Medicine*, 80:1215, 1980.

268. Taub S: Malpractice countersuits: succeeding at last? *Law, Medicine, and Health Care*, December, 1981 pages 17–20.

269. *Textbook of Advanced Cardiac Life Support.* Dallas: American Heart Association, 1981.

270. Todd JS: Professional liability insurance: a long way to go. *Journal of the Florida Medical Association*, 212, Mar 1982a.

271. Todd JS: MDs hit, attorneys defend tort system, contingency fees. *American Medical News*, Dec 3, 1982b.

272. Tougher COBRA fines may increase documentation. *Hospital Risk Management* 10(4):41–44, 1988.

273. Trafford LP: Career protection. *Ohio State Medical Journal*, 187, Mar 1982.

274. Tyler JS: A verbal promise to cure may be a debt unpaid. *Legal Aspects of Medical Practice* 16(2):6, 1988.

275. Van Pernis PA: *The Physician's Liability in Patient Care.* Chicago: Illinois State Medical Society, 1976.

276. Waggoner DM, Jackson EB, and Kern DE: Physician influence on patient compliance: a clinical trial. *Annals of Emergency Medicine,* 10(7):348, Jul 1981.

277. Walsh CH and Walker M: Shield yourself from malpractice suits. *Physician's Management,* 293, Feb 1983.

278. Waltz JR: The rise and gradual fall of the locality rule in medical malpractice litigation. *DePaul Law Review,* 18:408, 1969.

279. Warnes H: The traumatic syndrome. *Canadian Psychiatric Association Journal,* 17:391, 1972.

280. Warren DG: Problems in Hospital Law. Germantown, MD: Aspen Systems Corp, 1978.

281. Werber R: The duty to report a patient's condition to medical authorities. *Physician's Management,* 128, Jan 1983.

282. Where peer review led to guns, burglary, and lawsuits. *Medical Economics,* March 17, 1988.

283. Whitty CW and Zangwill OL: *Amnesia—Clinical, Psychological and Medicolegal Aspects.* Woburn, MA: Butterworth, 1977.

284. Who's best to handle malpractice defense? *Medical World News,* July 14, 1986, pages 12–14.

285. Williams EH: *The Doctor in Court.* Baltimore: Williams & Wilkins, 1929.

286. Wise MG: Posttraumatic stress disorder—the human reaction to catastrophe. *Drug Therapy,* 210, Mar 1983.

287. Woodside FC: Physician's advocate. *Legal Aspects of Medical Practice* 14(11):5, 1986.

288. Yochelson L: Traumatic neurosis. In *Reading in Law and Psychiatry,* edited by RC Allen. Baltimore: John Hopkins University Press, 452, 1975.

289. Zuck TR: Adverse reactions to blood transfusions. In *Current Therapy,* edited by HF Conn. Philadelphia: WB Saundres, 1981.

Among other references that can help you prepare and defend you case against a malpractice charge are those listed in the Medical/Legal/Personal/Injury Directory published by Matthew Bender & Company (P.O. Box 989, Department DM, Albany, NY 12201).

Case citations

The following citations point to information about court cases that may be similar to your own. Although discussions of cases in this book are brief, limited to the issue in question, and incomplete, the terms cited can help you find more thorough discussions and summaries by following the directions given below.

Before finalizing your verdict on any of the suits noted in the text and annotated below, remember that the "v." can mean another "view" as well as "versus." There are two sides to every story. So when you look up a case, withhold your judgment on the people and evidence cited until you have examined the court records for further detail. Remember that people are accused of, tried for, and convicted of things they do not do.

Case descriptions are located in federal, state, and regional books called reporters. They detail evidence, defenses, and decisions. The citations listed here tell you how to use the reporters, following the standard legal format (some citations given two references to the same case, separated by a comma):

Jones v. Smith	**514**	**SW 2d**	**345**	**(Mo Ct App**	**1978)**
Parties	Volume	Reporter	Page	State Court	Date

Here are the abbreviations for cited reporters you can find in a law library (others are listed in the back of law dictionaries):

Abbreviation	Reporter
A&A 2d	Atlantic Reporter
ALR & ALR 2d & ALR 3d	American Law Reports Annotated
ALR Fed	American Law Reports, Federal
Cal Rptr	California Reporter
F & F 2d	Federal Reporter
F Supp	Federal Supplement
Ill Dec	Illinois Decisions
L Ed & L Ed 2d	Lawyers' Edition, US Supreme Court Reports
Misc 2d	Miscellaneous Reports (New York)
NE & NE 2d	North Eastern Reporter
NW & NW 2d	North Western Reporter
NYS & NYS 2d	New York Supplement
P & P 2d	Pacific Reporter
S Ct	Supreme Court Reporter (West)
So & So 2d	South Eastern Reporter
SW & SW 2d	South Western Reporter
US	US Reports
USLW	US Law Week

1. *Abraham v. Zaslow* ,no 245862 (Cal Sup Ct. Jun 30, 1972).
2. *Adams v. Veggeberg* , Dist Ct Harris Co (Tex 1981).
3. *Aengst v. Board of Medical Quality Assurance* , 167 Cal Rptr 796 (Cal App 1980).
4. *Aetna Casualty & Surety Co v. Evers* , 590 F 2d 600 (CA La 1979).
5. *Albritton v. Bossier City Hospital Commission* , 271 So 2d 313 (La 1972).
6. *Alvis v. Ribar* , 85 Ill 2d 1, 421 NE 2d 886 (1981).
7. *Amdur v. Zim Israel Navigation Co* , 310 F Supp 1033 (SD NY 1969).
8. *Anclote Manor Foundation v. Wilkinson* , 263 So 2d 256 (App Ct 1972).
9. *Arana v. Koerner* , 735 S.W.2d 729 (Mo. Ct. of App., July 14, 1987; rehearing and/or transfer to Mo. Sup. Ct. denied, Sept. 1, 1987).
10. *Arnold v. Loose* , 352 F 2d 959 (3d Cir 1965).
11. *Arthur v. St Peters Hospital* , 405 A 2d 443 (NJ 1979).
12. *Bach v. Long Island Jewish Hospital* , 267 NYS 2d 289 (NY 1966).
13. *Badeaux v. East Jefferson General Hospital* , 364 So 2d 248 (La App 1978).
14. *Bainhauer v Manoukian* , 520 A.2d 1154 (N.J. Super. Ct., App. Div., Jan 20, 1987).
15. *Baird v. Sickler* , 69 Ohio St 2d 652, 433 NE 2d 593 (Oh 1982).
16. *Barber v. Reiking* , 411 P 2d 861 (Wash 1966).

17. *Baxstrom v. Herald* , 383 US 197 (1966).

18. *Berger v. Weber* , 303 NW 2d 424 (Mich 1981).

18a. *Berlin v. Nathan* , 64 Ill App 3d 940, 62 L Ed 2d 390, 100 S Ct 470

19. *Bing v. Thunig* , 163 NY 2d 3, 11 (NY 1957).

20. *Bleiler v. Bodnar* , 477 N.Y.S. 2d 780, 102 A.S.2d 266.

21. *Bowman v. Davis* , 356 NE 2d 496 (Ohio 1976).

22. *Brewington v. Raksakulthi* , 584 SW 2d 112 (Mo App 1979).

23. *Brisco v. LaHue* , 460 U.S. 325 1983.

24. *Brown v. Decatur Memorial Hospital* , 393 NE 2d 84 (Ill App 1979).

25. *Brown v. Guy* , 144 Cal App 2d 659, 301 P 2d 413 (1956).

26. *Brown v. Moore* , 141 F Supp 816 (WD Pa 1956), 247 F 2d 711 (Ed Cir 1957).

27. *Bryant v. St Paul Fire & Marine Insurance Co* , 272 So 2d 448 (La App 1973).

28. *Buckner v. Physicians Protective Trust Fund* , 376 So 2d 461 (Fla App 1979).

29. *Bull v. McCuskey* , 615 P.2d 957 Nev 1980.

30. *Burciaga v. St. John's Hospital* , 232 Cal. Rptr. 75 (cal. Ct. of App., Dec. 2, 1986).

31. *Burks v. The Christ Hospital* , 249 NE 2d 829 (Ohio 1969).

32. *Bussanich v. Douglas* , 733 P.2d 644; Ariz. Ct. of App., Nov 18, 1986; review denied, Feb. 24, 1987.

33. *Campa v. Sellers* , 292 SE 2d 532 (Ga App. Jun 21, 1982).

34. *Campbell v. Emma Laing Stevens Hospital* , 499 N.Y.S. 2d 993 (N.Y. Sup. Ct., App. Div., March 20, 1986).

35. *Capan v. Divine Providence Hospital* , 430 A 2d 647 (Pa Sup, Oct 10, 1980; reargument denied, June 12, 1981).

36. *Carrasco v. Bankoff* , 33 Cal Rptr 673 (1953).

37. *Cathey v. Williams* , 718 S.W.2d 98 (Ark. Sup. Ct., Oct 17, 1986).

38. *Cerol v. Arena* , 337 N.W.2d 618 (Wis. Ct. of App., Oct 2, 1985).

39. *Chapman v. Carlson* , 240 So 2d 263 (Miss 1970).

40. *Ciaccio v. Housman* , 412 NYS 2d 557 (NY 1979).

41. *Ciprut v. Moore* , 540 F Supp 817 (DC Pa, Sep 18, 1981).

42. *Clark v. Grigson* , 579 SW 2d 263 (Tx Civ App 1979).

43. *Clarke v. Hoek* , 219 Cal. Rptr 845 1985.

44. *Cobbs v. Grant* , 8 Cal 3d 229, 502 P 2d 1 (1972).

45. *Cockrum v. Baumgartner* , 425 NE 2d 968 (Ill App 1981).

46. *Coffran v. Hitchcock Clinic Inc* , 683 F 2d 5 (CA 1 NH, Jun 29, 1982).

47. *Cohen v. State of New York* , 382 NYS 2d 128 (1976).

48. *Cohen v. Weber* , 36 AD 2d 921, 320 NYS 2d 759 (1971).

49. *Correll v. Goodfellow* , 255 Iowa 1237, 125 NW 2d 745 (1964).

50. *Crouch v. Most* , 432 P 2d 250 (NM 1967).

51. *Damsker v. Berger* , 506 N.Y.S.2d 354 (N.Y Sup. Ct., App. Div., Sept. 15, 1986).

52. *(Darling v. Charleston Community Hospital 211 NE2d 2533; Ill 1965).*

53. *Darling v. Charleston Community Memorial Hospital* , 200 NE 2d 149, 211 NE 2d 253 (1965); 33 Ill 2d 326, 211 NE 2d 253 (1965); cert. denied, 383 US 946 (1966).

54. *Davis v. Marshall* , 693 SW 2d 359 (Tex App 1980).

55. *Dickinson v. Mason* , 18 Utah 2d 383, 423 P 2d 663 (1967).

56. *Dincau v. Tamayose* , 182 Cal Rptr 855 (Cal App. May 18, 1982).

57. *Dini v. Naiditch* , 20 Il 2d 406, 170 Ne 2d 881 (1960), 86 ALR 2d 1184 (1962).

58. *Doctors Hospital Inc v. Kovats* , 494 P 2d 389 (Ariz App 1972).

59. *Drago v. Buonaguiro* , No. 561 (N.Y., Dec 20, 1978), 404 N.Y.S.2d 250 1978.

60. *Embrey v. Borough of West Mifflin* , 257, 390 A 2d 765, 771 (Pa Super Ct 1978).

61. *Evans v. Newark-Wayne Community Hospital* , 316 NYS 2d 447 (App Div 1970).

62. *Felice v. St Agnes Hospital* , 65 App Div 2d 388, 411 NYS 2d 901 (1978).

63. *Ferrara v. Galluchio* , 5 NY 2d 16, 152 NE 2d 249 (1958).

64. *Ferriter v. O'Connell's Sons Inc* , 413 NE 2d 690 (Mass 1980).

65. *Fitzgerald v. Caplan* , 362 S. E. 2d 103 (Ga. Ct. of App., Oct 5, 1987); rehearing denied, Oct 19, 1987; cert. denied (Ga. Sup. Ct, Nov 19, 1987).

66. *Fjerstad v. Sioux Valley Hospital* , 291 NW 2d 786 (SD, Apr 30, 1980, commented on in American Medical News,, Oct 10, 1980).

67. *Flannery v. President and Directors of Georgetown College* , 679 F2d 960 (CA DC, Jun 8, 1982).

68. *Foil v. Ballinger* , 601 P2d 144 (Utah 1979).

69. *Forlaw v. Fitzer* , 456 So.2d 432s (Fla. Supr. Ct 1984).

70. *Foster v. Harris* , 633 SW 2d 304 (Tenn, May 17, 1982).

71. *Gates v. Jensen* , 595 P 2d 919 (Wash 1979).

72. *Gonzales v. Nork* , Cal. App Supp Sacramento County (Nov 27, 1973); 60 Cal App 3d 728 (1976).

73. *Gooden v. Tips* , 651 S.W.wd 364 (Tex 1983).

74. *Graham v. Roberts* , 441 F 2d 995 (DC Cir 1970).

75. *Graze v. Lawless* , 389 NE 2d 957 (Ill App 1979).

76. *Grindstaff v. Tygett* , 698 S.W.2d 33 1985.

77. *Gross v. Haight* , 496 So. 2d 1225 (La. Ct. of App., Oct 14, 1986.

78. *Hammer v. Rosen* , App Div 2d 216, 181 NYS 2d 805 (1959); 7 NYS 2d 376, 198 NYS 2d 65 (1960).

79. *Hannola v. City of Lakewood* , 426 ME 2d 1187 ((Ohio App. March 27, 1980).

80. *Hansch v. Hackett* , 66 P 2d 1129 (1937).

81. *Hardy v. Brantley* , 417 So.2d 358 (Miss. Sup. Ct. 1985).

82. *Hareng v. Blanke* , 279 NW 2d 437 (Wis 1979).

83. *Hasenei v. US* , 541 F Supp 999 (DC Md, April 8, 1982).

84. *Heller v. Medine* , 50 App Div 2d 831 (NY 1975).

85. *Helling v. Carey* , 519 P 2d 981 (Wash 1974).

86. *Henderson v. Milobsky* , 595 F 2d 654 (CA DC 1979).

87. *Hensley v. Heavrin* , 282 S.E.2d 854 1981.

88. *Holloway v. Robertson* , 500 So 2d 1056 (Ala. Sup. Ct., Oct. 31, 1986; rehearing denied, Dec. 5 1986).

89. *Honey v. Barnes Hospital* , 708 S.W.2d 686 (Mo. Ct of App Feb 18, 1986; rehearing of transfer denied April 1, 1986; transfer denied, May 13, 1986).

90. *Huene v. Carnes* , 175 Cal Rptr 374 (1981).

91. *Jane Doe v. Victory Memorial Hospital* , et al., No 86 CV 107 (Chippewah Co., Wisconsin reported Nov. 30, 1987).

92. *Jefferson v. Griffin Spalding County Hospital* , 247 Ga 86, 274 SE 2d 457 (1981).

93. *Johnson v. St Paul Mercury Insurance Co* , 219 So 2d 524 (La App 1969).

94. *Johnston v. Black Company* , 91 P 2d 921 (Cal 1939).

95. *Jones v. Smith* , 278 So 2d 239 (Fla 1973).

96. *Jones v. Walgreen Co* , 265 Ill App 308 (1932).

97. *Jutzi v. County of Los Angeles* , 242 Cal Rptr. 74 (Cal. Ct. of App., Nov. 24, 1987).

98. *Roger N. Kahn, M.D. v. Sheldon O. Burman* , M.D. 763 F. Supp 210 (E.D. Mich. 1987).

99. *Kaplan v. Central Med Group of Brooklyn* , 419 NYS 2d 750 (NY App Div 1979).

100. *Kelly v. Carroll* , 36 Wash 2d 482, 219 P 2d 79 (1950).

101. *Killgore v. Argonaut-Southwest Insurance Co* , 216 So 2d 108 (La App 1968).

102. *King v. Williams* , 279 SE 2d 618 (SC 1981).

103. *La Caze v. Collier* , 416 So 2d 619 (La App, Jun 15, 1982).

104. *Landeros v. Flood* , 131 Cal Rptr 69, 551 P 2d 389 (1976).

105. *Lehman v. Stephens* , 499 N.E. 2d 103 (Ill. App. Ct., Oct 9, 1986).

106. *Lieberman v. Employers Insurance of Wausau* , 407 A 2d 1256 (NJ App 1979).

107. *Lomayestewa v. Our Lady of Mercy Hospital* , no 78-SC-536-D (Ky Oct 1979).

108. *Lowry v. Henry Mayo Newhall Memorial Hospital* , 185 (Cal. App. 3d 188, 1986).

109. *Luka v. Lowrie* , 36 NW 1106 (Mich 1912).

110. *Malone v. City of Seattle* , 600 P 2d 647 (Wash App 1979).

111. *Maloney v. Wake Hospital Systems Inc* , 262 SE 2d 680 (NC App 1980).

112. *Matts v. Homsi* , 308 NW 2d 284 (Mich App 1981).

113. *Mays v. U.S.* , 806 F.2d 976 (C.A.10, Col., Dec 5, 1986).

114. *McGee v. US Fidelity & Guaranty Co* , 53 F2d 953 (1st Cir 1931).

115. *McHugh v. Audet* , 72 F Supp 394 (DC Pa 1947).

116. *McIntosh v. Milano* , 403 A 2d 500 (NJ 1979).

117. *McKenna v. Cedars of Lebanon Hospital* , 155 Cal Rptr 631 (Cal App 1979).

118. *Medical Center Hospital Authority v. Andrews* , 292 SE 2d 197 (Ga App, Jun 9, 1982).

119. *Mehlman v. Powerll* , 378 A.2d 1121 (Ct. App. Md. 1977).

120. *Meiselman v. Crown Heights Hospital* , 34 NE 2d 367 (1941).

121. *Mitchell v. Caraway Methodist Medical Center* , 507 So. 2d 498 (Alabama 1987).

122. *Mitchell County Hospital v. Joiner* , 189 SE2d 412 (Ga 1972).

123. *Ferguson v. Gonyaw* , 236 NW2d 543, 550 (Mich App 1976).

124. *Moore v. Francisco* , 583 P 2d 391 (Kan App 1978).

125. *Moore v. Webb* , 345 SW 2d 239 (Mo App 1961).

126. *Morrison v. MacNamara* , 407 A 2d 555 (DC App 1979).

127. *M.S.S. v. Demato* , 503 So.2d 1384 (Fla. Dist Ct. of App., March 19, 1987).

128. *Muller v. Likoff* , 225 111 310 A 2d 303 (Pa Sup 1973).

129. *Murray v. McFarland* , 3d Dist Ct No 170920 Salt Lake County (Utah 1969).

130. *MW v. Jewish Hospital Association of St. Louis* , 637 SW 2d 74 (Mo App, May 4, 1982; *rehearing denied*, Jun 18, 1982; *transfer denied*, Sep 13, 1982).

131. *Nelson v. Miller* , et al. 227 (Kan 271 P.2d 1980).

132. *Nevils v. Aberle* , 730 P.2d 729 (Wash. Ct. of App., Dec. 29, 1986).

133. *Newberry v. Tarvin* , 594 SW 2d 204 (Tex Civ App 1980).

134. *Oksenholt v. Lederle Labs* , 625 P2d 1357 (Or App 1981).

135. *O'Neill v. Montfiore Hospital* , 202 N.Y.S.2d. 436 (Supreme court, Appellate Division, 1960).

136. *Ooft v. City of New York* , 429 NYS 2d 376 (NY 1980).

137. *Patrich v. Menorah Medical Center* , 636 S.W.2d 135 (Mo. Ct. of App., June 15, 1982).

138. *Pederson v. Dumochel* , 431 P 2d 973 (Wash 1967).

139. *Peerman v. Sidicane* , 605 S.W.2d 242 (Tenn. App. 1980).

140. *Perkins v. Fitwell Artificial Limb Co* , 514 P 2d 811 (Utah 1973).

141. *Petyan v. Ellis* , 510 A.2d 1337 (Conn. Sup. Ct June 17, 1986).

142. *Pierce v. De Gracia* , 431 NE 2d 768 (Ill App 1982).

143. *Pierce v. State* , 254 SE 2d 838 (Ga 1979).

144. *Pizzalotte v. Wilson* , 411 So 2d 1150 (La App, March 2, 1982; *rehearing denied*, April 13, 1982).

145. *Polischeck v. US* , 535 F Supp 1261 ED (Pa 1982).

146. *Posey v. Medical Center West, Inc.* , 350 S.E.2d 259 (Ga. Ct. of App., Oct 9, 1986; *rehearing denied*, Oct. 27, 1986).

147. *Priest v. Lindig* , 583 P 2d 173 (Alaska 1978).

148. *Priolo v. Baxter* , no 187882 Cal App Supp Sacramento County (1971, reported in *The Citation*, 24:92, January 1, 1972).

149. *Purcell v. Zimbelman* , 500 P2d 225 (Arizona 1972).

150. *Racer v. Utterman* , 629 S.W.2d 387 (Mo. Ct. of App., Sept 22, 1981; transfer denied, Jan 18, 1982).

151. *Ravenis v. Detroit General Hospital* , 234 NW 2d 411 (Mich App 1975).

152. *Reese v. Nelson* , 598 F 2d 822 (CA Pa 1979).

153. *Reid v. Pratt* , Kennebec Journal, Augusta, Me (Aug 14, 1971, reported in *The Citation*, Jan 1, 1972).

154. *Reiser v. Prunty* , 717 p.2d 538 (Mont. Sup Ct., Oct 30, 1986).

155. *Richardson v. Lutheran Hospital of Brooklyn* , 417 NYS 2d 526 (NY App Div 1979).

156. *Richardson v. Richardson-Merrell* , Inc., 649 F. Supp 799 (D.C., Dec 19, 1986).

157. *Rizzo v. Edwards Laboratories* , NY App Div (Oct 1979).

158. *Roark v. St Paul Fire and Marine Insurance Co* , 415 So 2d 295 (La App, May 10, 1982).

159. *Robak v. US, 658 F 2d 471 (Ill 7th Cir 1981).*

160. *Roberts v. Wood* , 206 F Supp 579 (SD Ala 1962).

161. *Rogers v. Robson* , Masters, Ryan, Brummund, and Belom, 392 NE 2d 1365–1373 (Ill App 1979), *affirmed* 407 NE 2d 47 (1980).

162. *Ross v. Schubert* , 388 NE 2d 623 (Ind App 1979).

163. *Roy v. Hartogs* , 85 Misc 2d 891, 2d 587 NYS (1976).

164. *Salonia v. Samsoi Homes* , Inc, 507 N.Y.S.2d 186 (N.Y. Sup. Ct, App. Div., Oct 20, 1986).

165. *Samii v. Bay State Medical Center Inc* , 395 NE 2d 455 (Mass App 1979).

166. *Sandhofer v. Abbott-Northwestern Hospital* , 283 Northwestern Hospital, 283 NW 2d 362 (Minn 1979).

167. *Satz v. Perlmutter* , 362 So 2d 169 (Fla 1979), *affirmed* 379 So 2d 359 (1980).

168. *Schliesman v. Fisher* , 97 Cal App 3d 83, 158 Cal Rptr 527 (1979).

169. *Schroeder v. Perkel* , 87 NJ 53, 432 A 2d 834 (1981).

170. *Schuster v. US News and World Report Inc* , 459 F Supp 973 (DC Minn 1978).

171. *Seibel v. Kemble* , 631 P 2d 173 (Haw, July 13, 1981).

172. *Shulz v. Rice* , 809 F.2d 643 (C.A. 10, Kan., Dec 19, 1986).

173. *Siegel v. Mt. Sinai Hospital of Cleveland* , 62 Ohio App 12 (1978).

174. *Skelton v. Druid City Hospital Baord* , 459 So.2d 818 (Sept 1984).

175. *Smith v. Courter* , 575 SW 2d 199 (Mo App 1978).

176. *Smith v. United States* , 58 7 F 2d 1013 (CA Pa 1978).

177. *South Highlands Informary v. Camp* , 180 So 2d 904, 907 (Ala 1965).

178. *Speed v. State* , 240 NW 2d 901 (Iowa 1976).

179. *Stacy v. Williams* , 253 KY 353, 69 SW 2d 697 (1934).

180. *Stafford v. Louisiana State U.* , 448 So. 2d 852 (La Ct of App, March 26, 1984).
181. *St. paul Insurnace Companies v. Talladega Nursing Home Inc* , 607 F 2d 631 (Ca Ala 1979).
182. *State, Cardinal Glennon Memorial Hospital v. Gaertner* , 583 SW 2d 107 (Mo 1979).
183. *State v. Perricone* , 37 NJ 463 (1962).
184. *Stogsdill v. Mannor Convalescent Home Inc* , 35 Ill App 3d 634 (1976).
185. *Sullivan v. O'Connor* , 363 Mass 579, 296 NE 2d 183, 99 ALR 3d 294 (Mass 1973).
186. *Sutton v. Calhoun* , 593 F 2d 127 (Ca Okla 1979).
187. *Swanson v. Hill* , 166 F Supp 296 (DC ND 1958).
188. *Tarasoff v. Regents of the University of California* , 3d 275 (1973), 529 2d 553 (1974), 551 P 2d 334 (1976).
189. *Thompson v. Fox* , 326 Pa 209, 192 A 107 (1937).
190. *Thompson v. US* , 368 F Supp 466 (DC La 1973).
191. *Thornton v. Charleston Area Medical Center* , 213 SE 2d 102 (WV 1975).
192. *Truman v. Thomas* , 155 Cal Rptr 752 (Ga App 1979).
193. *Truman v. Thomas* , 611 P2d 902 (Cal 1980).
194. *Tubbs v. Campbell* , 731 F. 2d 1214 (C.A.5, Tex., May 14, 1984).
195. *Viland v. Winslow* , 34 Mich App 486, 191 NW 2d 735 (Mich 1971).
196. *Weinshenk v. Kaiser Foundation Hospitals* , no 480278 (Cal App Supp 1970).
197. *White v. US* , 510 F Supp 146 D (Kan 1981).
198. *Whitehurst v. Boehm* , 255 SE 2d 761 (NC App 1979).
199. *Wilczski v. Goodman* , 73 Ill App 3d 51, 29 Ill Dec 216, 391 NE 2d 479 (1979).
200. *Wiles v. Myerly* , 210 NW 2d 619 (Iowa 1973).
201. *Williams v. Bennett* , 582 SŒ 2d 577 (Tex Civ App 1979).
202. *Willis v. Western Hospital Association* , 182 P 2d 950 (Idaho 1947).
203. *Wilson v. Stilwell* , 309 NW 2d 898 (Mich 1981).
204. *Zipkin v. Freeman* , 436 SW 2d 753 (Mo 1968).

Index

285

Captain of the ship, 19, 31, 245
Case precedent, 245
Casts, 31, 166
Catheter, 185
Cause. See Proximate cause
Cerebral palsy, 174, 176
Child abuse, 245. See also Abuse
Chiropractor, 71
Circumstantial evidence, 245
Civil, 245
Civil lawsuit, 246
Claimant, 246
Claims-made policy, 226, 246
Closing arguments, 246
Co-defendants, 17, 66, 246
  attorneys of, 18
Collateral source rule, 110, 181,
    222, 246
Committment, psychiatric, 162
Common law, 246
Comparative negligence, 113, 246
Complaint, 29, 247
Complications, unavoidable, 133
Confidential, 247
Confidentiality, 15
  AIDS and, 147
  breach of, 143
Conflict of interest, 21, 53, 209,
    247
Congenital malformation
  due to X-ray exposure, 161
  Rubella syndrome, 149
Consent, 152, 247
  alcohol and, 155
  conditions sometimes claimed
      to invalidate, 160
  emergency treatment, 157
  informed, 155
  videotapes for, 166
  waived, 158
Consolidated Omnibus Budget
    Reconciliation Act, 154,
    177–179
Consortium, 37
Contingency fee, 34, 247
Contract, 247
  breach of, 138
Contractor, 247
Contributory negligence, 113, 114,
    116, 247
Counterclaim, 30, 247

Countersuits, 199–209, 248
Crime, 248
Cross-examination, 63, 106, 248

DSM-III, 40
Damage, 8, 248
Damages, 36, 203, 248
Damaging evidence, 95
Darling v. Charleston Community
    Hospital, 23, 31
Deadlocked jury, 248
Defamation, 206
Deep pocket, 7, 248
Defamation, 248
Defendant, 248
Defenses. See also specific
    accusation, such as breach
    of contract
  absence of duty, 134
  best treatment not required, 133
  conditional-occasional
      privilege, 142
  emergency case, 120
  for not filling prescriptions, 154
  Good Samaritan Laws, 119
  involving other defendants,
      180–198
  involving the patient, 113–136
    assumption of risk, 137
    comparative negligence, 113
    contributory negligence, 113,
        116
    denial of symptoms, 115
    inaccurate history, 134
    noncompliance, 114
    refusal of treatment, 121
    uncooperative, 129
  to specific charges, 137–179
  statute of limitations, 117
  unavoidable complication, 132
  unusual anatomy, 132
Demurrer, 30, 248
Denial, 115
Dentists, 118, 152, 182
Deposition
  preparation for, 62
Deponent, 249
Depose, 249
Deposition, 77–82, 249
Deposition transcript, 249
Depression, 162

RELATED TITLES OF INTEREST
